WILD

WATERS

C000214680

Also by Richard Nairn

Wild Wicklow: Nature in the Garden of Ireland

Ireland's Coastline: Exploring its Nature and Heritage

Bird Habitats in Ireland (joint editor)

Dublin Bay: Nature and History

Wild Woods: The Magic of Ireland's Native Woodlands

Wild Shores: The Magic of Ireland's Coastline

WILD WATERS

THE MAGIC OF IRELAND'S RIVERS AND LAKES

RICHARD NAIRN

Gill Books

Gill Books
Hume Avenue
Park West
Dublin 12
www.gillbooks.ie

Gill Books is an imprint of M.H. Gill and Co.

© Richard Nairn 2023
978 07171 9757 6

'Against the Flow' from *The River* (Bloodaxe Books, 2015) and 'The Dipper',
'Rowan' and 'Refuge' from *A Change in the Air* (Bloodaxe Books, 2023)
by Jane Clarke, reproduced with permission of Bloodaxe Books. www.
bloodaxebooks.com
Extracts from 'A Soft Day' and 'The West Wind' from *Songs from Leinster*
(1913) by W.M. Letts, reproduced with permission of Oriana Conner.

The author and publisher have made every effort to trace all copyright holders,
but if any have been inadvertently overlooked, we would be pleased to make the
necessary arrangement at the first opportunity.

Designed by Bartek Janczak
Print origination by O'K Graphic Design, Dublin
Map by Derry Dillon
Edited by Bríd Nowlan
Proofread by Jane Rogers
Indexed by Cliff Murphy
Printed and bound by ScandBook AB, Sweden
This book is typeset in 12.5 on 21 pt Sabon LT Pro.

*The paper used in this book comes from the wood pulp of sustainably managed
forests.*

All rights reserved.
No part of this publication may be copied, reproduced or transmitted in any
form or by any means, without written permission of the publishers.

A CIP catalogue record for this book is available from the British Library.

5 4 3 2 1

For Rowan, Derry, Hazel and Tim,
now paddling their own canoes

Preface and Acknowledgements

Rivers and lakes are the veins, arteries and beating heart of Ireland. To our ancestors these wetlands were their highways, as well as providing valuable sources of food such as water plants, fish and wildfowl, vital materials such as reeds for thatching and willows for basket-making. Today they supply us with drinking water and cleanse our waste. Their energy is harnessed to provide power, from the water mills of old to the hydroelectric stations of modern Ireland. They have a rich heritage of history, folklore and distinctive wildlife. They give us beautiful, peaceful places for recreation, including active field sports such as angling and canoeing, and inestimable attractions for tourists. Just think about the value to this country of the River Shannon, the Lakes of Killarney or Glencar Waterfall. And yet we repeatedly undervalue them, ignoring their unique wildlife, turning natural channels into lifeless canals and allowing agricultural discharges to pollute their waters.

My own interactions with waterways have been spread over half a century, from surveying the birds that breed among them to exploring the river that runs through our farm. I am fortunate to live in Wicklow, the 'Garden of Ireland', through which flows the beautiful Avonmore River. With my friend the poet Jane Clarke, I have explored many stretches of the Avonmore, which drains most of east Wicklow including the mountain lakes. I thank Jane for her insight and her company. On these adventures we have been joined by a range of other people including Cormac Byrne, Mairead Kennedy, Helen Lawless, Isobel O'Duffy and Paddy Woodworth. These friendships became deeper with our common endeavour to explore the valley in all its moods.

Jane Clarke and her publishers Bloodaxe Books are acknowledged for permission to reproduce her poems 'Against the Flow' from *The River* (2015) and 'The Dipper', 'Rowan' and 'Refuge' from *A Change in the Air* (2023). We thank Oriana Daphne Conner for permission to publish extracts from two poems, 'A Soft Day' and 'The West Wind', from *Songs from Leinster* (1933) by W.M. Letts.

As well as my own photographs, others were kindly provided by Ann Fitzpatrick, John Fox, Will O'Connor, Aoife O'Rourke, Brian O'Toole and Karl Partridge. Fáilte Ireland and the Irish National Heritage Park are acknowledged for the use of several other images.

I am especially grateful to a number of experts for reviewing different chapters. These include Jane Clarke (Chapter 1: Meeting of the Waters), Evelyn Moorkens (Chapter 2: Rivers), Julian Reynolds (Chapter 3: Lakes), Declan Little (Chapter 4: Wet Woodlands), Rob Gandola and Aoife O'Rourke (Chapter 5: Artificial Waters) and Padraic Fogarty (Chapter 6: Rewilding the Waters). I would also like to thank many other people for their help, information and expertise in connection with this book. They include Mark Boyden, Brian Burke, Mary Bourke, Darragh Byrne, Brian Caffrey, Diane Carton, Declan Cooke, John Cross, Barry Dalby, Berian Davies, Christine Davies, David Davies, Oonagh Duggan, John Feehan, Kathryn Finney, Ann Fitzpatrick, Amber Godwin, Rory Harrington, Feidhlim Harty, Colin Kelleher, Angie Kinsella, Stephen Heery, Ian Herbert, Daniel Kelly, Mary Kelly-Quinn, Mark McCorry, Allan Mee, Declan Murphy, Lorcan O'Toole, Karl Partridge, Craig Somerville, Michael

Stinson, Courtney Tyler, Graeme Warren and Ken Whelan. With thanks to Nicki, Teresa, Laura, Kristen, Charlie, Paul and all the hardworking team at Gill Books. My special thanks go to Rachael Kilduff, editor with Gill Books, for her tireless attention to detail. My son, Tim Nairn, prepared the map of the Avonmore River System.

Contents

Where dips the rocky highland

Of Sleuth Wood in the lake,

There lies a leafy island

Where flapping herons wake

The drowsy water rats;

There we've hid our faery vats,

Full of berrys;

And of reddest stolen cherries.

Come away, O human child!

To the waters and the wild

With a faery, hand in hand,

For the world's more full of weeping

Than you can understand.

From 'The Stolen Child' (1889) by W.B. YEATS

Introduction

I often sit by the bank of the small river that flows through our farm in County Wicklow, fascinated by its many moods. After an overnight storm it can be a roaring torrent, racing along with a load of sticks as passengers until it merges with other tributaries and finally reaches the sea. During summer droughts it is reduced to a quiet trickling stream, starved of moisture from the boggy fields on the hill. But most of the time it just flows steadily past, peacefully winding between the ancient trees that line its banks. My thoughts mirror these moods, sometimes bursting with inspiration, at others devoid of ideas, but most days just rumbling along in my chosen path, creating bits and pieces of work that gradually merge into a book.

My early experiences of rivers and lakes were wet and wonderful. As a child in Dublin, I played in a stream that flowed through our fields, using a hand net to catch small minnows and frogs. I loved to construct stick dams to make the water deeper so that I could sail little home-made boats around in the pools and generally mess about in the mud. Occasionally the stream would overtop its banks and flood the basement of our old house and we spent some exciting times wading about the rooms downstairs. During the summer holidays I would go to visit my cousins who lived close to one of the midland lakes where we went on fishing expeditions in a wooden boat. These formative experiences gave me a fascination for water and how it can enrich our lives.

Some nights after dark I stand outside the door of the house in the Wicklow valley where I live now. On cold winter nights with clear skies the landscape is lit only by the moon, the stars and a few twinkling lights from distant farmhouses. Just a short walk away at the foot of the slope I can hear the sound of the river rushing past through the woodland. It is a familiar sound. I can see in my mind's eye the places where the water rushes around bends and over fallen tree trunks, and others where it trickles over gravel banks as the river widens out. I can picture the otter that I once saw in the fading light, making its way upstream in search of the trout that spawn in the headwaters. The river marks the boundary of our land and the division between two townlands, and it has done so for centuries. I often reflect on the importance of this waterway in the landscape, passing through different farms and touching the lives of so many people in the valley. I would miss it if I could not hear its reassuring sounds.

Getting to know a river is like reading the story of a person's life from childhood to their inevitable end. The life of a river mirrors our human lifespan, from its young, energetic stages in the hills to the slower-moving mature river, through to the tranquil water of lakes and finally to its resting place in the sea.

Since coming to live in Wicklow more than forty years ago, I have been to visit most of its rivers and lakes – mostly the better-known places like Glendalough and Powerscourt waterfall. During the lockdowns of the Covid-19 pandemic in 2020, I began to explore the biggest river system in the county, appropriately called the Avonmore (*Abhainn Mhór* meaning big river). Its catchment covers most of the east side of the Wicklow Mountains from its source near the border with Dublin to the sea at Arklow, close to County Wexford. It has

ten main tributaries and four major lakes, many of
which begin in the classic glacial valleys or glens. So
I set out to walk the entire length of the Avonmore
system, from its source to the sea, over one year, to
meet people connected with the rivers and lakes and
to learn more about the nature and history of these
fascinating places. This led me to submerge myself
in the nature, history and legends of lots of other
freshwaters in Ireland, or at least those that became
the subjects of this book.

After heavy rainfall, the Avonmore River swells with
brown, peat-stained water and powers along filling its
channel to the brim. In 1986, torrential rain following
the passage of Hurricane Charlie led the river to burst
its banks in many places and tore away the supports
of several old stone bridges, causing them to collapse.
Today, rain is still one of the main talking points
among Irish people. Located as we are on the edge of
the Atlantic Ocean, we tend to get too much of it at
once as the moisture-laden winds empty their contents
on the green landscape below. A poor summer usually
means a wet one, although most tourists who come to
Ireland are not here for the sunshine. Every morning I
stop whatever I am doing to listen to the day's weather

forecast. Will it bring heavy rain, scattered showers or a dry day? Will I need to water the tender saplings that I grew from acorns last autumn? The weather forecasters frequently talk about wintery showers, persistent rain and flooding.

Our native language has no shortage of expressions when it comes to describing precipitation. Rain may simply be described as *báisteach* or *fearthainn* but there are plenty of other words for different types of wetness. The words *ceobhrán* and *brádán* describe drizzle or misty rain. *Ceathanna, múrtha* or *scrabhanna báistí* suggest showers of rain while *aimsir cheathach* or *aimsir spairniúil* describe showery weather.[1] The twelfth-century Welsh author Giraldus Cambrensis wrote, after his travels in Ireland, 'there is, however, such a plentiful supply of rain, such an ever-present overhanging of clouds and fog that you will scarcely see even in summer three consecutive days of really fine weather'.[2] The comedian Hal Roach famously said, 'you know when it is summer in Ireland as the rain gets warmer'. 'A soft day' in the country is one where the atmosphere is humid and moisture is held in the air. Or, in the words of a poet:

A soft day, thank God!

The hills wear a shroud

Of silver cloud;

The web the spider weaves

Is a glittering net;

The woodland path is wet,

And the soaking earth smells sweet

Under my two bare feet.

And the rain drips,

Drips, drips, drips from the leaves.

Extract from 'A Soft Day' from *Songs from Leinster*
(1933) by W.M. LETTS

The result of all this water falling from the skies is that Ireland is one of the wettest parts of Europe. Annual rainfall totals in the west of Ireland generally average between 1,000 and 1,400 millimetres per year and in many mountainous districts this may exceed 2,000 millimetres per year (enough to cover a tall person). A lot of this moisture is absorbed by the soil or finds its way into groundwater, more runs off in streams and rivers to the sea, while a large proportion of it is held in lakes, marshes and bogs. These waterways and wetlands are occupied by a dizzying variety of native plants both above and below water. They also hold a good variety of fish species, and Ireland is well known as an international destination for angling. There are wonderful wetland insects, such as dragonflies and water beetles, and one of the healthiest populations of otters in Europe.

The prevalence of rivers, lakes and other wetlands, especially in the midlands and north-west of Ireland, is one of the principal attractions for the great flocks of migratory waterbirds that arrive here in the autumn and depart again in spring for their breeding grounds in the Arctic. I have many happy memories of watching flocks of whooper swans, recently arrived from Iceland, trumpeting out their loud calls across flooded fields in the Shannon valley. Vast swirling flocks of golden plover circle above lake shores, their bright plumage picked out in the low winter sunlight. The stirring sound of a drumming snipe above a marsh in early summer will be etched in my memory for ever.

Surprisingly, rivers and other wetlands offer some of the best conditions for the preservation of historical and archaeological remains. The archaeologist Aidan O'Sullivan wrote:

In the past, some of the most striking archaeological discoveries on this island have been made in its wetlands, whether they are Iron Age human remains or trackways in bogs; early medieval crannogs and dwellings in lakes with their abundant collections of objects; or intact late medieval wooden fish-traps and baskets quietly eroding out of estuarine mudflats. Archaeological survey and excavation in wet environments can uncover spectacularly well-preserved dwellings with their occupation and midden deposits present; or wooden vessels with their tool-marks surviving and traces of their last contents within them. Protected from the annihilation of time by their anaerobic, waterlogged environments, the sense of wonder that these discoveries evoke is often traceable to the fact of their unlikely survival and existence.[3]

There are many different definitions of what comprises a river or lake, but a broad understanding is a piece of land that is inundated by water for at least part of every year. This can include moving water such as rivers and canals or still water as in ponds, lakes, lagoons or special temporary lakes known as turloughs. Wetlands, by definition, are transitional habitats between open water and dry land. They include marshes, bogs, reedswamps and wet woodlands. They often contain a number of parallel zones into which the plants and animals are organised. Some international agreements, such as the Ramsar Convention, include shallow coastal waters and tidal estuaries as wetlands, but as these are saltwaters I have not included them in this book.

The frequency of words for different types of wetlands in the Irish language underlines the historical importance of these features in the landscape. Examples are *abhainn* meaning river, *loch* meaning lake, *móin* a bog, *caladh* a river meadow, *seascann* a marsh, *saileán* a willow grove and *tuar loch* a dry lake (or turlough).[4] Historically, these areas were treated with respect because they yielded valuable resources – fish and shellfish for food, reeds for thatching, willows for basket-making, waterpower for mills and many other things that were useful in everyday life. In the twenty-first century there is a growing realisation that rivers and lakes have an important role to play in the fight against climate change. Freshwater for domestic and industrial use has become one of the more valuable commodities as our consumption levels continue to escalate and the climate becomes increasingly warmer and drier. Water shortages are more frequent in summer and there is an active proposal to lay a pipeline across half of the country to transfer water from the River Shannon to Dublin. Undisturbed peatlands can store much more carbon than forests on the same area of land. Filtration of pollutants through the root systems of wetland plants such as common reed and bulrush is a valuable nature-based solution to water pollution. The conservation of Ireland's rivers and lakes demands our attention in the future.

Throughout most of my adult life I have been visiting wet places around Ireland to seek out their wildlife, understand their archaeology and history or simply enjoy the sense of a lost wilderness that they can convey. I always bring wellington boots because even walking through wet vegetation can be a miserable experience in normal shoes. A change of socks is another useful standby for the times when water levels are over the top of my boots. I love to follow the course of a river, walking on the banks or wading in the shallows, discovering the source at a tiny spring bubbling out of the soil. Or I might take a boat out onto one of our larger midland lakes where it feels like a trip on an inland sea with the landscape all around reflected in the water surface. As well as the familiar lowland lakes and rivers, we have a number of very special wetland types in Ireland such as turloughs, coastal lagoons and deep mysterious mountain lakes. Following my exploration of the Avonmore catchment in Wicklow, this book dives into a series of other watery features throughout Ireland – the rivers, lakes, wet woodlands and artificial waters such as ponds and canals. The final chapter surfaces again in an honest appraisal of the threats to these wetlands and what can be done to ensure their survival.

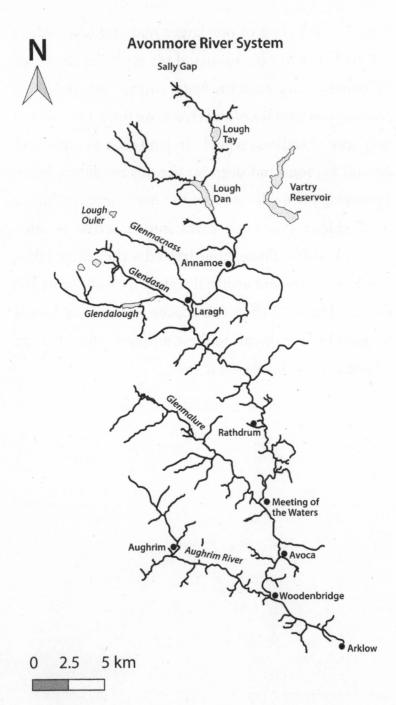

Avonmore River System

Sally Gap

Lough Tay

Lough Dan

Vartry Reservoir

Lough Ouler

Glenmacnass

Annamoe

Glendasan

Glendalough

Laragh

Glenmalure

Rathdrum

Meeting of the Waters

Aughrim

Aughrim River

Avoca

Woodenbridge

Arklow

0   2.5   5 km

Meeting of the Waters

There is not in the wide world a
    valley so sweet
As that vale in whose bosom the
    bright waters meet;
Oh! the last rays of feeling and life
    must depart,
Ere the bloom of that valley shall fade
    from my heart.

Yet it was not that nature had shed
    o'er the scene
Her purest of crystal and brightest of
    green;
'Twas not her soft magic of streamlet
    or hill,
Oh! no, – it was something more
    exquisite still.

'Twas that friends, the beloved of my
    bosom, were near,
Who made every dear scene of
    enchantment more dear,
And who felt how the best charms of
    nature improve,
When we see them reflected from
    looks that we love.

Sweet vale of Avoca! how calm could
    I rest
In thy bosom of shade, with the
    friends I love best,
Where the storms that we feel in this
    cold world should cease,
And our hearts, like thy waters, be
    mingled in peace.

'The Meeting of the Waters' (1807) by THOMAS MOORE

Thomas Moore, poet and songwriter, was certainly in
a romantic mood when he wrote these words about
the Vale of Avoca in the centre of County Wicklow
where the Avonmore and Avonbeg rivers converge.

At a younger age he was somewhat more daring, as a collection of his verse included a celebration of kisses and embraces that was considered to be on the verge of erotic in the British Empire of the early 1800s. After an extended dalliance with British politics, Moore returned to Ireland, where he wrote the lyrics to a number of Irish melodies that became immensely popular. Among the best known of these songs was 'The Meeting of the Waters', which he wrote in 1807 after a visit to the famous beauty spot near Avoca village.

I went there again recently to see what inspired Moore, and I too felt that this was an important meeting place where friendships might grow as common interests outnumber differences. So, as a source of inspiration for this chapter, I decided to walk the entire length of the river from the source to the point where it enters the Irish Sea. I hoped in this way to gain some understanding of the evolution of the river, the stages of which reflect the span of a single human life. Fortuitously, I discovered that another person I knew had the same ambition. This was Jane Clarke, a poet who lives in Glenmalure, one of the Wicklow valleys, and who was already engaged in writing a series of poems about the river.

Others joined us at intervals, all of us united by a common aim to explore the river valley in depth and to understand its secrets. This was a meeting of minds as well as a meeting of the waters.

With these friends, all experienced hill walkers, I set out to explore the Avonmore and its tributaries, the lakes fed by the rivers and the beautiful habitats that fill many of the valleys. The main channel of the river is some sixty-five kilometres in length. Downstream of the Meeting of the Waters it is known as the Avoca River. The entire catchment contains many different landscape types: mountain bogs, beautiful valleys carved by glaciers, deep ribbon lakes and waterfalls, old woodlands, modern forestry plantations and beauty spots, some scarred by mine waste and industrial pollution of the past. I wanted to see the wild plants and animals that live in these places and that make the riverbank their home. There are many public riverside paths but there are also some stretches of waterside that are protected by landowners who value their privacy. Along the river there is a scattered community including sheep farmers, foresters, large landowners, conservationists and people who value the peace and tranquillity that the river valley offers. To explore nature in such a peaceful setting, with a group of like-minded friends, was a privilege indeed.

The source

On a cold winter's day I set off with my friends to reach the source of the main river high in the Wicklow Mountains. As we left the road and trekked uphill along the rushy banks of the White Sand Brook, we were accompanied by a dipper, a plump little bird perching on rocks in the fast-flowing stream and diving into the water to catch insect larvae. Our objective was to reach the source of this mighty river on the flat bog between the mountain peaks of Kippure and Tonduff. In the surrounding landscape, as far as the eye could see, unbroken vistas of acid grassland were dominated by tussocks of purple moor-grass and heather. Occasionally, we came upon isolated birch and rowan trees, clinging onto steep slopes where the nibbling teeth of sheep could not reach them. The poem 'Rowan' by Jane Clarke captures the harsh conditions in which rowan trees survive in the mountains:

When grief
like a river

is set
to burst its banks

the rowan
has already lost

its berries
and leaves;

it sways
in the wind,

steadies,
sways.

On the slopes around us, herds of deer bounded away from the greener grasslands along the river where they had been grazing. The granite and quartzite rocks, everywhere to be seen, lead to acid conditions and low productivity in the river. But this paucity of nutrients is compensated for by the sheer energy of the water, powering along through the bog, around boulders and over small waterfalls. As we climbed higher, patches of snow appeared on the banks and some of the slower-flowing sections were covered with a layer of ice. Then the bog became more level and we were no longer climbing. Among still pools filled with colourful mosses we paused to marvel while the river that drains most of a county emerged in a quiet trickle. There was no gushing from the earth or dramatic waterfall. Just the gentle sound of water running through the soil. With satisfaction and vivid memories, our little group descended the mountain in the setting sun.

The blacksmith

Later, at a small waterfall in the mountains, we sat for a while marvelling at the power of the water and the clouds of spray that constantly filled the air around the pool where it landed. The low cliffs were damp and clothed in mosses, liverworts and ferns. My attention was caught by a dark little bird, flying into the crevice with beakfuls of winged insects – maybe stoneflies or caddisflies. It was here that a dipper had made its nest among the slippery wet rocks. Like the wren, the dipper has a jaunty posture with a cocked tail, but it is slightly larger in size than a robin. Its black and brown plumage, with a striking white bib, have given it the Irish name *Gabha dubh* or blacksmith. This poem,

'The Dipper' by Jane Clarke, evokes the character of
the dipper that we watched in the mountain stream:

You fly upstream while I tramp

    among snow-dusted rushes
    along the suckering edge.

True as a mandrel

    you dive, flickering
    into the narrow rill.

I think I've lost you –

    but beyond clumps of sedge
    and withered asphodel,

little blacksmith,

    you bob on an anvil.
    Droplets fall from your bib.

Hammer to chisel,

    you hurtle notes
    higher and higher

above the river,

your treble bell

pealing across the heath.

When hunting, the dipper flew rapidly along the river, perching occasionally on boulders in midstream wherever there was broken white water in riffles. Here it bobbed up and down, dipping its tail, apparently to get a better view of potential insect prey flying over the water. It often dived into the water, where it swam or walked on the riverbed, turning over small stones to pick off the larvae underneath. The dipper has been intensively studied for many decades in Munster, where most nests are built under stone bridges with only a small number on natural bank, rock or tree root sites. When the rivers are flooded, the dippers feed more on terrestrial insects, but they never fly far from the water unless they take a shortcut across a meander in the channel. Dippers are widespread across Ireland but concentrated in the uplands and foothills of the mountains where there is fast-flowing water. They are absent from most of the midlands, presumably because the rivers are slower and deeper and there is less opportunity for finding their preferred prey.[1]

The origin of the dipper's English name may be connected with its 'dipping' habit when standing on a rock or with the feeding behaviour of dipping in the water. Older English names include the 'water ouzel' or 'water blackbird', and this similarity also emerges in its alternative Irish name, *lon abhann*, meaning 'river blackbird'. The dipper was once believed to be the female kingfisher. This is not surprising as both species can be found on the same stretch of river and both fly low over the water. In Victorian Britain the dipper was persecuted, as it was mistakenly believed to feed on the eggs of salmon and trout. Many dippers were killed by overzealous gamekeepers as a result. In nineteenth-century Ireland a sighting of a number of dippers was believed to foretell the arrival of a malignant disease in the area. The skin of a dipper, when worn on the stomach, was said to be a cure for indigestion.

The Irish dipper *(Cinclus cinclus hibernicus)* is a unique subspecies found only in Ireland. It is distinguished from its cousins elsewhere by a rusty brown band where the bib ends on the breast. The ecology of dippers is intimately linked to river ecosystems, as they rely on them for food and nesting sites. They rarely leave the river even in winter. Researchers at University College

Cork have found that breeding occurs earlier than in other songbirds, with egg-laying often beginning in March, because it is synchronised with the peak of aquatic insect abundance.

Today, the dipper has an important role as an indicator of good water quality, and the birds may decline where pollution or acidification occurs. Streams overlying acidic rocks like granite and quartzite and with catchments that are extensively planted with conifers are especially vulnerable to acidification. When it rains, a weak acid is formed on the needles and drips onto the ground, running down drainage channels and into streams. Aluminium in the soil is mobilised by the acidic water and this is dissolved in streams and rivers where it becomes highly toxic to fish and some invertebrates like mayflies. The absence of prey resources makes such rivers poor breeding grounds for dippers. Those that do attempt to breed have fewer eggs and smaller chicks than dippers on good-quality waters. This leads to poor survival of the birds and inevitable decline. I will be keeping an eye out for the young birds during the summer as they zip up and down the river here. On the Avonmore River, dippers are the commonest river birds, occupying a

series of adjacent breeding territories from the lowland
stretches right up into the higher hills.

Water twisters

My companions and I were following a section of the
Avonmore River in east Wicklow that flows off the
Sally Gap Bog and plunges into the deep, spectacular
valley of Luggala. As it descends over multiple
cascades and around moss-covered granite boulders,
the river gathers speed. In the 1930s this natural power
was harnessed with the installation of a small dam
and turbine to provide renewable energy for Luggala
House and estate. Situated in a bend of the river, the
gothic-style house was built in the 1780s by the La
Touche family and then passed into the ownership of
the Guinness family and its heir Garech de Brún. The
house is nestled in the natural amphitheatre of Luggala
valley, which must be one of the most spectacular
settings for a residence in Ireland. As we walked past
the classic house I could imagine the entertainment put
on by its wealthy owners over the centuries. It has now
been acquired by the family of Luca Padulli. Writing
about the land here, this committed conservationist
remembered a Native American mystic who once

visited Luggala and remarked that he could hear the ancestors whistling through the trees. Padulli says, 'I often hear these words echoing through my mind and feel the weight of them on my shoulders. In the end they epitomise my goal with Luggala – it is a place to be saved and treasured for eternity.'[2]

Close to Luggala House are the deep, dark waters of Lough Tay, whose setting is one of the most iconic views in the east of Ireland. As the wind whipped across the surface of the lake it snatched the water into a swirl and sucked it vertically into a twister that skated across the lake at high speed like a kite surfer. Then it was followed by another and another in a natural show of movement and light that would rival any fireworks display. If I half-closed my eyes, I could imagine it was a column of water nymphs dancing across the lake. The image reminded me of a painting of dancing fairies by the Swedish painter August Malmström, where a swirling line of ethereal female forms sweeps across the surface of a moonlit lake.

By the shores of the lake we walked along a pristine beach of white sand beneath the impressive cliffs and scree slopes of Fancy Mountain. On the steep eastern slopes above the lake is an impressive stand of pure native oakwood fringed by giant beeches and Scots pines, planted by the previous estate owners. A red squirrel scampered up a trunk in the winter sunshine. Some of these centuries-old trees are approaching the end of their natural lifespan and showed many rot holes and broken limbs. They also had the twisted spiral form so characteristic of veteran trees, as if mirroring the twisters that danced across the lake below us.

Riffles and glides

Lower down the valley between Lough Tay and Lough Dan I sat on the bank of the river, savouring the peace and quiet, broken only by the babbling of the water as it flowed between overhanging trees. The constant sound and movement of the river was mesmerising. It was hard to take my eyes off the sunlight glinting on the water surface. In places there were riffles or rapids where the fast-flowing water was broken by shallow banks of gravel and cobbles, in others deep pools where the flow was slower and resting trout waited to lay their eggs. I thought about the tale of Mole in *The Wind in the Willows*, discovering a river for the first time:

By the side of the river he trotted as
one trots, when very small, by the side
of a man who holds one spell-bound
by exciting stories; and when tired at
last, he sat on the bank, while the river
still chattered on to him, a babbling
procession of the best stories in the
world, sent from the heart of the earth
to be told at last to the insatiable sea.

From *The Wind in the Willows* (1908)
by KENNETH GRAHAME

This sequence of riffle, glide and pool is common
to most rivers in their middle or lower reaches. It
reflects the varied gradient, sometimes level, sometimes
descending over a series of rapids where gravel bars
reach the surface. These features are important for the
wildlife in the river. The faster-flowing water in riffles is
well oxygenated and ideal for the larvae of many insects
that live beneath the stones holding tight in the fast flow
by some ingenious methods. The larvae of the caddisfly
develop from eggs that are laid in a mass of jelly. On
hatching, the larvae make a kind of protective case or
tube to protect their soft bodies from fish and other

predators. This case may be made of small stones, sand or plant material. These tiny animals are no pushovers for predators, though, as the only thing that protrudes from the case is a set of biting mouthparts. The riffles are also a favourite spot for foraging dippers and grey wagtails. Pools are generally quieter places. In late summer, dragonflies dip the surface, while swallows and sand martins feed on the abundant insects that hatch from the water. Occasionally, a heron pays a visit and stands motionless with its feet in the water, waiting to stab an unsuspecting fish or frog.

Brown waters

The section of the main river called the Cloghoge carries a large amount of peat silt in suspension from the mountains, giving it a dark brown colour. It enters a series of sweeping meanders and then, surrounded by dramatic mountain landscapes, it discharges into Lough Dan (*Loch Deán*), the largest natural lake in the county. We crossed the river by a slippery line of stepping stones, before walking along a sandy beach that would grace any holiday resort. I had arranged permission to access this very private estate called Ballinrush, which is owned by an extended family called Archer. Ancient oak and birch trees grow from the lake sand, their twisted knarled trunks witness to centuries of human change. We paused here for a while to enjoy the 'lake water lapping' and to take in the immense views.

The archaeologist Chris Corlett described the valley above Lough Dan as 'the largest example of a fossilised 18th/19th century farming landscape in Wicklow, if not in the country'. Scattered across its heathery face are the tumbled remains of several small settlements. On one of the few level areas of ground at the western side of the valley we walked among the walls of a ruined sod house with lazy bed cultivation ridges stretching up the slopes all around. In the 1841 census of Ireland the townland of Cloghogue was home to 148 people living in 19 households. Just twenty years later, following the convulsions of the Great Famine, there were only fourteen people living here in two houses. In the intervening years, the landlords had initiated a wholesale clearance of the tenants to make way for a new sheep farm with imported Cheviot sheep 'from the purest flocks in Scotland'.[3]

I tried to imagine life here, isolated from neighbours by the hills, with mostly relatives for company. Beside these houses there is evidence that cereals, probably oats, were grown here, as there were the remains of corn ricks: four upright stones on which a platform would have been placed to dry the crop and keep it free from rodent damage. In one small group of ruined houses we found the remains of a well, with its characteristic flat stones. The location of the farm buildings was thus not random. They were built along the spring line to avail of a ready source of fresh water. Where the Inchavore River joins Lough Dan at its western end there is an area of flat grassland that is still farmed today. This is essentially a floodplain across which the river meanders to empty into the lake at a beautiful sandy beach covered with old birch trees. Close to a small stream is another cluster of six ruined cottages. Here there are the remains of a series of circular and rectangular hay ricks, which suggests that the area was used for extensive grazing and the saving of hay.

The waters of Lough Dan are dark and mysterious – up to forty metres at their deepest point. One experienced angler described 'a hatch of sedges here with trout rising everywhere.' This was once one of Ireland's best-known lakes for Arctic char, a very rare species today. This relative of the trout is a relic of a time when Ireland still had an Arctic climate, but it is now thought to be extinct in this valley. Records of char in Lough Dan date back to 1822. The last authenticated specimen was lodged in the Natural History Museum of Ireland in 1988, although an angler by the name of Tom Sutcliffe is reported to have caught one in 1991. Repeated attempts since then to find them have drawn a blank. Increasing acidity of the water caused by modern forestry in the lake catchment may be the cause of their decline, as there has been little change in the variety and abundance of invertebrate food.[4]

Further south along the shores of Lough Dan we entered some very old oakwoods that reach right down to hang over the lake water. The 1760 map of County Wicklow by Jacob Neville shows woodlands in this very location, so it is probably ancient woodland that has stood here for many centuries. Huge moss-covered boulders line the lake shore and among them is a fine traditional boathouse, painstakingly restored by the present owner of the property, Simon Pratt. He kindly showed me around the woodlands and the lake shore. His family home, nestled among the giant trees, is called Lake Park House, a fishing lodge built around 1835. A

Topographical Dictionary of Ireland described Lake Park in 1837 as 'the admired residence of Gerard Macklin Esq ... formerly a wild and barren spot, which has been reclaimed and formed into a handsome demesne commanding fine views of Lough Dan and the adjacent mountains'. Previous owners of this romantic location include the poet Richard Murphy and the novelist Edna O'Brien.

Historic estates

From Lough Dan we walked along the river through a wooded area with old oak trees, which were multi-stemmed as a result of past coppicing. Through the wood runs a track called the Old School Road. Walking along it, I imagined groups of schoolchildren passing along by the river from their homes in Annamoe a century ago. They would have learnt first-hand about nature in their local area as they made their daily journey to the schoolhouse at Oldbridge.

The right bank of the river is fringed by a number of large estates, the first of which belongs to Glendalough House. This property, originally named Drummeen, was built around 1760 and belonged to Thomas Hugo, a former high sheriff of Wicklow and a firm supporter of the British government. He was notorious for repressing the rebellion in Wicklow and was described as 'a cruel and inhuman tyrant'. There was once a 'hanging tree' near the river. In revenge, the house was burnt by the rebels in 1798. Following reconstruction, the house and lands were purchased in 1838 by Thomas Barton. Erskine Childers, a relative of the Bartons, was arrested at the house in 1922 during the Civil War and later executed in Dublin because his gun was a prohibited weapon and to carry it a capital offence. Robert Barton farmed the estate benevolently during his long life; it was then inherited by Robert Childers, brother of Erskine Hamilton Childers, who later became President of Ireland.[5]

Further downstream at Annamoe we walked along the river near The Glebe, originally a Church of Ireland rectory and later owned by the film director John Boorman, who lived here for over fifty years. In recent years Boorman wrote several books including a *Nature Diary* and a series of poems about trees and the river that flows through his land. He would sit for long periods beneath a favourite tree, the twin oak that still overhangs the riverbank. I sat on his wooden bench and I too found a sense of peace here, watching the waters swirling by. Although Boorman has become seriously disabled in later life his son Lee helped him to continue swimming in a favourite deep pool. In an addendum to the *Nature Diary*, Lee wrote that, when his father was waist-deep, magic happened. 'In the river he stood without my aid, supported only by his arms paddling in the water and by the gentle embrace of the current. After a few minutes of swimming, the river gave another gift. It returned to Dad his confidence.'[6] This river is continually giving gifts to all who know it.

The next section of the river runs through a large, wooded estate owned by Paul McGuinness, former manager of the Irish band U2. The water is overhung by old oak and ash trees but is also overgrazed by deer and infested with invasive rhododendron, which will shade out any significant regeneration. I was accompanied along this stretch of the river by a local naturalist, Declan Murphy. He has written about his personal quest to find a kingfisher here:

Flying towards me from further downstream, its call heralded its approach long before I saw it. Seconds later my eyes picked it up flying low over the water, tilting its body this way and that, before coming to land on one of the rocks that formed the weir in front of me. I was able to regard its plumage in intricate detail. Each of its blue feathers revealed itself to be composed of endless tints and shades within that one colour.[7]

Walking further along the bank we came upon the flat stepping stones that cross the river at Trooperstown Wood. Here I was able to jump from stone to stone across the flowing river to reach the other bank. The townland is so named because it is said that British troops camped here during the 1798 rebellion. Nearby is the headquarters of the Wicklow Mountains National Park, suitably hidden in dense woodland, as well as a base of the Dublin and Wicklow Mountain Rescue team. From here the river makes several turns before it meets another tributary, the Glenmacnass, at Laragh.

Valley of the falls

> Across the Wicklow Hills he came,
> The herdsmen heard his great wings
> > beat,
> The waves of Lough Nahanagan
> Were ruffled by his flying feet;
> The Vale of Clara felt him pass
> Swift-foot across the meadow grass:
> They heard him where the waters
> > meet,
> He made the pines and larches sway;
> He crossed the stream at
> > Glenmacnass,
> And blew the falls to silver spray.

Extract from 'The West Wind' from *Songs from Leinster* (1933) by W.M. LETTS

Glenmacnass (*Gleann Log an Easa*, meaning 'the valley of the hollow of the waterfall') has an eighty-metre-high waterfall situated at the head of a deep glacial valley through which this tributary of the Avonmore flows. We approached the top of the falls from the Military Road, hopping from rock to heather-covered rock. This old road runs north–south along the spine of the Wicklow Mountains. It was constructed in the first few years of the nineteenth century, in the wake of the 1798 rebellion. Its purpose was to open up the mountains to the British Army to assist them in putting down insurgencies and capturing any rebels who were hiding there. I could imagine battalions of red-coated soldiers marching along in tight formations beside the river with loaded muskets over their shoulders. This was, in fact, one of the first purpose-built roads across the mountains. Four large barracks were built along the way at Glencree, Laragh, Glenmalure and Aghavannagh.

Above the waterfall a small stream flows down the sides of Tonelagee mountain. We crossed the stream and trekked uphill through wet boggy ground and long heather. High on the north-east side of the mountain is a dark mountain lake, Lough Ouler. Shaped like a heart, this lake is one of the most photographed in the Wicklow Hills. It is a classic example of a corrie lake where a patch of ice left behind by the last Ice Age finally slipped downhill, taking parts of the mountain with it and creating the steep cliffs around the lake in the shape of a giant armchair. The water is peat-stained and cold enough to freeze the fingers of any brave swimmers.

River of two lakes

Another tributary of the Avonmore flows from the valley of Glenealo, high in the Wicklow Mountains. It plunges down a steep slope into the Upper Lake at Glendalough, a classic glacial valley set in the heart of County Wicklow and probably its best-known tourist attraction. The most striking features here are the steep slopes carved by ice and now clothed in woodland as they might have appeared in prehistoric times. This landscape was very different in more recent centuries when, as etchings and black and white photographs show, the valley was stripped of timber to provide fuel and wood for making charcoal used in smelting. In those days, the famous monastic remains of Glendalough stood out 'like ruined teeth in a bare gum'.[8]

The monastery was established here in the sixth century at a key location where the valleys of Glendalough and Glendasan converge. It is believed that the monastery was established by St Kevin, who sought out the remoteness of the valley to avoid the company of his followers. Here he lived as a hermit in a hollowed-out cave in the rock face above the Upper Lake. The cave (sometimes incorrectly described as a

Bronze Age tomb) is now known as St Kevin's Bed, and it is recorded that he was led here by an angel. The cave is still quite visible, looking across the lake from the north side. There have been accidents here when modern sightseers, clambering along the cliffs to reach the cave, have fallen down the rocks. They are usually rescued by boat from across the lake. The legends tell that St Kevin lived the life of a hermit here for seven years wearing only animal skins, sleeping on stones and eating very sparingly. Here he was surrounded by forests and wildlife, his only companions. One of the most widely known poems of Nobel prize-winner Seamus Heaney, 'St Kevin and the Blackbird', relates the story of the saint holding out his hand with such stillness and for so long that a blackbird built a nest in it and laid eggs from which the chicks fledged. While this legend is hard to believe, it does suggest the undisturbed nature of the valley in the sixth century.

From here, we walked up the track that parallels the Upper Lake through tall pine trees that were planted here over a century ago. They were originally intended to be harvested and used as pit props for the lead mines that flourished in the valley in the nineteenth century. This is where the eastern margin of the Leinster granite meets the surrounding rock, where heat and pressure caused mineralisation and veins of heavy metals to form. These veins stretch from Glenmalure to the Dublin border, but the main centre of mining was in Glendalough and the neighbouring valley of Glendasan. The Glenealo River powers its way through the old spoil heaps from the mine, comprising bare gravel and sand where few plants grow because of the toxic presence of heavy metals from the historic mining.

During the nineteenth century this valley was a busy place, with up to a hundred people living and working here throughout the year. In the mining village, the river entered a millrace where it poured over a millwheel that drove the rock-crushing machinery. Gunpower was used to blast out the rock and the people worked in the deep mine shafts, using just candles for light. The mines at Glendalough were abandoned in 1880 but opened again for a short time in 1919. The enormous waste heaps around the mines are a visible scar on the landscape, but there are also invisible impacts on the water in the valley which persist a century later. The content of lead in the marshes at the head of Glendalough Upper Lake is many thousands of times higher than normal upland water, and there have been cases of swans dying of lead poisoning in this area.

The river feeds two lakes, which are each very different in character. The Upper Lake is deep and surrounded by cliffs while its smaller companion is shallow and fringed by extensive reedbeds and marsh. We walked around the edge of the Lower Lake, along a fine wooden boardwalk, surrounded by willow trees and flocks of small birds feeding on the abundant insects here. In a short distance the river skirts the cluster of monastic ruins with their distinctive round tower and flows down past Derrybawn Wood to join with the main Avonmore.

Fishing duck

It was late evening, and the sun had set by the time my friend Paddy Woodworth and I returned to the Upper Lake at Glendalough. We walked through the old Scots pine trees that cast deep shadows on the track along the lakeshore. Beside us the lake water lapped gently as there was little wind. We were full of anticipation because this is one of the locations where a flock of goosanders gathers to spend the night on the deep, dark lake waters. Peering out into the gloom with my binoculars it took a few minutes for my eyes to readjust to the shadowy shapes on the water, and, slowly but surely, we began to pick out a few dozen birds bobbing on the small waves that disturbed the lake surface. They spend the nights here where they are safe from predators before taking off at dawn and flying to nearby lakes and rivers to breed.

The goosander is a medium-sized duck, different from most of the wildfowl species, which are mainly vegetarian, in that it feeds primarily on fish. To do so it has evolved a serrated edge to the long red hooked bill which it uses to hold on to slippery fish before swallowing them. This puts it in the worldwide group of birds called sawbills. Goosanders have a light breast and underside which makes them just about visible in the dusk light. The green head feathers of the males distinguish them from females, which have dark chocolate brown heads.

The Irish birds are fairly scarce residents at larger lakes and rivers in County Wicklow but are occasionally joined by some winter visitors from abroad. One pair was first found to be breeding in County Donegal in 1969, and they remained in this area for the following decade before disappearing again.[9] Goosanders are frequently seen on the Avonmore River, not far from Glendalough, but they are highly secretive. They are quite elusive birds and I have only had occasional glimpses of them in the water. Local ornithologist Declan Murphy, who knows this river well, writes, 'Rarely do you see goosanders by design – chance encounters are the norm, usually while walking along a well-wooded stretch of river. During April and May, sightings are usually of single birds, often the male guarding the territory as the female, hidden from view, incubates the eggs in the nest.'[10]

Breeding of goosanders along the Avonmore River has been facilitated by the National Parks and Wildlife Service (NPWS) which provides wooden nest boxes attached to large trees close to the river. The female bird will lay eight to fourteen large creamy white eggs in a nest that she lines with down plucked from her breast. Ann Fitzpatrick, a conservation ranger with the NPWS, told me:

Once the chicks start to hatch out, everything happens in a flurry as the whole brood hatches within a 24-hour period. In those first hours the chicks form a bond to the female and to each other, learning the sound of their mother. When it's time to go, the female will leave the box and sit on the water below, calling with a harsh cackle to the chicks, encouraging them to follow her and launch themselves into the unknown. It's a truly amazing phenomenon to witness these tiny bundles of feather and energy hurtling into the river.

Vale of Clara

Just downstream of Laragh, the Avonmore plunges over a series of rocky steps and powers through some narrow gaps in the bedrock. This is known as Jackson's Falls, which reflects a very short period when the landowner on one side of the falls was a man called Jackson. According to map-maker Barry Dalby, the old name is Poulamurrish. Jane Clarke and I walked here in the late autumn when the rusty leaves of the overhanging oak trees littered the water's edge. The falls are a favourite training ground for adventurous kayakers who want to 'shoot the rapids'. Within a short distance the river is joined by two more tributaries, the Glendasan and the Glenealo, the latter flowing from the Glendalough valley. It has now become a substantial body of water, stained brown with peat washed off the hills. Despite its maturity, the river still moves with a strong flow as the gradient of the land continues to fall towards the south.

The old stone bridge at Clara is one of the most picturesque on the entire river, with a small church built almost on the bank. We sat in the field beside the bridge for a lunch break and watched the river rushing under the stone arches. The earliest definite record of a church building here is in the map produced by Jacob Neville in 1760. In those days, the building would have been thatched. Parish record books reveal that there was a major reconstruction of the church in 1838 with the mud floor later tiled and the ceiling plastered, all costing the princely sum of £128.

From Laragh to Rathdrum the river is almost entirely surrounded by mature woodland, most of it within the Vale of Clara Nature Reserve. This woodland is a remnant of the once extensive forests of east Wicklow, which may have occupied this site since the end of the last Ice Age. However, most of the commercial trees have gradually been removed, allowing natural regeneration with native species to occur. As we walked through the trees the sound of the river alongside was a constant companion.

Occasionally, we glimpsed a dipper perching on a rock by the water's edge, especially where it was broken by rocky shallows.

Nearing the end of this stretch of woodland we walked through the area known by the strange name Stump of the Castle. The structure after which the townland is named is Kilcommon Castle, built by Sir Hugh Lawless of Anglo-Norman origin. For walkers there is the welcome addition here of a modern suspension bridge crossing from one bank of the river to the other. The bridge was opened in 2021 and is named after Samuel Hayes, a member of the Irish parliament and a large landowner in County Wicklow, who wrote a remarkable *Treatise on Planting and the Management of Woods and Coppices* in 1794.[11] Hayes was a resident of Rathdrum, where he owned the estate of Avondale. The bridge led us into Ballygannon Wood, another native woodland that was selected in 2000 as one of the People's Millennium Woodlands. A path leads out of the wood past a famine graveyard and some fine old yew trees that must be centuries old. In recent years, a waymarked route known as The Avonmore Way has been laid out here, stretching from Trooperstown Wood near Laragh to Rathdrum.

Railway meetings

After a welcome coffee break at Mocha Joe's café, in the village of Rathdrum, we set off down the track to the local railway station from where a narrow path enters the woodland high above the river. The ground was lit up with wildflowers – celandines, anemones and bluebells. Arching ferns gave a mystical look to the place. From here we entered the riverside path through Avondale Forest Park. This mainly wooded estate is spread over 200 hectares and is now managed by the state forestry company Coillte, mainly for visitors. At its centre is Avondale House, built in 1777 for Samuel Hayes, a barrister and a pioneer in forestry methods. He bequeathed it to his friend and fellow MP Sir John Parnell in 1795 and the latter's great-grandson Charles Stewart Parnell was born here in 1846. Also elected as an MP, the younger Parnell is best known for his work on land reform in Ireland. In the early twentieth century the estate was sold to the government and the house was subsequently used as a forestry school. The grounds were planted with a great variety of trees, many in experimental blocks, with the most successful being conifers from the Pacific coast of North America.

The sounds of birdsong and the river rushing over shallow rapids were occasionally interrupted by the clatter of a passing train. The railway and river here are intertwined like the strands of a rope, with the track crossing six bridges between Rathdrum and the Meeting of the Waters. Several of these crossings are on nineteenth-century viaducts high above the water. At times the path leads upwards, so that we were high above the river, with almost aerial views of the water. At others the path runs alongside the riverbank, allowing us to stand beside the peat-filled water. From time to time we saw the darting movement of a dipper flying upstream like a missile fired from a cannon. On the lower sections of the river they mainly nest under bridges.[12]

We emerged from the woods for a short walk across a flat riverside field known as the Bottoms. Suddenly, without warning, two horses plunged into the river from the opposite bank and ploughed across the powerful flow to emerge from the water and gallop away into the field. I couldn't tell if they had escaped or if this was part of their normal daily routine, but there was no one nearby to ask. Jane Clarke evokes the excitement of this encounter in her poem 'Refuge' (2023):

a filly tracks her mother
    on the far side of the river

splashing and scrabbling
    through rocks along the edge

at a moss-mantled boulder
    impervious as a border post

the mare turns
    into the current

water swirls
    around her belly

churns high as her withers
    the Avonmore in spate

unwavering she trains her eyes
    on the other side

a clearing among hazel and birch
    flecked yellow with celandines

the foal traces her mother's steps –
    when the river reaches her breast

she raises her long and lovely head
    supple as willow

We then crossed the Lion Arch Bridge, which was
built in the early nineteenth century at the entrance
to the Castlehoward Estate. In 1986, following the
infamous Hurricane Charlie, this was one of four
bridges on the Avonmore that collapsed under the
weight of floodwater. The others were at Sally Gap,
Annamoe and Avoca village. It was said that large
hay bales being carried down in the flood caused the
initial damage to the stone structure.[13] As I leaned on
the stonework, an orange and blue flash shot out from
below the bridge: a kingfisher flying upstream, calling
loudly with a single note. There must be some suitable
earthen banks near here where the birds make their
nest burrows. Kingfishers are found mainly on the
central lowland section of the river.[14]

This section of our walk finished at the Meeting
of the Waters, made famous by the balladeer Thomas
Moore in his *Moore's Melodies*. Here the Avonmore is
joined by its sister river, the Avonbeg, flowing out of
Glenmalure. Looking into the water at the confluence,
it is quite obvious that water quality in the latter is
superior to that of the main channel, where the stones
are coated with green algae indicating that excess
nutrients are entering the water. The Waters of LIFE is

a European Integrated Project that aims to help reverse the deterioration of Ireland's most pristine waters, and the Avonmore has been selected as one of six catchments in the country for this innovative approach. The objective is to involve landowners, local authorities, local communities and homeowners in modifying land use practices such as farming, forestry and other activities that impact the upper reaches of the river.

Little river

Among the many tributaries of the Avonmore, the river that flows from the wide U-shaped valley of Glenmalure is one of the most beautiful. The upper section of the Avonbeg (*Abhainn Bheag*, meaning little river) is dominated by the towering slopes of Lugnaquilla, one of the highest mountains in Ireland. There is a wide ford across the river at Barravore, which we crossed on our way to the high rocky valley of Fraughan Rock Glen. This glen is bisected by a stream coming from the slopes of 'Lug'. Near the ford is what has been described as 'the last house in the glen'. This isolated building was owned and played host to some well-known characters from Irish literature and history. Maud Gonne bought the house in 1919 and entertained many people there

including Éamon de Valera, Erskine Childers and Sean
McBride. She was imprisoned for her part in the War
of Independence. She was also associated with the poet
William Butler Yeats and inspired many of his poems.
In 1937 the house was acquired by Dr Kathleen Lynn,
who was best known for her part in the 1916 Rising. It
later became a youth hostel.[15]

Further downstream, the Avonbeg River winds its
way past the ruins of an early nineteenth-century British
Army barracks at Drumgoff. This was one of a string
of military installations built to accommodate soldiers
sent to County Wicklow after the 1798 rebellion. These
barracks were strung out about a day's march apart,
along the Military Road that led from Dublin city into
the heart of the Wicklow Mountains. Until this last
section of road was built in 1809, there were only two
possible approaches to this isolated valley, from the
west across Table Mountain or from the east through
the town of Rathdrum.

Close to the old stone bridge at Drumgoff Barracks
is the steep cliff known as Dwyer's Rock. It is named
after Michael Dwyer, a small farmer in the valley and
one of the leaders of the 1798 rebellion. He had joined
the United Irishmen the previous year and was quickly

given a prominent role with the rebels. He fought in the Battle of Arklow and subsequently at Vinegar Hill in Enniscorthy, County Wexford, where the insurgents were defeated by a better-equipped British force. With a group of surviving rebels, Dwyer escaped to his mountain hideout in Glenmalure, from where he carried out raids on the authorities long after all other rebels had been captured or killed. With Robert Emmet he began plotting a new uprising and undertook to raise 5,000 men from County Wicklow. But the 1803 Dublin rising collapsed within a day, and Emmet was quickly executed. Yet such was the stature, real or imagined, of Dwyer that he was able to negotiate a remarkable surrender deal that exiled him to Australia.[16]

Near to Dwyer's Rock is the Glenmalure Lodge, once known as Drumgoff Inn, and opened by an Englishman named Wiseman who expected substantial business from the billeted British officers. Some famous writers, including Thomas Moore and Evelyn Waugh, stayed here and the hotel is now a well-known stop for hillwalkers. Down by the river, there is a mobile sauna called *Bosca Beatha*, which was hand built in Ireland with natural materials that give it a unique character. All the lights run on solar energy, and the sauna is heated by a wood-fired stove which creates a cosy authentic atmosphere. Enthusiasts find it a refreshing and sociable way to spend an hour or two, sitting in the sweltering heat of the sauna and then plunging into the icy waters of the river.

Ballinacor

Ballinacor, at the eastern end of the valley, was for centuries a stronghold of the powerful clan the O'Byrnes, whose best-known leader was Fiach McHugh O'Byrne. From the remoteness and relative safety of Glenmalure, this clan played a cat-and-mouse game with the Elizabethan English who, more or less, ruled Ireland in the sixteenth century. McHugh O'Byrne and his allies ambushed and massacred a substantial Elizabethan force here in 1580, inflicting a rare defeat on the Crown, although their leader was captured and killed seventeen years later. Today Ballinacor is still a large, wooded estate and farm, bordered on the east by the Avonbeg River, which here descends in a series of picturesque cascades and pools. My friend Paddy Woodworth, who lives beside the river, regularly watches from his deck as dippers and grey wagtails feed on this stretch. Very occasionally he also sees goosanders and kingfishers here. Together Paddy and I explored the extensive old woods in Ballinacor with the permission of their owner. Despite the presence of many fine oak trees and swathes of bluebells in spring, the woods are essentially dying due to lack of regeneration, as the large numbers of deer browse any young trees. We listened to great spotted woodpeckers drumming and saw some of the young fledglings in the trees.

From here the Avonbeg flows downstream to a bridge at Greenan where Byrne's traditional pub, unchanged over decades, has been turned into a small grocery shop. With the gradient levelling out, the river begins to meander until it passes beneath a lovely old stone bridge in the small village of Ballinaclash – locally known simply as 'Clash'. The village is mentioned in J.M. Synge's play *The Tinker's Wedding*: 'And a big fool I was too, maybe; but we'll be seeing Jaunting Jim to-morrow in Ballinaclash, and he after getting a great price for his white foal in the horse-fair of Wicklow.'

Shortly before reaching the confluence with the Avonmore, Paddy and I came on a beautiful wet meadow, known as the Bottoms, in a large bend of the river. Here we found some traditional hay meadow plants such as yarrow, knapweed and marsh thistle, while clouds of meadow brown butterflies rose up as we walked. We met the owner of this special field, Darragh Byrne, who is also a fly fisherman. He took us to look at the riverbank where he was busy removing heaps of rubbish and all the remaining barbed wire fences. He told us that his love of the place began when, as a boy, he caught a large trout in the river. On our visit, we saw lots of small trout in the crystal-clear water, and a kingfisher flashed by on the way to its nest in the riverbank upstream. Darragh has decided to remove grazing livestock from the meadow in summer to allow its wildflowers and insect life to prosper. I commended Darragh on his commitment to enhancing nature here.

Not far away, where the Avonbeg joins the Avonmore River, we stopped for a welcome coffee at the Meetings Pub, where the owners Daireacha and Derek Fulham also run a delightful little shop selling local crafts. As we gazed at this famous beauty spot from the pub veranda, a dipper emerged from beneath the old three-arch stone bridge nearby, where it had its nest. It was time to resume my exploration of this fascinating river valley.

Paddling past the mines

From here downstream the waters are known as the Avoca River. As access to the riverbank becomes more difficult further on, I resolved to take to the water in a canoe with my friend Cormac Byrne. This is the ideal way to see the river from a kingfisher's perspective. But we had to wait for the autumn rains to come, to swell the river and provide the consistent depth that we needed for the canoe. The concrete plinth at the Meeting of the Waters provided an ideal launching place, so we loaded on a few provisions and some drinking water for the day and pushed off. I had done some canoeing a long time ago but mastering the art of guiding this lightweight craft was like learning to ride a bicycle backwards. Balance is one thing but guiding the canoe between rocks and under low-hanging branches took some learning. John Connell described it well in his book *The Stream of Everything*:[17]

> After some careful work we figure out our own method of steering. We call them the hard lefts and the hard rights and when we want to turn, we both pull outwards on the same side. It's early days, but the hard turns work and, when we

need to, I call out the instructions like a race car navigator.

As we paddled down the river between wooded banks, we saw chimneys and other ruined buildings on the valley sides. These are all that remains of the historic Avoca mines that once provided much-needed employment in this rural area. Copper mining began in Avoca around 1720 and continued, with some breaks, for the next 260 years. The mining of high-grade seams using only hand tools in the eighteenth and nineteenth centuries gave way to mechanised mining of relatively low-grade copper ore in the second half of the twentieth century. Historically the mine was subdivided into a series of small properties, or setts, although in modern times the site has generally been divided simply into east and west of the valley. Unfortunately, throughout the period of mining operations and for long after, acidic metal-rich mine water has drained directly into the river, causing severe contamination and disruption of the aquatic ecosystem. This led to the unwelcome classification of the Avoca as one of the six most polluted rivers in Ireland. Various attempts have been made in the past to clean up the mine waste, but none has been entirely successful.

Discharge of poorly treated wastewater from various towns and villages along the river has also been an ongoing problem. In 2022 the semi-state agency Irish Water unveiled plans to upgrade the water treatment plant in the village of Avoca with the inclusion of a new reedbed to process treated sludge. It is estimated that the new reedbed will reduce the current transport of sludge, thereby reducing carbon emissions. Efforts are being made in the planning for a new treatment plant to enhance biodiversity at the site through habitat creation. The new treatment plant is expected to have the capability to serve 1,900 houses, treating a large volume of raw sewage per day before safe discharge. This will mark a big change from the current process where wastewater is discharged directly into the river from a storm overflow pipe in the village.

Weavers and kites

Just upstream of the village of Avoca we stopped for a break at the famous Avoca weaving mill. A quick visit to the old weaving shed proved to be a fascinating introduction to the heritage of this local industry. It all

started in 1723 when a cooperative weaving mill was set
up along the banks of the Avoca River, the wheels driven
by the power of the water. Here, local farmers could
have their corn milled and their wool spun and woven.
At first only uncoloured yarn was used for weaving
at the mill. Later, though, this would all change when
coloured dyes came to the valleys. Natural vegetable
dyes in reds, greens and yellows began to be used.
These would become the signature hues of Avoca. The
old hand loom is still in use here, but the skill of the
handweaver is a trade that is in danger of dying out. By
the end of the eighteenth century, the valley of Avoca
was a busy and vibrant community mining copper,
zinc, lead and gold.

As we passed slowly down the river we were
accompanied by several large birds of prey overhead.
These were all red kites, distinguished by the rufus
colour of their plumage and a forked tail. They
seemed to glide effortlessly on their long narrow
wings, occasionally twisting their tails to change
direction, like the way a pilot uses rudder flaps. Kites
were once common throughout Ireland, feeding on
small mammals and birds while also performing a
useful function in scavenging carrion, including dead

rabbits and rats. They were even known to scavenge in towns and cities. However, their reputation for taking poultry and young game birds did not do them any favours, and they were persecuted by shooting and poisoning until they became extinct around the seventeenth century.[18] In 2000, plans were drafted for a reintroduction programme steered by the Golden Eagle Trust, and Avoca in the centre of Wicklow was chosen for the release site as it closely resembles the wooded valleys and small farms of central Wales where the last native red kites in these islands survived. By now over a hundred pairs are breeding in the east of Ireland in one of the most successful rewilding projects ever undertaken in this country.

The wooden bridge

At Woodenbridge, I left the canoe for another adventure on land. The townland takes its name from several timber bridges in the area which were swept away by a flood in 1770, although the Irish name *Garraí na nGabhlán* means 'garden of the river fork'. Here the Avoca River is joined by two tributaries. The Aughrim River drains from south-west Wicklow while the smaller Goldmine River flows from the south. Near the confluence is the

Woodenbridge Hotel which was established as long ago as 1608. This building overlooks the spot where, in September 1914, the MP John Redmond called on local Irish volunteers to postpone their struggle for Home Rule and join the British Army on the battlefields of France. There is a memorial on the banks of the Aughrim River which commemorates the 1,192 Wicklow men who sadly lost their lives in the subsequent Great War. They did not live long enough to take part in the historic 1916 Rising and Irish independence.

Here I met my friend Paddy again, and together we walked upstream along the old railway line that runs inland, following closely the Aughrim River as far as Shillelagh in the extreme south of County Wicklow. The track itself closed in the 1950s, but the hardcore stones are still present on some substantial embankments running through the wet ground along the river. There is a proposal to create a shared cycleway and footpath for pedestrians here. The proposal is to use the old railway line between Woodenbridge and Shillelagh for parts of the greenway, as it offers a flat, ready-made route. Some historical buildings associated with the old railway line are still in place in Shillelagh, Aughrim and Woodenbridge.

On the north side of the river, not far upstream from Woodenbridge, is a fish farm that diverts water from the Aughrim River. The long parallel ponds are packed with rainbow trout which are fed daily to fatten them for market. In 2020 an inspection of the fish farm by the Department of Agriculture, Food and the Marine reported that these ponds held a total of eighty-four tonnes of trout. To deter fish-feeding birds such as herons and cormorants the ponds are covered with lines of fine wires. However, both bird species were present on the Aughrim River, suggesting that they may benefit from the occasional escaped trout. We also saw a large dead trout in the river below a bridge. I worried that the fish farm might have negative impacts on water quality downstream or that rainbow trout might escape to compete with the wild fish populations here.

Following the old railway line upstream towards Aughrim proved to be a challenge in places as it is heavily overgrown. We struggled through fallen trees and brambles and over barbed wire fences while passing a stand of the invasive Japanese knotweed on the riverbank. Undoubtedly fragments of the plant have floated down the river and lodged here in the bank. This is one of the most difficult invasive plants to remove, and it is best not to disturb it as it can grow back from even tiny fragments. Eventually, we reached the large tree nursery run by the Van der Wel family. From here we passed the old flour mill in Aughrim which dates back to the seventeenth century and was fully powered by water diverted from the Aughrim River. The mill was owned by the Fogarty family and provided much-needed local employment for many years. There was even a railway siding leading into the mill. The rail branch was closed in 1952, and in 1963 the flour mill ceased production.

At Aughrim, the river is joined by two tributaries, the Tinnakilly River and the Ow River, the latter flowing off the flanks of Lugnaquilla. The main channel upstream of Aughrim is known as the Derry Water (from the Irish word *doire*, meaning oakwood). The entire valley between here and Shillelagh was once filled with old woodlands, many of which were managed by the Coolattin Estate as 'coppice with standards'. This means that the oak and hazel trees were cut on a long rotation with the regrowth coming up as multiple stems. The harvested stems were used for many purposes on farms, from fence posts to roofs of buildings. Some of the 'standard' oaks were left to

Meeting of the Waters

grow to maturity, ultimately providing quality timber for long boards, much of which was exported through the port of Arklow.[19]

Lower valley

From Woodenbridge, the enlarged Avoca River holds deep water in most months of the year. Not far downstream we passed between two large estates and the stately homes of Glenart Castle and Shelton Abbey. The abbey was built in 1770 and became the ancestral seat of the Earls of Wicklow, originally serving as a mansion house. By 1951, Shelton Abbey had been purchased by the Irish State and repurposed as a residential training facility for forestry workers. In the early 1970s, it once again changed its role, this time serving as a low-security prison for men. Across the valley, Glenart Castle was originally built as a hunting lodge around the same time as the abbey, but in the 1800s it was enlarged and redesigned as a castellated house by John Proby, the first Earl of Carysfort. It later became a hotel but today is used as a holiday home and is closed for much of the year. I made a visit here one day as I was curious to see the present condition of the castle. Walking up a long, winding driveway through the woods, I finally came to an enormous castellated mansion surrounded by towering oak and lime trees. Sadly, the building was partly abandoned, and there was a collection of vintage cars parked outside the grand front door, each with grass growing through the wheels.

Both the abbey and the castle are surrounded by extensive woodlands reaching right down the riverbanks on both sides. This gives the valley a quiet secluded atmosphere broken only by the clatter of a passing train on its way to the station in Arklow. After a short distance, the woods give way to a large industrial site, much of which now lies vacant and derelict. This was the site of a major fertiliser factory owned by the state. It became quite controversial in its early years as the sulphurous emissions from its chimneys killed off a large number of trees in the area, leaving a devastated landscape. In recent times it has been partly revived as a business park, and it was here that I went in the early 2000s to carry out a bird survey as a prerequisite for the development of wind turbines on the site. To get a good vantage point over the whole valley I was given access to one of the disused towers and climbed a winding staircase inside to emerge on a high platform. Scanning the area with a telescope I was able to record a wide variety of bird species including buzzard, red kite and peregrine while herons and an occasional cormorant flew up the river.

The great estuary

On the northern outskirts of Arklow town, there is a large marshland fringed by oak trees. The marsh is bisected by an old road that once served as a driveway linking Shelton Abbey with the town. Much of the western end has been drained and dried out, but the lower end, nearest the town, still retains an extensive reedbed. On this marsh I undertook a range of ecological studies in the early 2000s in support of plans for a flood relief scheme. The long stone arched bridge across the river in the town was built on a concrete plinth that acts as a dam for floodwaters, and properties on the northern side of the town have been frequently flooded in past years. Arklow native Jackie Burke described a vivid recollection from the 1930s and 1940s:

> The floodwaters covered the marsh so that only the tops of the bushes were visible. Dead cattle, sheep and pigs were seen being swept down in the flood.

The flood walls were known to reach the hall door
of Shelton Abbey. When the floods subsided, I have
seen salmon and trout left in the remaining pools of
water and dead rabbits caught up in the bushes.[20]

Unfortunately, the river has also been on the
receiving end of untreated sewage discharges from
the town over many years, adding to the pollution
problems caused by mine waste from further upstream.
For decades the water was so contaminated that
migrating salmon could only pass through in extreme
flood conditions to reach their spawning grounds in
the upper reaches of the Avonmore catchment.

The Irish name of Arklow, *An tInbhear Mór*, means
'the great estuary'. Arklow Harbour was once a
thriving fishing port with hundreds of small sailing
smacks tied up along the keys. As I walked among the
small houses and narrow lanes leading from the main
street down to the quaysides, I imagined a time when
the livelihoods of many local families depended on the
sea. As well as hundreds of fishermen and fish sellers,
local women worked on processing fish for export and
on the manufacture and repair of fishing nets. Since
at least the 1770s, the Tyrrell family designed, built or

skippered boats out of Arklow. The shipbuilder John Tyrrell founded a family business here in 1864 and, after building dozens of fishing smacks and other sailboats, he and his son built the firm's first motor-powered yacht in 1904. The Arklow Maritime Museum on the North Quay is full of fascinating historical information on the town and its links with the sea including the building here in 1981 of the traditional sail training ship *Asgard II*, which eventually sank in the Bay of Biscay in 2008.

On the lower part of the river is a sheltered harbour known locally as The Dock. This is still a place for small inshore trawlers and lobster boats but is increasingly being taken over by the tugs and workboats that service Ireland's only existing offshore wind farm on the Arklow Bank. In one corner is the Lifeboat Station where many local fishermen served as volunteers over the centuries.

A river remembers

My arrival in Arklow marked the end of this marathon exploration of the great Avonmore River system in its many forms from the source to the sea. I have seen its lifespan, from the vigorous rushing streams of the mountains to the sluggish, silty tide of the estuary.

But the river has existed for many thousands of years more than I can comprehend, from the melting of the glaciers, through the removal of its woodland cover and the mining of minerals throughout the valley, to modern times when some efforts are at last being made to bring nature back here. Following the river has led me to a rich treasure trove of hidden histories. It has also taught me how the river links the communities along its banks and how some visionary individuals can change the narrative from exploitation to restoration.

This journey has given me the first-hand experience I needed to understand how a whole river system works together. The river water merges into the lakes, slowing down for a quiet rest before resuming its urgent journey to the sea. Where streams converge, they mix their loads of peat and sediments and much other debris picked up along the way. I have seen the river system in winter, where trickling streams emerge from the snow cover of the mountains, and when the full, peat-stained flow fills the lower channels. I have seen it in spring when the woodlands along its banks take on their green mantle and bird life busies itself with another breeding season. In summer, the water drops so low that I can wade across from one bank to another and gravel bars, formed after thousands of years of erosion, are exposed to the air. By autumn, the water surface carries the messages contained in millions of leaves and tree seeds as they float downstream to their next resting place. This is just one of the thousands of river–lake systems in our wet country, some of which I will explore in the next two chapters.

Rivers

Smooth it glides upon its travel,
Here a wimple, there a gleam –
O the clean gravel!
O the smooth stream!

Sailing blossoms, silver fishes,
Pave pools as clear as air –
How a child wishes
To live down there!

From 'Looking-Glass River' (1885)
by ROBERT LOUIS STEVENSON

When I stand beside the clear bubbling water of the river that flows through our farm, I look up to the hill where it rises, a rocky summit called Carrick covered in heather and gorse. Here the water trickles from springs and boggy hollows to coalesce in several small streams that eventually form a single channel. Generations of local farmers used the river to water their livestock and drained their wetter fields to ensure that the water ran more quickly down the slope. In times of heavy rainfall, the river becomes a raging torrent, carrying brown peaty water off the hill, down the valley and through the village. The debris of fallen branches and leaves is washed downstream, gravel beds are washed clean of silt, and the floods allow trout and salmon to move upstream to their traditional spawning grounds. It is likely that the river has been running here, just like this, since the last glaciers retreated many thousands of years ago.

There is a legend that all the Irish rivers were created by a single hailstorm. It is an example of the mythology that surrounds many of our natural waterways, the rivers and lakes, streams and springs. Even the names of Irish rivers have their origins in folklore. There are religious overtones too as the goddesses of the Tuatha Dé Danann were worshipped as symbols of life while others derive from legendary characters such as Fionn mac Cumhaill, the Fir Bolg and the Children of Lir. The goddess Boen is the character after whom the River Boyne is named. The Shannon is named after the goddess Sionnan, granddaughter of Manannán Mac Lir the Son of the Sea. Sionnan means 'possessor of wisdom'. She is said to have eaten the Salmon of Knowledge and thus became the wisest person in the world. Whatever about the origin of these stories, the facts surrounding Irish rivers are equally fascinating.

River facts

When you look at a map of Ireland showing all of the rivers, each one appears like a cluster of upturned tree roots with a massive and complicated network of channels. Moving upstream, the larger roots divide again and again into more and more tributaries so that the smallest streams are like the mass of fibrous roots that gather water for a tree. These first- and second-order streams make up three-quarters of the river network, with only about 85,000 kilometres of these smaller watercourses mapped so far. Tiny drainage ditches that do not feature on the map at all would probably double the total length of the channel.

Because of the saucer shape of the island most rivers, just like the one that flows through our farm, are relatively short, rising on coastal hills and mountain ranges and flowing directly to the sea. Those that flow across the relatively flat midland counties tend to be the longest rivers with the largest catchments. The Shannon is by far the longest river network in Ireland with over 10,000 kilometres of measured channel. It can be claimed by eleven counties, with rainwater landing on around one-seventh of the entire island flowing into it. Following the Shannon, the other most important rivers, in order of catchment size, are the Bann, Erne, Suir, Munster Blackwater, Corrib, Barrow, Foyle, Boyne, Nore and Slaney.[1]

Bill Quirke is a freshwater biologist who worked for many years in Killarney, County Kerry. He wrote:

As is the case in the woods and mountains, an intricate web of life thrives in the world of water. This web of life is sustained by a constant supply of nutrients dissolved in the water and in the form of soil, peat and plant debris washed into the rivers. The greater the supply of nutrients, the more abundant the growth of plant life in the water, both visible and microscopic. The more plentiful the plant growth, the more abundant are the animals which feed on them: a menagerie of strange and wonderful animals, mostly tiny clinging, crawling and burrowing animals. The lakes are home to even more mysterious communities of plants and animals. Here, as in the rivers, the supply of nutrients is a vital factor.[2]

The most abundant forms of animal life in river water are the invertebrates (animals without backbones) that range in size from tiny organisms, visible only under a microscope, to large shellfish such as the freshwater pearl mussel. Some invertebrates are found living on the beds of all types of rivers, from fast-moving mountain streams tumbling over waterfalls to the slow-flowing, meandering stages of a mature watercourse. Turning over a large stone in the riverbed is the best way to see these. Here you will find larval stages of caddisflies, stoneflies, mayflies, true flies and beetles, freshwater shrimps and crayfish, leeches and worms, as well as snails and freshwater shellfish. Some of these animals, such as the worms and molluscs, spend all of their lives in the water while the insect larvae will metamorphose into delicate winged adults that fly about laying eggs to produce the next generation.[3]

The life in a river is directly related to the rock types over which it flows and the nature of the land in its catchment or watershed. Naturally acidic rivers, such as those flowing off granite or quartzite, are low in nutrients and support a limited range of animals. Their origins are often in open peatland habitats such as blanket bogs and wet heaths. These habitats soak up water at times of high rainfall and release it slowly during drier months in the same way that continental catchments store water as snow in winter and release it slowly in spring and summer as snow melt. Lowland waters, winding through lime-rich soils, are often more alkaline in nature with abundant nutrients that support many forms of plant and animal life. They are found in landscapes with more productive mineral soils that would typically support woodlands, most of which have been cleared over the millennia for agriculture.

The prehistoric waterways

The earliest settlers in Ireland arrived during the Mesolithic period (Middle Stone Age) about 10,000 years ago. Archaeologists in previous centuries noted that coastal locations – particularly dunes and raised beaches – were good sources of ancient artefacts and

this led them to believe that Mesolithic settlements were
confined to the coastal strip. The antiquarian R.A.S.
Macalister even argued that the first settlers were
'content with the molluscs of the shores, with trapped
birds or captured fish. Thus, easily satisfied, they made
no effort to explore the interior of the country, where
all was unknown and full of dread'.[4] More recently
this misinterpretation has been exploded as sites of
Mesolithic date are now known across the full extent
of Ireland, including many locations some distance
from the coast.[5] The early settlers probably followed
the course of the larger rivers in canoes, right into
the interior of the island. Here they found a watery
wilderness, a maze of lakes, braided rivers, islands and
wet woodlands the like of which has largely vanished
from the landscape today. In these habitats they
encountered an abundance of wild mammals and birds
to hunt, and fish to catch in basket traps.[6]

The houses of Mesolithic people were probably
made from wood, bark, reeds and animal skins. They
moved home frequently as the waters rose and fell
and as their prey species migrated or became wary
of the hunters. Between more permanent settlements
on the drier hills, the wetlands stretched for many

kilometres, and these Stone Age people lived here largely in harmony with their surroundings, just like the animals that they hunted. Survival often depended on the ability not only to hunt and forage for food but also to preserve some of that food for the harsher times of year.

Fishing would also have been an important food-gathering activity for these Stone Age peoples, as evidenced by the recent discoveries of wooden fishing structures on the lower reaches of the River Liffey in Dublin[7] and fish baskets from Clowanstown, County Meath. The Liffey structures are of particular importance in the current context as it has been suggested that the material used in their construction was derived from woodland that had been coppiced. The Clowanstown baskets were located on the edge of what was a small lake during the Mesolithic but is now the edge of a cutover raised bog. Four almost-complete baskets were identified alongside some additional fragments that may have belonged to other baskets. The baskets were manufactured from alder, birch and other locally available woodland material.

There is evidence that sea levels in the Stone Age were very different from today so that the lower reaches

of the River Shannon would have flowed through a
complex mosaic of estuarine and freshwater wetlands
with mudflats, saltmarshes, reedswamps, fens and
bogs giving way inland to a scrubby landscape of wet
woodland. The settlements were probably located on
the drier ground of intervening hills, but the people
would have foraged, hunted and fished extensively in
the wetland areas. Excavations in a peat deposit beside
a stream at Ballycahane Lower, County Limerick
produced burnt, heat-shattered stones and wild boar
bones dating from around 6,000 years ago.[8]

I can imagine these early people living in the
lowlands in a diverse, mainly forested environment,
interspersed with braided streams and rivers winding
between multiple lakes and fens. One of the few
remaining examples of this type of habitat is at the
Gearagh, located within a large reservoir confined
by two dams at Inniscarra and Carrigadrohid on the
River Lee. This unusual area formed where the river
divides into a complex network of channels weaving
through a maze of wooded islands. Just like natural
predators, early hunters stalked their prey, such as
ducks, and fished in the channels to supplement their
diet of mainly foraged plant foods.[9] There were other

mammal predators too, such as the brown bear, that almost certainly preyed on migrating salmon moving up the streams. The earliest fossil remains of the otter were found at a site in County Galway and are from the Bronze Age, approximately 4,000 years ago.[10]

Water dog

One of the Irish names for the otter, *an madra uisce* meaning 'the water dog', perfectly describes its lifestyle. With a preference for living in water, otters are among the few surviving large carnivores that have managed to find a niche living alongside intensive human use of the landscape. Another name is *dobharchú*, a combination of the two words *dobhar* and *cú*, meaning 'water hound', in reference to its dog-like appearance and aquatic lifestyle. They are opportunistic predators that can take advantage of whatever is available in a particular season or in whatever habitat they live. In rivers their favourite prey includes sticklebacks, salmon, trout, eels and freshwater crayfish.[11] I remember some years ago walking on the banks of the River Shannon in County Longford. The grass close to the end of a series of weirs was littered with the distinctive droppings (or spraints) of otter, many containing the unmistakable remains of the crayfish – tiny claws, carapace and antennae. These slow-moving crustaceans must be relatively easy for the otters to catch in shallow waters near the bank. Frogs are also an easily caught prey item at certain times of year, especially when they are spawning in the spring.

From the house where I began writing this book, I looked out on a network of artificial ponds and lakes that drain into the Murrough wetlands in east Wicklow. From there I could see a pair of mute swans, the female sitting tightly on her large nest of reed stems and the male (or cob) patrolling around the water, his wings raised to make him look formidable to any competitor or predator. He had good reason to be afraid. The previous year the pair raised five cygnets and, when they were fully grown, they were each killed in a series of attacks by an otter under the cover of darkness. Piles of brown and white feathers on the water's edge told a sad tale, for the swans.

On land the otter moves in sinuous bounds, arching its back like a stoat. Its short legs are clearly not designed for the land, the webbed feet revealing its true habitat. Although for much of year it travels widely within its home range, when the time approaches to give birth a female will seek out a cavity on the riverbank called a holt. Muddy slides on the riverbank are signs that the otter is here quite often. Once in the water, its powerful tail becomes the engine propelling it through the water.

In Ireland, the otter occurs throughout the freshwater networks from upland streams to lowland lakes and rivers and right down to the coast. Although they seldom travel too far from water, otters can cross stretches of dry land between river valleys where, unfortunately, they sometimes become road casualties. A male (or dog) otter may have a territory involving tens of kilometres of river tributaries and even several catchments, with larger areas exploited in the uplands where river prey is scarce. In a diverse lowland river with a wide variety of prey, the core territory may be as little as a few kilometres. Survey work on otters concentrates on the distinctive spraining sites which tend to be at consistent and traditional locations, such as large boulders in rivers and streams or on the supporting buttresses of old stone bridges. Once found, it is easy to confirm an otter has been here by a quick sniff of the black, spiky dropping which gives off a musky or fishy odour. I have found these spraints all over the country – even under bridges in city centres. I call them 'smellograms' as they contain the scent from a special gland under the otter's tail that identifies this individual to other otters and provides key information on age, sex and breeding status for a population that is widely dispersed and where individuals rarely meet.

I regularly see small trout in the river that runs along the boundary of our own farm in County Wicklow. So I decided to do a simple experiment to see what else was using the watercourse. From my local fishmonger I got the head and tail of a large trout and placed these on a boulder in the centre of the river with an infrared sensor camera mounted on a nearby tree to watch the site. After just a few hours, I saw the distinctive images of an adult otter emerging from the water to take the fish remains before diving back in again. The otter was followed shortly afterwards by a fox that scavenged the few remaining fragments. I had no idea that the otter was so close to our land and probably patrolled up and down the river on its regular hunting expeditions.

In his classic book *Tarka the Otter*, first published in 1927, Henry Williamson described the life of a wild otter and the wonderful natural habitats that then existed in the rivers Taw and Torridge in north Devon. 'The eldest and biggest of the litter was a dog cub, and when he drew his first breath, he was less than five inches long from his nose to where his tail joined his back-bone.'[12] By the 1970s otters had all but disappeared from England and had even become extinct in a number of countries across Europe. This was linked with a post-war rise in the use of agricultural pesticides (such as DDT, dieldrin and aldrin) which became concentrated in their fish prey. The declines were much less marked in Ireland where farming was then generally less intensive, although there were some signs of decline between 1980 and 2006. With the banning of the worst of these chemicals, the otter population has now recovered and there are few rivers or lakes where it is not present. Today, the Eurasian otter has a very wide distribution right across the northern hemisphere. Calculating the population size of an animal that is widely distributed but rarely seen can be tricky, but the best current estimate for the island of Ireland is about 16,000 to 20,000 individuals.[13] The future of these beautiful animals depends on clean water, undisturbed areas for breeding and, most of all, a healthy population of fish.

Fish kill

One winter's day, I was gazing into the clear water in the river running through our farm when I noticed a silvery reflection from the sand on the riverbed. Wading into knee-deep water, I reached down and picked up a small trout about the size of my middle finger. It was dead but still had a beautiful, speckled appearance to its miniature scales. Then I noticed more and more of these little fish at different places on the riverbed. I walked downstream along the bank searching carefully in the water, and after an hour I had a bucketful of dead trout, some big enough to fill my hand. Talking to a local fisheries inspector later, I learnt that there had been a spill of slurry in a field that borders our river further up the valley and this pulse of polluted water had made its way downstream and into the main river a kilometre away. It was too late to do anything about it then, but I resolved to be more vigilant in future, especially when slurry was being spread on the local fields.

Fish kills usually occur because a sudden rise in the level of nutrients, such as nitrates or phosphates, in the water causes depletion of oxygen and the fish literally suffocate to death. Other causes are the release of toxic chemicals, including pesticides, or the presence of large volumes of silt washed into the river from surrounding land. All of these threats are preventable by good land management but in the 1980s there were fewer controls on farming and forestry and fish kills were a frequent occurrence. Fortunately, most fish populations can recover naturally, provided their habitat and the water quality return to normal and that there are no further pollution incidents.

A more insidious cause of fish kills is the enrichment of a riverbed over a long time. This is due to increased nutrient loadings, primarily an increase in the concentrations of phosphorous from fertilisers. The enrichment results in a multiplying of plant life – both higher plants and bottom-dwelling algae. Such a superabundant growth of plants gives rise to not only very high oxygen concentrations during the day (more than 120 per cent is not unusual) but also the release of high concentrations of carbon dioxide at night. This results in very low oxygen levels around dawn, which can cause localised but pernicious fish kills. Such fish kills often go unnoticed, but over time they can denude a stretch of river or stream of its salmon and trout. As we encounter more extremes in water temperatures and much lower water levels due to climate change, the level of organic pollution in our rivers needs to be reduced to an absolute minimum to avoid such disasters.

Trout, such as those that I found in my local river, are among the very few species of freshwater fish that we can call truly native to Ireland. That is, they have been present in our rivers since the end of the last Ice Age. Salmon, eel, shad and lamprey are in the same category and all of these fish share the characteristic that they are migratory, spending parts of their life cycle in the sea and part in freshwater. When the glaciers finally receded from the land some 12,000 years ago, Ireland was already an island, separated from Britain and the continent of Europe. So, freshwater fish moving through rivers and lakes from the south were unable to cross the sea to Irish rivers unless they had evolved a phase of their lives like the salmon in which they naturally took to the ocean.

This is confirmed by evidence from archaeological sites. A good quantity of fish bones was found at Mount Sandel on the Bann Estuary in County Derry, the earliest known human settlement in Ireland, dating from more than 9,000 years ago. Apart from coastal fish such as bass and flounder, the only freshwater species identified from these bones were salmon, trout and eel.[14] In the millennia that followed a wide variety of fish were introduced to Irish freshwaters by the people who lived along their banks. These included popular angling targets such as bream and perch, while dace and roach are both considered invasive alien species requiring control. Despite these invaders, brown trout, salmon and eel are still widespread in Irish rivers, with trout in particular found in almost every stream, river and lake where they have not been displaced by introduced species.[15]

Against the flow

The salmon and sea trout that appear in Ireland every year from their maritime travels return exclusively to their natal rivers which they can sense from the water in the estuaries. These have been described as 'families of spawners that distribute themselves throughout the river according to the best spawning sites'.[16] The individual tributaries where they hatched have distinctive characters, unique like our fingerprints, that the fish recognise instinctively. As they move up the freshwater channels, they must negotiate many hurdles and hazards such as waterfalls, weirs, low water levels,

water pollution and drainage schemes that speed the
flow. But they press on regardless to reach the tiny
tributaries where they must lay their eggs. This innate
urge to reach the headwaters is captured in Jane
Clarke's poem 'Against the Flow' (2015):

> One day you knew you must turn,
> begin to swim against the current,
>
> leave the estuary waters, brackish
> with sediment, head upstream
>
> through riffles and deeps,
> millraces that churn in spate,
>
> over sheets of granite, across weirs,
> into rapids that thunder-pound,
>
> squeeze between boulders
> to the upper reaches of the river,
>
> those waters of blanket-bog brown,
> where you'd find a place in gravel and silt
>
> to hollow a dip,
> to spawn a life of your own.

Sadly, populations of Atlantic salmon have plummeted in Irish waters over the last three decades. I asked Dr Ken Whelan, fisheries expert and angler, why this has happened. He explained that, 'In the past, we might have expected up to thirty grilse, or one-sea-winter salmon, to return from every 100 salmon smolts migrating to sea. Currently most rivers are lucky to see five to eight salmon return to their native waters.' On the River Bush on the north coast of County Antrim, for example, overall survival from smolt to adult is less than 10 per cent, although thirty years ago it was 30 per cent.[17]

Work is ongoing to find out why so many fish are dying at sea. Whelan says that 'at present, it would seem that warming oceans, due to the effects of climate change, are the most likely cause of the stock collapse. In these circumstances it is more important than ever to eliminate the man-made pressures impacting on rivers where they spawn and to maximise the numbers of wild healthy salmon smolts heading back for the ocean.' Whelan also says:

Sea trout populations are stronger across the country, except in the Connemara area where, in

the early 1990s, populations were decimated by the
effects of sea lice from salmon farms. Tragically
many of the more seriously affected fisheries have
seen little if any improvement in their sea trout
stock levels. Facing into the full impacts of climate
change, high water temperature levels in the small
streams where sea trout spawn may well become
a very serious issue and major programmes are
required to revegetate the banks of streams in order
to provide welcome shade to these delicate habitats.

The importance of small coastal streams for salmon
and sea trout has often been overlooked in favour of
the larger angling rivers such as the Moy, the Boyne
and the Shannon. Because of their size, small streams
are particularly at risk from the predicted changes in
temperature and flow regimes resulting from climate
change. Already these small acid rivers have suffered
from peatland drainage, resulting in a reduced sponge
effect (a loss of temporary storage) and less stable flows.
It has been argued that recruitment of fish hatched
in such streams may be of critical importance to the
abundance of sea trout in the neighbouring coastal
margins. There is evidence that the bulk of sea trout

eggs are provided by the one- and two-year old sea trout. This adaptation is ideally suited to the physical nature of these transitory coastal streams.[18]

Salmon and trees

The miracle of salmon returning each year from the sea to their natal rivers happens all around the globe. The yearly return of salmon from the open Pacific Ocean to coastal rivers of western North America is one of nature's grand displays, and recent investigations by researchers in Washington State, British Columbia and Alaska indicate that the salmon's signature marks both aquatic and terrestrial ecosystems, as far inland as the Rocky Mountains. The most widespread predators associated with these formerly immense schools of salmon are black and grizzly bears, which migrate from alpine and distant habitats to congregate along streams and rivers during the spawning migration of salmon.

Recent studies show that these predators play a much more significant ecological role in coastal forests than was previously recognised. During an investigation into the foraging behaviour of black bear on Queen Charlotte Island in Canada, Tom Reimchen found that individual bears captured up to 700 largely spawned-out salmon over the six-week spawning period. They carried the majority of these into the forest where they could feed relatively undisturbed by competitors. In all, 8 bears transferred 3,000 salmon into the forest from a 1-kilometre length of stream where the fish spawned. On average, about one-half of each salmon carcass was consumed by the bears and the remnants were scavenged by eagles, martens and flocks of crows, ravens and gulls. A diversity of insects, including flies and beetles, were found with the carcasses and typically within five days, all carcasses were a seething mass of maggots which consumed all remaining soft tissues, leaving the bone. Amazingly, the cumulative effect of all these decomposing carcasses combined with the faecal and urine discharge from bears and other animals has been detected in the vegetation.[19]

Researchers in Alaska and Washington State have shown evidence of nitrogen enrichment in aquatic and streamside vegetation. One study sampled needles or leaves from ten riparian plant species, including the native tree western hemlock and a further ten plant species from some twenty watersheds throughout the British Columbia coast that differed in abundance of salmon. They demonstrated that up to 40 per cent of the nitrogen used by the riparian plants is derived from salmon nutrients, with values dependent on the salmon density in the stream, abundance of bears, plant species and distance from the stream. These nutrients originated in the sea where the salmon spend more than half their lives.

Although larger predators, such as eagles, wolves and bears, were exterminated in Ireland many centuries or millennia ago it is likely that a relationship between these animals and the formerly abundant populations of salmon and sea trout had a similar impact on riverside vegetation here. A few thousand years ago, extensive broadleaved forests clothed the country, stretching along the banks of our lowland rivers and lakes. The trees also had beneficial effects for the salmon, as they cast shade and dropped considerable amounts of organic matter into the water, and fallen trees in the channel slowed down the flow allowing easier fish migration upstream.

The angler's view

The famous filmmaker Éamon de Buitléar (1930–2013) grew up on the banks of the River Dargle in County Wicklow, where he learnt to fish from the tender age of

five years old. His father gave him a rod with a worm
for bait, and Éamon began to fish from the edge of the
weir pool near his home. He later recalled:

> It must have been beginner's luck, because a
> sizeable brown trout, a pound in weight, grabbed
> my bait. Knowing nothing of what was happening
> down below me in the darkness of the murky pool,
> I attempted to lift my rod for another cast. It felt
> heavy and, as I pulled and pulled again, suddenly
> the large trout came splashing and kicking and
> hurtling towards me. It was too much. With a gasp
> and a scream I fled! In my wild panic I forgot to
> drop my rod, so instead of leaving the monster
> behind, it followed me as I tried to run backwards
> up the dry slope of the weir.[20]

Since de Buitléar was a boy in the 1930s, the River
Dargle has sadly changed due to drainage and flood
protection works. The weir was removed and most of
the fishing on the river is controlled by the local angling
club and private individuals. Peter O'Reilly (1940–2018),
who published successive editions of the standard
manual on *Rivers of Ireland: A flyfisher's guide*, wrote that:

We have seen more changes happen to the natural environment in the last sixty years than in the thousand years that preceded them. Top of that sad list is arterial drainage and the 'maintenance' work that follows it; fish-farming and the sea lice that they generate; and the annihilation of salmon runs by hydro dams of some of our finest rivers. When I was a child, hundreds of salmon spawned in the rivers and streams close to our farm (in County Cavan). One of my earliest memories is of watching their grey shadows in the river by my father's corn mill. Today there is not one pair of salmon left. Even the eels are disappearing![21]

To find out how an experienced modern fly fisherman sees the current crisis in the Atlantic salmon population I met Dr Declan Little, a native of Limerick now living in County Wicklow. He says that he only started flyfishing in his twenties, but from then on he fished a lot of rivers, as his job took him all around the country, and he always carried with him a copy of O'Reilly's book. Declan says:

Since the late 1980s when I started, there has
been a decline, particularly in salmon. I did think
that by the 2000s there would be no salmon left in
Irish rivers. I am actually amazed by the resilience
of salmon and sea trout to be able to survive the
onslaught against all the odds.

Declan is a member of the management committee
for the Owenduff River in County Mayo, and he notes
that there is now an automatic fish counter on the river.
'This tells us that there are fairly stable levels of spring
salmon but that grilse numbers (summer salmon) are
falling all the time.' I asked Declan how he thinks the
river itself had changed over the time he has known it.
He says:

One change is that the amplitude of the floods has
reduced. This has been helped by revegetation in
the mountains when the high sheep numbers of
previous years were reduced. As a result, the floods
are coming up slower and going down slower.
There may be only a few hours in the difference but
it means that the river is cleaner and not filled with
peat silt. As a result, the window of opportunity to

catch fish on a rod is actually less as the salmon can see the angler and they are less vulnerable.

One of the additional pressures on salmon is higher water temperatures in the spawning rivers. Declan reminded me that the Owenduff River flows through open blanket bog with few trees, so it is very exposed to high summer temperatures and there have been fish kills in some years. 'The salmon also have to contend with many other threats such as water pollution, overfishing and difficulties at sea.' If the bog were intact it would not result in higher temperatures or peat silt. Drain blocking and bog restoration should be key objectives here. Declan recalls, 'when I started fishing in the 1980s, less than 10 per cent of the fish landed were put back after catching but this has increased to about 50 per cent now as anglers become aware of the plight of the salmon'. Even small changes like this can make a difference.

Little crayfish

Standing quietly flyfishing in a river is a great way to see other wildlife. Anglers tend to be excellent naturalists, intimately familiar with their favourite stretch of river and its inhabitants. They may be lucky enough to see a miniature relative of the lobster hiding beneath the banks. The freshwater crayfish is widespread in Irish lakes and rivers that flow over limestone or glacial gravels containing lime-rich stones. It needs the calcium to form its shell, and acid waters, such as those in many of the coastal mountain ranges, do not provide this. It is thought that the crayfish was brought to Ireland by French Cistercian monks as food for the abbeys, and genetic analysis supports this theory.

I once lay down beside a slow-flowing section of the River Barrow and looked under the water using a specially made pipe with a glass lens at the bottom. In a crevice in the bank, I could see some tiny pincers poking out in a threatening fashion to warn off the pipe. The crayfish only emerge from their hiding places in darkness for fear of being eaten by a whole suite of predators including eels, trout, otters, mink, herons and lots of other water birds. In this role as a food item they are connected in a freshwater web to a whole complex of other creatures. They are considered to be a 'keystone species' linked to many others via food webs and through their burrowing activities. They are omnivores themselves, eating small amounts of plant and animal material and detritus. They also act as engineers of their own ecosystem, disturbing the riverbed while feeding at night and burrowing in the riverbank. Who knows what other creatures depend on this digging and disturbance for their ecology? The white-clawed crayfish – to give it the full name – is found in both large rivers and small streams and also in about twenty large lakes. Slow-flowing or still waters are preferred, as the species is not a strong swimmer.[22]

Ireland has one of the last widespread populations of the crayfish in Europe, but it faces a number of threats and pressures in its natural habitat here. Deterioration in water quality and engineering works on rivers can have damaging effects on the crayfish. In England and other countries the introduction of the American signal crayfish has brought outbreaks of crayfish plague, with decimation of the native population. There have been outbreaks of the plague in a variety of Irish rivers too, stretching from the Bann and Erne in Northern Ireland to the Boyne, Barrow and Suir and the Deel and Lorrha tributaries of the Shannon. According to ecologist Dr Julian Reynolds, an Irish authority on the subject, this has been 'closing a ring of disease' around Ireland's best populations of the native crayfish. So far there have been no confirmed records of the signal crayfish in Ireland, but if this invasive species can be kept out of Irish rivers and lakes, the native crayfish can continue to be a key inhabitant of our waters.[23]

Gatecrashers

Unfortunately, there are plenty of other invasive species on rivers in Ireland. On a riverbank close to my home in County Wicklow, where I have often watched the blue and orange flash of a passing kingfisher, there is a huge stand of a shrubby plant that is covered in exotic pink blooms in summer. This is the Himalayan balsam, a native of northern India. As the flowers mature and produce seeds, these small packets of DNA literally explode from the plant and may land several metres away. Many land, of course, in the river and are carried downstream, eventually coming ashore on some bend where there has been disturbance to the sandy bank. Here they will extend the invasion of this alien species.

Ireland is full of introduced plants and animals – in gardens and parks, in city streets and derelict sites, in hedgerows and woodlands, on sand dunes and sea cliffs and in rivers and lakes. Most of these aliens are here to stay and there is little that we can do about it. Some are aggressive invaders – displacing and disrupting native species, even causing major economic impacts. Some are predators of native species; for example, the North American mink hunts native water birds and fish. Others compete with native species, often through sheer weight of numbers.

African curly waterweed escaped from garden ponds into Lough Corrib in County Galway, filling the entire water column in shallow bays with a dense mass of plant growth and shading out any submerged plants and animals on the lake bed. Nuttall's waterweed is an invasive plant species, originally from North America, from where it has spread, and is a major problem in Lough Arrow and other lakes. The plant was probably brought in on the underside of boats or on boat engines. It forms dense mats of vegetation that shade and kill the beneficial stonewort plant species, prevent boats from navigating in the waters, make angling very difficult, and damage the natural ecosystem of the lake.

Likewise, the zebra mussel grows in such dense encrustations that it excludes all other plant and animal life on the bed of lakes such as Lough Derg on the Shannon system. Zebra mussels are smaller versions of our native blue mussel, although they never meet each other as the invasive mollusc occurs only in freshwater and the blue mussel only in the sea. Zebra mussels were first discovered in Ireland in Lough Derg in 1997, but probably arrived a few years earlier attached to the hulls of imported second-hand boats. Today they are well established in the Shannon, Boyle and Erne navigations, and to date they have spread to over fifty lakes including Lough Neagh, so they seem to be here to stay. The zebra mussel has a very distinctive striped shell, and individuals are small; each shell would fit comfortably in a teaspoon. They settle on a wide range of surfaces including rocks, anchors, boat hulls, intake pipes, other shells and plants, often forming dense beds that exclude other bottom-dwelling animals. Zebra mussels were originally from the Caspian and Black Sea region but have become invasive in Europe since the late 1700s after the construction of an extensive canal network.

A non-native fish species called chub was illegally introduced into the River Inny in County Westmeath in the late 1990s or early 2000s, reputedly by anglers. The habitat in this tributary of the Shannon is quite suitable for chub and, had it established more widely, it would very likely have competed with the indigenous fish communities and impacted on other flora and fauna. It took more than seven years of intensive work by fisheries personnel, using electrofishing equipment, to completely eradicate this invasive species before it had time to spread to other rivers in the Shannon system or beyond.[24]

There are many introduced waterbird species, often brought into the country as part of wildfowl collections and subsequently escaping into the wild. It is quite common to find feral Canada geese on riverbanks, in town parks and wetlands in the midlands area. They are noisy, especially when breeding, as they display to one another with loud honking calls. Large flocks of Canada geese can dramatically change grassland habitats around rivers through trampling, grazing and enrichment caused by their droppings. In parkland this is often more of an aesthetic problem but it can still pose a challenge to the management of amenity grassland. They are often quite aggressive towards people. In Northern Ireland the feral population has increased to nearly 1,000 birds, most of which occur at two main sites, Lough Erne and Strangford Lough. In the Republic of Ireland breeding occurs mainly in counties Cork, Cavan and Monaghan.

The coypu is a large rodent that lives along riverbanks in South American countries. They dig burrows that can undermine the banks of rivers and dykes, causing instability. These are herbivores that can impact negatively on aquatic vegetation, including rare and threatened species. They are pests in agricultural areas, feeding on a variety of crops including root crops. Coypu are also thought to impact on aquatic birds by decreasing nest habitat. They have been shown to carry a number of diseases of importance to humans and domestic animals. They were first introduced into Europe in the nineteenth century for fur farming. The species has since colonised coastal marshes, swamps and other wetland areas in no fewer than nineteen member states of the European Union. Since the first modern sighting in 2010, coypu have been seen and reported from seven locations in Ireland including Cork, Tipperary and Limerick. Their introduction into Europe is linked to fur farming, but it is not known how they got to Ireland. Following a report of an unusual animal in the Cork city area in 2011, the NPWS issued a public call for people to report suspected sightings of the invasive coypu. A rapid response was initiated in October 2016 in Curaheen, Cork city, and ten animals were removed, but a verified sighting of a coypu in the River Lee in 2017 raised concern that this species may have spread further.

There are few wild animals in Ireland that produce a more vitriolic reaction in Irish anglers than the feral American mink. They are small dark mammals with a long bushy tail, superficially like the native otter but smaller and darker in colour. Before the 1950s the mink was unknown in Ireland. The species was introduced to Ireland in 1951 when the first fur farms were established. By the time legislation to regulate mink farming was introduced in 1966 there were at least fifty-eight farms in Ireland, mostly in the north and midlands. There were many backyard mink-breeding operations too, which, predictably, led to frequent escapes into the wild. By the end of the 1960s, some thirty-one mink had been trapped or spotted in the wild.[25] By 2009 they were considered to be highly prevalent in the east of the country but less widespread in the west, though modelling suggested that the mink still had considerable potential to increase their range and population in western areas.[26] Studies of the food of this invasive mammal suggest a varied diet dominated by whatever prey happens to be available in the home range area. An analysis of 2,510 scats (droppings) from the midlands revealed that over 90 per cent of the prey was made up of freshwater crayfish, fish, birds, rabbits, rats, mice, shrews, frogs and insects.[27]

For the smaller aquatic gatecrashers, the best form of control is preventing spread in the first place. Many would be confined to small areas but for the transport of fragments attached to boats, equipment and clothing to other rivers and lakes. A cross-border campaign under the title 'Stop the Spread' urges water users to check their belongings for living plants and animals and to clean and dry all items and disinfect them where necessary.

Water mills

Long before anyone ever spoke of renewable energy, Ireland had thousands of tiny generating stations producing energy from the 'free' supply of waterpower. At one time virtually every river had its own water mill for grinding corn, for sawing timber or for many other heavy jobs in a pre-industrial country. Deep in the woods near my home in Wicklow, there is a crumbling ruin covered with ivy. On the high side wall a massive iron wheel lies rusting; the wooden paddles that once turned in the water are long since rotted and useless. This was a sawmill that was used to turn the local pine and oak trees into rough timber spars and planks that still form the older supports in local buildings, including my own house. The water that turned the millwheel was diverted from the Vartry River, a mile upstream, into a large artificial millpond to provide a 'head' of water above the mill. Here a sluice was used to control the flow over the old mill wheel. The pond today is surrounded by trees, with moorhens calling from the reeds that grow in the shallower water.

Corn mills were built to replace the rotary hand-powered querns that were used from ancient times to grind corn into flour. There is a legend that the water mill was introduced to Ireland in the third century by King Cormac Mac Airt out of pity for his beautiful hand maiden who laboured grinding corn with a hand quern. Corn mills were often built beside monasteries, which were centres of farm trade in earlier centuries. Early mills were operated by small water wheels that rotated in a horizontal plane, pushed around by the pressure from the river on the blades. These horizontal mills were described in everyday Irish speech as *muileann tón le talamh* (mill with backside to the ground). The larger mills were given extra power by diverting water from the river into a millpond and channelling it down a millrace (or headrace) to the wheel, so that water from the pond could still be used in drier periods. By the early nineteenth century there were almost 2,000 corn mills in Ireland, most of them located on rivers and streams. Their history still lives on in placenames such as Millstreet in Cork or Milltown in Donegal.

In 2003, a survey of the sites of almost 200 mills, distilleries, breweries and maltings was undertaken throughout County Offaly at the behest of Offaly County Council. These were mostly water-powered and dating from the late eighteenth and nineteenth centuries. They ranged from small corn mills where oats were dried and ground into oatmeal to much larger flourmills in which wheat was milled. Although most such sites are long gone or exist only as ruinous shells, some retain virtually all their plant and machinery, albeit inoperative. Forty-three sites were involved in distilling, malting and brewing. Woollen mills were also important in Offaly where weaving, fulling and spinning were practised. Flax processing and linen production was carried on at scutching mills and bleach works respectively. There was one purpose-built jute mill at Clara, one of the few that existed in Ireland. Fourteen sawmills, five threshing mills, two bone mills and two hydroelectric mills were also recorded.[28]

I went to visit the site of one of these old mills, deep in the heart of County Offaly. On the banks of the picturesque Silver River, the impressive ruins are hidden away in a dense overgrown woodland. Massive stone walls loomed up out of the shade, reaching the height of the surrounding tree canopy. The corner blocks and wooden window and door lentils were still intact, but some of the masonry had fallen inside in piles. Old rusting ironwork littered the floor of the mill, resting where it had landed after falling from the wheel and other machinery. Outside the walls a deep mill race, now dry and filled with trees, led back through the woodland to link with the river upstream. This is Ballinacarrig Mill near Tullamore where, for centuries, local farmers brought their grain to be turned into flour. A mill was present here as far back as the Down Survey of 1655–58. The present owner, Berian Davies, intends to restore the mill and the woodland around it as a contribution to the preservation of historic sites.

Just a few kilometres upstream of Gorey in County Wexford is a beautifully restored corn mill on the banks of the Lask River in the townland of Craanford. The timber-beamed, flagstone-floored mill, with its massive grinding stones, its cogged wheel gearing and four-metre diameter waterwheel, are over 400 years old and still in a good state of preservation. The mill was restored by Michael Lyons, a retired local farmer who had learnt the miller's trade as a child in the 1930s. His grandfather, Michael, bought the mill 150 years ago and later his uncle, David Lyons, became the miller. From the age of six, Micheal brought tea to the miller and his assistants, who operated the machinery around the clock. Later he learnt his trade here, becoming familiar with every stage of the milling process.

With the advent of rural electrification, the Craanford Mill became redundant and closed in 1948. When Michael returned there, he found the three-storey building overgrown and crumbling, but with its machinery still intact. Working alone, he started the long job of restoration. Typically, a corn mill served an area up to twenty kilometres around it. It would have been one of the most important buildings in the area, providing food for humans and animals, and often serving as a meeting place for far-flung farmers when they brought their corn for grinding. The placenames in this locality, such as Milford, Mill Lands and Millquarter, record the importance milling once held for the local community.

Placenames

Being major features in the landscape, rivers feature strongly in the names of townlands, the smallest unit of land marked on most Irish Ordnance Survey maps. In previous centuries, those who lived in a townland were often related to one another, as few people travelled far outside their home area. Rivers were also of great importance to rural dwellers as sources of water for drinking and irrigating crops, for powering mills and for transport through heavily wooded areas. According to cartographer Barry Dalby, 'some river names seem to be very ancient. Being crucial features for many reasons, the names appear to carry over time.' The best source of information on Irish placenames is logainm.ie.

The simplest description is 'place of the river', *Baile na hAbhann* (Ballynahown, County Galway). Some common townland names are 'place between two rivers', *Baile idir Dhá Abhainn* (Ballyderown, County Cork; Ballyederowen, County Donegal; Ballynadrone, County Down). Other natural features associated with rivers include 'hill between two rivers', *Drom idir Dhá Abhainn* (Dromderaown, County Cork; Dromdiraowen, County Kerry) and 'wood between two rivers', *Coill idir Dhá Abhainn* (Killadrown, County Offaly; Killederdaowen, County Galway).

The colour of the water in the river has commonly been included in its name as in 'white river', *An Abhainn Bhán* (Whiteriver, County Louth), 'streaked or grey river', *An Abhainn Riabhach* (Owenreagh, County Derry); 'black river', *An Abhainn Dubh* (Owenduff), 'yellow river', *An Abhainn Bhuí* (Owenboy) and 'green river' *An Abhainn Ghlas* (Owenglass), both in County Mayo. The common enough river name Douglas originated as *Dú Ghlaise*, 'the dark (or poor) river'.

The larger rivers sometimes formed barriers to travel between neighbouring townlands so fords *(áthanna)* were common in shallow stretches. These also led to hundreds of placenames such as 'ford of the paths', *Áth na gCasán* (Annagassan, County Louth); 'ford of the slaughter', *Áth na nUrlainn* (Urlingford, County Kilkenny); 'ford of the cattle', *Áth na mBó*

(Annamoe, County Wicklow); 'ford of the ash', *Áth na Fuinseoige* (Ashford, County Wicklow); and even cities such as 'town of the ford of the hurdles', *Baile Átha Cliath* (Dublin). Other natural features of the landscape include 'river of the marsh', *Abhainn tSeiscinne* (Owenteskiny, County Donegal).

As water mills played such a key role in rural life over the centuries many townlands are known by this label such as 'mill of the cave', *Muillean na hUamhan* (Mullinahone, County Tipperary), 'mill of the cross', *Muillean Cros* (Mullincross, County Louth) and 'the mills of Farannan', *Muilte Farannáin* (Multyfarnham, County Westsmeath). Some of these may conceivably date back to the introduction of water mills in the Early Christian period. A widespread belief in the supernatural in previous cultures led to such names as 'mill of the fairies', *Mullach na Sí* (Mullanashee, County Sligo).[29]

Other placenames associated with parts of a river include many townlands called 'mouth of the river', *Bun Abhann* (Bunowen). The Irish word for a waterfall is *eas*, a term that appears in many placenames as waterfalls were prominent landmarks. Examples include *Eas Géitine* (Askeaton, County Limerick), 'hollow of the waterfall', *Gleann Log an Easa* (Glenmacnass) and 'milking place of the waterfall', *Buaile an Easa* (Boleynass, both in County Wicklow). The 'bridge of the grey falls', *Droichead Eas Liath* (Aasleagh Bridge, County Mayo), is the location of the famous Aasleagh Falls, a popular tourist destination.

Waterfalls

Waterfalls certainly have a mystical attraction for people, partly because of the sheer power of the water, where gravity becomes the dominant force. They also tend to occur in some magical places – deep ravines covered in mosses and ferns or cliffs surrounded by high mountains. Sometimes the misty conditions under the falls are associated with fairies and other imaginary beings. Waterfalls often occur where there is a sudden change in rock type, with a hard formation overlying a softer rock that has been eroded by the water and caused an overhang to develop. Equally, the unconformity in the rocks may have been caused by a geological fault or by the action of a glacier scraping away the sediments at the base of a cliff.

The Devil's Chimney is at Glencar, on the borders of Sligo and Leitrim. This is officially the highest waterfall in Ireland with a drop of 150 metres. In strong westerly winds the avalanche of water can be driven back to the edge of the cliff, giving it the Irish name *Sruth in Aghaidh an Aird*, which translates as 'the stream against the heights'. Made famous by the poetry of William Butler Yeats, the waterfall attracts thousands of visitors every year to see 'where the wandering water gushes from the hills above Glencar'. That beautiful verse of the poem 'The Stolen Child' takes the reader high into the hills above the waterfall to meet mischievous fairies, tiny pools and stars, weeping ferns, trout and 'unquiet' dreams. Having been carried into this magical space by Yeats, the reader (the 'human child') is seduced to come away with the fairies.

The second highest waterfall is at Powerscourt in my home county of Wicklow. Here the Dargle River plunges from the hanging valley of Glensoulan some 121 metres down the rock face into a deep basin that was carved out in the last Ice Age. The land through which the Dargle River flows is owned by the Powerscourt Estate. In August 1821, Richard Wingfield, Fifth Viscount Powerscourt, was hosting King George IV on a royal visit to Ireland. To make the famous beauty spot more dramatic for the monarch, Lord Powerscourt had a dam constructed above the waterfall so he could release a spectacular torrent while the two luminaries stood on the bridge below the falls. Fortunately, the king decided not to leave the banquet at Powerscourt House to view the waterfall as the eventual release of river water washed away the bridge completely.

The permanently damp atmosphere around a waterfall creates a special habitat for plants and animals. The water is generally too fast flowing for many plants to be able to hold on, so instead we find a mix of a few true aquatics and emergent vegetation in the surrounding spray zone. Lower plants such as long-beaked water feather-moss, greater water moss and St Winifred's liverwort are fairly common in waterfalls and are the most obvious plants seen there. Mosses attach to the rocks with tiny hairs much smaller and more numerous than the familiar roots of higher plants. Ferns are quite common in the surrounding habitat, and waterfalls are also 'hotspots' for the Killarney fern, a rare and legally protected species. In the animal kingdom, most of the typical small creatures that live in streams cannot hold on in the fast flow of waterfalls. One of the largest stoneflies, *Perla*, often lives beside waterfalls. These may take up to three years to develop from egg to adult. Some birds, such as dippers and grey wagtails, nest in rocky crevices at the side of waterfalls, often within the spray zone. They will even fly through the falling water to feed their chicks with beakfuls of insects.

In many beauty spots, waterfalls are the main focus for visitors, with a 'selfie' photo in front of the falls the essential memento. Large crowds are often present at places like Poulanass in Glendalough, Powerscourt waterfall, County Wicklow and Glencar waterfall, County Sligo. Getting wet in the spray is all part of the waterfall experience.

Vampire fish

I stood on a bridge over the River Fergus in the County Clare town of Ennis and looked down into the clear water flowing over gravels below. There was some commotion going on here as a number of large eel-like fish appeared to be moving the gravel and stones about to create depressions in the riverbed. They were spawning sea lampreys, each fish measuring up to a metre in length. These are very primitive fish that have an oral sucker disc instead of a mouth with jaws. Adult sea lampreys have a dark mottled colour, with rows of curved teeth in their suckers, which gives them a sinister appearance. Their gills have no covers, so water taken in through the mouth passes through the pulsing pouches, and is then expelled through a line of seven round holes along each flank. There are no scales and there are no proper bones either, just cartilage, which gives the fish a robust, rubbery form.

The lamprey is a member of a small group of animals called the jawless fish – descendants of the primeval fish-like progenitors that eventually evolved into true fish hundreds of millions of years ago. The jawless fish were once the pinnacle of evolution, the most advanced and revolutionary creatures in the sea. They used their jawless mouthparts to scrape away at their food or swallow huge chunks of meat whole. However, it wasn't long before true fish appeared in the oceans. They grew proper jaws and were able to outcompete their jawless rivals. Today, only a few jawless species remain – the strange, slime-producing hagfish and the lampreys.

Sea lamprey spawn annually, in summer, in the lower reaches of large rivers, in nests called redds, using their suckers to move stones about on the riverbed. Adult lamprey die after spawning, and their carcasses can sometimes be seen in rivers. After hatching, larval lamprey drift downstream until they find a suitable muddy or silty part of the riverbed to burrow into. Lamprey then spend several years in a blind, worm-like, juvenile form known as ammocoetes, which filter feed microscopic organisms from the water and mud. After about six to eight years, sea lamprey ammocoetes develop eyes and turn silvery, transforming into free-swimming adults as they make their way downstream and migrate to sea. Fisheries, stock surveys and anecdotal reports from anglers have shown that there are landlocked populations of sea lamprey in several lakes in Ireland.

Although the lamprey is not very attractive to look at, it was once eaten as a luxury food. The flesh of the lamprey is reputed to be very nutritious and tasty, albeit rather fatty, and during the Middle Ages they were widely eaten by the upper classes throughout Europe. In 1135, King Henry I of England is said to have died after eating 'a surfeit of lampreys', against his physician's advice, although many historians today believe that he died from food poisoning.

River and sea lampreys migrate downstream into the sea and become ectoparasites, latching on to marine fish and mammals and grating their flesh using their multitude of teeth to feed on their blood. As they tear through the skin and muscle of the victim, they secrete an anticoagulant that keeps the blood flowing freely. It's easy to understand why these primitive creatures have earned the nickname 'vampire fish'. Once attached to a host, a lamprey is almost impossible to detach, although it will fall off by itself when satiated. However, this leaves its victim with a gaping wound that is slow to heal and prone to infection. Host fish often die as a result of this parasitism.

The sea lamprey in Ireland is classified as 'near-threatened'. On rivers like the Shannon, lampreys have been severely impacted by dams and weirs, river regulation, canalisation, flood schemes and water quality decline. Migratory lampreys are now almost completely confined to below the Shannon dams, with their migration into tributaries of the old river impeded by weirs. Migratory lampreys are rare in the Corrib catchment, with their migration into Lough Corrib blocked by the Galway barrage and all spawning and nursery habitat downstream of the weir removed by drainage works. On the Lower River Mulkear, County Limerick, heavy rain can cause river levels to rise and this stimulates upstream migration of lampreys. However, their migration is blocked by an ornamental weir at Annacotty, despite the fact that a special pass was created here to allow free movement. Dr Will O'Connor has observed sea lampreys clinging to the bottom of this pass but, being unable to jump like salmon, they become exhausted and cannot climb the slope, and they are also exposed to predators.

Other fish passes have been constructed at Hanover Weir, County Carlow, and on the River Nore at Castletown, County Laois. However, Dr O'Connor says, 'both are salmonid passes and do not have features which can be used by lampreys and eels. Both passes have ledges and jumps at the top. Lampreys cannot climb or jump so having an upper ledge renders this design impassable for these species.' Special measures are required to restore their river habitats and remove barriers to migration. Watching them from a bridge in town offers an ideal opportunity for educating the public about these remarkable fish.

City river

The Minnowburn is a small tributary of the River Lagan that flows through the city of Belfast. The National Trust (Northern Ireland) first became involved here in June 1945, when the Minnowburn Beeches, the famous stand of trees alongside the Ballylesson Road in Belfast, came under threat. As Shaw's Bridge was a well-established retreat and walking destination for Belfast people, the trust stepped in to prevent the felling and buy the four hectares containing the trees to protect this special area from building development. As further land became available around the beeches, the trust took the opportunity to further protect the area, including the lands on either side of the river.

I walked around the paths in the Minnowburn with Craig Somerville, National Trust ranger for the Belfast area. He grew up in this city but worked overseas and in the UK as a forester and then as a tree surgeon in Northern Ireland before joining the National Trust, initially as a volunteer. Walking along the riverbank we looked over the wet meadows filled with meadowsweet, yellow rattle, flag iris and knapweed and dominated by a large alder tree in the centre. This grassland is flooded in winter and managed by hand-scything the vegetation in late summer.

This section of the River Lagan up to Shaw's Bridge was surveyed for breeding birds annually over seventeen years by my late friend Chris Bailey in the 1970s and

80s.[30] The Minnowburn offers a perfect habitat for grey wagtail, dipper and kingfisher, each species depending on aquatic life for their food. There is still a dipper nest under the old stone bridge on the Minnowburn, just as there was in Chris Bailey's surveys fifty years ago. A recent winter flood washed out the kingfisher nest in the riverbank, but this has now been replaced with an artificial tunnel that is hidden beneath the overhanging trees. There was a traditional pond near the river that had become completely silted up over the years. Craig called in a favour from the Rivers Agency and had the silt removed, creating open water again and restoring the habitat diversity of the pond. Craig explained that the Minnowburn holds a special place in his heart:

> It was through this landscape that I would cycle to the Giant's Ring, as a small boy, with my brothers. We would stop at the Minnowburn bridge and chuck a few stones into the river or have a paddle. During my teens the River Lagan between Stranmillis and Edenderry was where I hung out with friends. We built rafts, camped and courted along the tow path. It was a place to escape from the sometimes-oppressive atmosphere during 'the

Troubles' in Belfast. Now, all of the built structures from my childhood have long since been demolished and replaced with something else, the two schools where I was educated, the house I was raised in, even the church where I attended Sunday school. However, I still have the banks of the Lagan and Minnowburn rivers as my connection to the past, so I'm going to do everything I can to preserve this place. I feel that I have to.

River music

Human life is often compared with a river. It ebbs and flows. Sometimes it's calm, other times it's rough. It should come as no surprise then that musicians use water – and particularly the river – as a metaphor to describe love, resistance, serenity, sorrow and many other human traits. These themes have been used in some of the best songs about rivers ever written.

Probably the most famous river song is 'Ol' Man River', written for the musical *Show Boat* in the 1920s. The show was based on Edna Ferber's novel chronicling the lives of a group of travelling performers. Many consider the treatment by Paul Robeson the definitive version, but it has been covered by dozens of famous singers, including Sammy Davis Jr, Frank Sinatra, Judy Garland, Ray Charles, Django Reinhardt, and the Beach Boys.

'Big River' is a song written and originally recorded by Johnny Cash. It tells a story of the chase of a lost love along the course of the Mississippi River from St Paul, Minnesota, to New Orleans, Louisiana. Released as a single in 1958, it went as high as number four on the country music charts and stayed in the charts for fourteen weeks. Johnny Cash seems to have had a fascination for the river, which also features in his song 'Five Feet High and Rising'. When he was aged four, he experienced the 1937 Mississippi flood first-hand. He wrote this song about the ordeal he experienced when his family was forced to flee their home.

Joni Mitchell's song 'River' is set in Canada when the water is frozen. It tells of a broken love affair: 'I wish I had a river I could skate away on'. Rivers and religion often go hand in hand. They certainly do in 'Down to the River to Pray' which features in the great Coen brothers' movie, *Oh Brother, Where Art Thou?* It has been described variously as a traditional American song, a Christian folk hymn, an African-American spiritual, an Appalachian song and a southern gospel song. 'Moon River' sung by Audrey Hepburn was the theme song in the movie *Breakfast at Tiffany's*. It refers to a real place – Moon River in Savannah, Georgia, where the songwriter Johnny Mercer grew up.

Perhaps the most famous piece of Irish music associated with a river is *Riverdance*, a theatrical showcase of traditional Irish music and dance. With a score composed by Bill Whelan, it originated as an interval performance act during the 1994 Eurovision Song Contest, featuring Irish dancing champions Jean Butler, Michael Flatley and the vocal ensemble Anúna. 'Where the river foams and surges to the sea, Silver figures rise to find me, Wise and as daring, Following the heart's cry.' Shortly afterwards, this musical sensation was expanded into a stage show, which has since toured to over 450 venues worldwide and has been seen by over twenty-five million people, making it one of the most successful dance productions in the world.

Blueways

> Believe me, my young friend, there is
> nothing, absolutely nothing, half so
> much worth doing as simply messing
> about in boats.

From *The Wind in the Willows* (1908)

by KENNETH GRAHAME

I learnt to handle a canoe on the River Barrow some years ago on a two-day trip from Muine Bheag (Bagenalstown) to St Mullins in County Carlow, ending at the point where tidal water enters the river, an expedition that involved camping on the riverbank. The descent of some thirty-two kilometres meant dropping over a number of weirs, some of which seemed like small waterfalls. I capsized on many of them, spending most of the trip wet through. Seeing wildlife in the surrounding landscape from the river is a unique experience and a great way to appreciate the extensive areas of mature woodland that clothe the banks. However, it takes some time to get the hang of paddling a lightweight craft on moving water. The

writer John Connell and his friend Peter used a canoe
to explore the Camlin River in their native County
Longford. He wrote, 'to balance the canoe you must
rely on your arse. Leaning back and forth on our glutes
we hold the boat in position. Don't get me wrong, it's
not just sitting on your bottom; you have to work it.
Already, after about half an hour, our rears are getting
stiff.'[31]

Many Irish rivers are used by experienced canoeists.
One of the most challenging is the River Liffey, which
rises in the Wicklow Mountains and flows through
north Kildare and the city of Dublin to the sea. The
Liffey Descent is the best-known annual canoe event
in Ireland, attracting hundreds of competitors of all
ages and abilities. It all began in 1960 when a short
canoe race was held on the Liffey as part of the Dublin
Boat Show programme. From this small beginning
the annual Liffey Descent canoe marathon developed,
attracting paddlers from all corners of the globe, and
it is now a major event in the international marathon
racing calendar. A feature of the Liffey Descent is the
variety of challenges, which fully test the skills of
the paddlers as they make their way from Straffan
in County Kildare to Islandbridge in Dublin city – a

distance of over thirty-two kilometres. Soon after the start comes the first of ten weirs, followed by the dense vegetation known as The Jungle. At Leixlip reservoir, there are five kilometres of flat-water paddling, after which the kayakers must carry their craft around the ESB hydroelectricity dam. Downstream there are more weirs, the most notorious of them Wren's Nest, at Lucan, and finally Chapelizod. From there it is a lung-bursting race to the finish at the Garda Boat Club in Islandbridge.

Waterways Ireland is one of six north/south statutory bodies established under the British-Irish Agreement of 1998 and supported by both governments. It is the cross-border navigational authority responsible for the management, maintenance, development and promotion for recreational purposes of over 1,000 kilometres of inland navigable waterways, including the canals and a number of major rivers. It has established a number of 'blueways' that follow these watercourses and also 'greenways' allowing access along the banks. These are generally long-distance routes, ideal for activity holidays such as trekking and travelling slowly by canoe, kayak or paddleboard. They often give access to stretches of the countryside that would not be seen from a vehicle but do pass through towns and villages where overnight stops can be arranged.

Rainbow bird

A canoe is the ideal form of transport for undertaking a survey of river birds, giving access to parts that would be unreachable on foot. I once worked in an office in Wicklow Town where my window overlooked the Leitrim River, a short distance before it reached the Irish Sea. Sometimes, in autumn or winter, I would see a flash of blue and orange darting past, and I knew this was a kingfisher. To get a closer look at this colourful bird I paddled a kayak up the estuary and along the lower reaches of the Vartry River. I was rewarded when a kingfisher stopped right beside me to perch on a low branch before diving straight into the water after a tiny fish.

Commonly known as *cruidín* in Irish, *biorra an uisce* (water spear), another of its Irish names, is more descriptive, referring as it does to the kingfisher's dagger-sharp bill. In Irish folklore it was said that dead kingfishers preserved in a dry place would never decay and if put among clothes and other articles would ward off moths and give them a pleasant odour. Another old folk tradition in Ireland and Britain describes how a dead kingfisher hung by a thread from a post will always have its beak pointing in the direction of the prevailing wind.

Kingfishers are more widely distributed in Ireland than most people think. They are present on all the main lowland rivers, even in the centre of some towns and cities. Because they are quite small (about the size of a robin) and fly incredibly fast and low over the water, they are often overlooked. But the sight of one sitting still on the branch of an overhanging tree, watching for its fish dinner, is exquisite. The typical breeding habitat is on a large, slow-flowing river with woodland either side. Here, the birds seek out high banks where a vertical earth face is exposed. The eggs are laid deep within a burrow that the kingfisher excavates with its strong bill. When the chicks finally emerge, they drop straight out of the mouth of the burrow into the river below. In the first days after fledging, the chicks often line up in a comical queue on an overhanging twig to be fed by their hard-worked parents.

Because the kingfisher is such a popular and easily recognised bird, BirdWatch Ireland made an appeal to

members of the general public to send in records of any
sightings they had between 1998 and 2007. This produced
a total of over 2,000 records from more than 1,000
separate locations during the 10-year period. Almost all
sightings were from lowland rivers, with records from
every county in the island of Ireland. To supplement
this, in 2008 and 2010 a team of ornithologists undertook
dedicated surveys along nearly 1,000 kilometres of six
river systems, both the main channels and a number of
smaller tributaries. These were the Boyne, Moy, Clare,
Nore, Barrow and Munster Blackwater. A variety
of boats were used on the larger rivers including an
inflatable dinghy, a Canadian canoe and a double
kayak; there were also a number of visits on foot. The
results showed that good numbers of birds occurred
on all rivers; the highest densities were on the Boyne,
Nore and Moy rivers, with about one pair every ten
kilometres or less of the main channels.[32]

My local river in east Wicklow, the Vartry, has
fortunately been spared the worst effects of arterial
drainage. To search for river birds, I decided to
walk about ten kilometres of the banks from the sea
heading upstream to where the channel leaves the
Vartry Reservoir via some filter beds. On the way I

passed through reedbeds, under old stone bridges and through cattle-grazed fields. To avoid having to climb numerous fences or beat through dense thorny scrub, I occasionally dropped into the shallow water in my thigh waders, walking on the gravelly riverbed. There were plenty of moorhens in the bankside reeds, from where sedge warblers belted out their loud songs. Grey wagtails bobbed in the stony rapids, and occasionally I disturbed dippers near their nests under the bridges. More than once, I also startled local people as I appeared unannounced at the bottom of their gardens. Just past the old coaching stop of Hunter's Hotel, I also surprised a kingfisher which flew rapidly upstream away from me. Here were some ideal vertical earth banks and, in one bend of the river, I found a nest hole, marked with the giveaway white droppings around the entrance. On this quiet stretch of river the birds were undisturbed and left to breed in peace.

On some rivers, kingfishers face a variety of threats. The quality of the water is important to them as any form of excessive pollution from town sewage, industrial or agricultural run-off will have negative impacts on the fish species that form their prey. Occasionally, this can be catastrophic when, for example, slurry is washed into the river and a fish kill results. Introduced predators such as American mink can also impact on kingfishers as the birds have not evolved strategies to avoid this voracious mammal. However, the most permanent effects are felt when drainage work is undertaken; heavy tracked machines radically alter the riverbanks and rock armoury is often placed in the water to prevent bank erosion. In these areas kingfishers may disappear for ever.

Channels and challenges

Two types of drainage are detrimental to rivers: one is land drainage that results in more rapid loss of water from the land to the river, and the other is arterial drainage. The latter involves a permanent alteration of the channel to speed the flow of water to the sea, reducing flooding and lowering the general level of the river so that field drains can flow into it. Machines are used to straighten, widen and deepen the channel, remove obstacles such as large rocks and bankside trees and protect the banks from erosion with concrete or rock armoury. The arterial drainage programme of the mid-twentieth century was responsible for damage to a large number of rivers and their ecosystems in the name of agricultural progress. Major works had been carried out in the later nineteenth century, and between 1948 and 1995, the Office of Public Works (OPW) completed 34 arterial drainage schemes and five estuarine embankment schemes amounting to over 11,000 kilometres of river channel. This dried out a total area of land equivalent to the size of County Roscommon. Most of the natural features (meanders, riffles, pools and fords) as well as gravel substrates were removed from rivers during these arterial drainage programmes, leaving them more like straight, steep-sided canals.

Returning these channels to a semblance of their natural form, in order to recover the habitat for fisheries, was the basis for a campaign undertaken by Dr Martin O'Grady and his colleagues in Inland Fisheries Ireland (IFI). Under the Irish fisheries enhancement programme (1994–99), natural techniques were used to restore riverine habitats along over 400 kilometres of rivers and streams. Fish stock numbers increased in these rivers by up to thirty times greater than they were before the work began. Most of the techniques used natural materials such as timber, boulders, rocks and old Christmas trees. These methods had been pioneered in the USA from the

1930s, where the government employed the Civilian
Conservation Corps to begin restoration of stream
habitat in National Forests. The manual that resulted
from the Irish fisheries enhancement programme gives
practical advice on using the techniques in almost any
river system.[33]

In the early stages of these river habitat
enhancement programmes, EU funding was made
available through what was called the Tourism
Angling Measure. O'Grady's idea was to reintroduce
some variety of habitat to these modified channels. In
the early days, much of the work was experimental.
Dr Declan Cooke, a current fisheries inspector with
IFI, says: 'In some instances, too much intervention
resulted in less-than-ideal outcomes. As the programme
progressed, however, knowledge and skills advanced
and more subtle changes and structures began to yield
great results by gently nudging rivers into a natural
flow pattern rather than trying to force channels into
idealised configurations.'

Most of the recent habitat enhancement/restoration
work of IFI is now being carried out in conjunction
with the OPW as part of their drainage maintenance
programmes. They have the machinery and engineering

expertise and IFI have been training some of the OPW staff in fisheries conservation measures. While the ultimate aim of the OPW is to achieve faster discharge of river water for flood relief purposes, they are keen to work with IFI to also achieve habitat enhancement objectives, where possible. Cooke says:

> We meet early in the year with local OPW engineers and discuss channels that are ear-marked for drainage maintenance. We identify a few candidate sites where enhancement work is feasible. We then follow up with an on-site walkover survey where we measure and assess the enhancement possibilities, discuss appropriate structures and substrates which could be introduced. I will then draw up an enhancement plan and the OPW staff will implement this under IFI supervision.

However, Dr Will O'Connor, an independent fisheries and environmental consultant based in Limerick, has a different view of this recent work. He told me:

> I don't think that we are finished with communicating the bad news message for our rivers yet. I can't

think of any current river project that would fit into this category of restoring habitats for aquatic life. The work that IFI do filling in our rivers with rocks and gravel is not restoration – it is armouring and confining rivers for the OPW to reduce maintenance costs.

Land drainage, particularly the drainage of our open peat catchments for turf harvesting, agriculture and forestry have resulted in widespread riverbed habitat loss through scour during floods caused by fast movement of rainwater from the land to the river. During droughts, poor flow velocities and high temperatures cause a drop in oxygen and a concentration of nutrient pollutants, often resulting in blooms of filamentous algae on the riverbeds. Land drainage affects both upland acidic and lowland calcareous rivers, whereas arterial drainage problems occur mainly in lowland rivers. The restoration of upper catchments by drain blocking is essential for acid rivers and in lowland rivers would take away much of the need for ongoing in-stream works.

Barriers in rivers such as weirs and long dark culverts have long been a problem for migratory fish such as salmon, trout, lamprey and eels that need to move upstream to spawn in the tributaries. For example, IFI identified the bridge at Clashdog near Clonea, County Waterford as a serious barrier and started a pilot project to construct a rock ramp-type fish pass and bank protection works downstream of the bridge. This river is a tributary of the River Clodiagh, which is itself a tributary of the River Suir. A new fish pass at this barrier is now complete, opening a further six kilometres of habitat for salmon spawning and nursery. This work was conducted by Waterford City and County Council with direction from IFI under the Salmon Conservation Fund. Such measures could be repeated in river catchments all over the country.

A catchment approach

All water in a river system is connected and any conservation measures for fish and other aquatic creatures need to be approached on a whole-catchment basis. The Duhallow LIFE SAMOK programme is an innovative project that started in 2015. It is based on a conservation and restoration strategy for many endangered fish, mammals and birds found in the Munster Blackwater River Special Area of Conservation,

142

which includes farmland and in-stream works along the River Allow. Co-financed by the European Commission and the Irish exchequer, this €1.9m project is run in partnership with IFI. Key project on-the-ground actions are aimed at improving and protecting animal species of European importance – otter, kingfisher, Atlantic salmon and freshwater pearl mussel – all of which are found in the Upper Blackwater River and its tributaries.

The project is working with landowners, state organisations, angling clubs and the public to advance important on-the-ground works. River bank erosion is a major issue along rivers in the Upper Blackwater. Bare, unprotected banks are at risk of being washed away. The disturbed silt and sediments affect the spawning beds of Atlantic salmon, and excess bank erosion can lead to loss of land for farmers. To address this, many project actions are aimed at restoring and protecting riverbanks along farmland. Over 200 metres of riverbank have been re-profiled and protected with rock and trees. This type of restoration eases the pressure on riverbanks caused by flood events. The Christmas trees, donated by the public over the years, have been put to great use by protecting the newly restored Duhallow riverbanks and helping in the regeneration of native vegetation.

Native plants and trees are vital for the added protection of riverbanks. Rural Social Scheme and Tús participants were key to the LIFE Project, helping with the planting of over 4,000 trees along nearly 6.5 kilometres of river. The project has worked with landowners to help manage cows along riverbanks as they can cause erosion of the banks and siltation in the river. More than thirty-five kilometres of waterway bank have been fenced along the Allow and Dalua Rivers to prevent this happening. This delivers advantages to both the landowner and the environment. Along with the large-scale fencing scheme, direct dairy cattle access to the river has been replaced with alternative drinking water sources. This strategy replaces traditional cattle drinking methods rather than creating new ones, which would require planning permission. The project team has also continued to work with the landowners in improving the system of silt trapping to reduce the siltation of riverbeds. This will greatly benefit salmon and freshwater pearl mussel.

Thanks to dedicated work by many enthusiastic

volunteers and diligent local anglers, the invasive plant Himalayan balsam has been tackled along thirty-five kilometres of riverbank. Originating in Asia, it was planted as an ornamental flower in many gardens around Ireland. While the plant has been nearly eradicated from the Allow catchment area, continued monitoring of the riverbanks will be needed as seeds from the flower can still grow after two years in the soil. Since surveying began in 2013, over twenty-eight kilometres of riverbed has been surveyed for freshwater pearl mussel. These surveys have to be conducted under licence and by snorkelers who are trained by experts approved by the NPWS. A total of 12,895 individual mussels have been counted. Along with recording and mapping of each individual mussel, river conditions (substrate, vegetation, water depth etc.) have also been noted.

Pearls in the river

The pearls that my mother liked to wear were produced artificially, but few people today are aware that natural pearls from Irish rivers were once a valuable commodity traded for cash. Throughout the centuries, pearl fishing was a widespread if specialist activity that became a commercial concern in some areas. As only about one in 10,000 freshwater pearl mussels produces a pearl inside its shell, the fisheries that developed around this species led to massive and unsustainable exploitation of this natural resource. At one time this natural jewel became a powerful symbol in Irish folklore and art. While only rich customers could afford to buy them, it was the poor people along the rivers who hunted for the pearls in a similar way to prospectors panning for gold.

In late summer, when rivers were at their lowest levels, the pearl fishers waded in the water up to waist level and, bending underwater, tore the shells from the riverbed, placing them in baskets slung across their shoulders. As an alternative, the fisher would carry a slender stick which was jammed between the open shells, forcing the mussel to close so that it could be pulled from the sediment. As very few shellfish contained a valuable pearl, the surplus shellfish were probably discarded and died. But the population of these slow-growing animals could not sustain such exploitation and, like native oysters in coastal waters, they became rare or disappeared completely from some rivers.[34]

Today, the freshwater pearl mussel has been one of the main casualties of poor water quality, especially due to land drainage and forestry in headwaters causing the release of silt into rivers throughout Ireland. At over a hundred years of age, some individual molluscs may be among the oldest surviving animals in Ireland. The mussel has a large, heavy black shell and a complicated reproductive ecology that requires the immature stages to be attached to the gills of salmon or trout before they drop off to live in clean gravel beds washed by fast-flowing rivers and streams. Unfortunately, poor water quality in most of its traditional lowland river habitats means that the majority of the mussel populations have failed to reproduce in recent decades. Where living mussels are still present they are often just a group of geriatrics on life support with no younger individuals to replace them. I remember wading into a stretch of the River Eske in Donegal where there were thousands of empty mussel shells killed by pollution.

This sad sight is all too common around the country and has led to the pearl mussel being listed as 'critically endangered' in Ireland. The species is equally endangered across its global range, and Ireland happens to be a stronghold for the few mussel populations that remain in the world. This special responsibility is made even graver by the fact that the freshwater pearl mussel can be considered both an indicator of environmental quality and a keystone species whose welfare affects many others in the freshwater ecosystem. The species is relatively widespread here, being found in 124 rivers on the island of Ireland, all of which flow over non-calcareous rock. This requirement for water that is low in calcium separates the freshwater pearl mussel from a near relative, the Nore pearl mussel which, by contrast, lives in lime-rich water. The endangered status of the two pearl mussel populations relates partly to their complicated multi-stage life cycle which requires the presence of salmon or trout and clean gravels with a good flow of oxygen for the mussels to survive.

Unfortunately, the history of Irish rivers has not been kind to the pearl mussel, with widespread pearl fishing, land drainage, arterial drainage, water pollution and general siltation leading to a largely hostile environment for these molluscs. The decline of this keystone species is strongly related to deteriorating hydrological conditions, specifically to the threat of low flows during dry summers. Populations still capable of reproducing require a minimum discharge and flow velocity to support juvenile mussels, or else stress builds up and an entire generation may be lost.[35] If sufficient conservation effort is not applied quickly, the species will face worldwide extinction and, like the dodo before it, will be gone for ever. However, ensuring a clean, pollution-free habitat takes time, and so emergency measures such as captive breeding have been employed in Ireland to try to produce more juvenile molluscs that can ultimately be reintroduced to the wild when conditions improve.[36] The freshwater pearl mussel is very likely to become functionally extinct in the wild in the near future. If it does not get the complex clean conditions that it needs to reproduce in Irish rivers, it will disappear for ever. Then it will become what Georges Bizet described in his 1863 opera *The Pearl Fishers* as a 'goddess looming up in the shadow and holding out her arms to us'.

Some big efforts have been made to try to rescue the last remaining viable populations of the pearl mussel in our rivers. KerryLIFE was a demonstration project in south Kerry that ran from 2014 to 2019 with the primary objective of restoring two internationally important freshwater pearl mussel populations. Located on the Iveragh Peninsula, it included two large rivers, the Blackwater and the Caragh, separated by Macgillycuddy's Reeks. The project area covered about 221 square kilometres where the primary land use is agriculture. The project sought to develop and demonstrate sustainable land use management techniques and practices for local farmers and forest owners in freshwater pearl mussel catchments and focused on supporting sustainable farming and forestry activities within the two river catchments.

The work has also had a positive impact on the wider ecology of the river and its catchment. Getting the conditions right for the pearl mussel, the most sensitive species, ensures that that the conditions are also better for a wide range of other protected animals such as salmon, trout, river lamprey and otters. The farm measures implemented have also resulted in improved condition of wetland and peatland habitats that support a wealth of rare plants and animals. Engagement with the farmers and forest owners allows local knowledge and experience to be harnessed, which can then be brought together with scientific expertise to overcome some of the challenges faced in freshwater pearl mussel catchments. However, this was a very short-term measure, and Dr Evelyn Moorkens, an international expert on the mussel, is less optimistic. She told me:

> We are dealing here with drainage issues and these take a long time to reverse and recover – maybe decades. At the very best, we may be reducing the speed of decline of the species in the meantime. However, we have a small number of very large pearl mussel populations with relatively low levels of sediment and nutrient pollution where restoring adequate flows will secure their future. I am encouraged by the potential for rewarding farmers for bog restoration, which will provide long-term climate benefits as well as improvements for river flows and the reduction of downstream flooding.

Water quality

On a bridge over the Vartry River near my home, I often notice the distinctively marked vehicles of IFI as their inspectors check on the state of the river and its fish populations. All over Ireland experts from IFI, the Environmental Protection Agency (EPA) and local authorities take samples at fixed locations along our main river channels to monitor the water quality which underpins healthy biodiversity and fisheries. These sampling locations are mostly at road bridges where there is easy access to the channels. Information is collected from 2,355 rivers on a rotational basis with a continuous programme stretching back to the 1970s. At intervals, the EPA publishes a comprehensive review of the quality of surface waters, and the network of rivers is central to this as they supply the water to lakes, canals and other water bodies. Water quality is usually summarised in five categories (Q1 to Q5) indicating low to high quality. Unfortunately, the quality of our rivers has been on a steady downward slide for a long time.

There has been a substantial increase in polluted river waters, with over half now being of poor quality, an increase of one-third since 2007–2009, providing clear evidence that river water quality is getting worse. There has been a steady increase in the levels of slight to moderate pollution in a large proportion of channels, the main contributor being increased intensification of agriculture with a rise in the use of fertiliser in particular. Nitrogen levels are growing in concentration at 38 per cent of river sites, while volumes of phosphate are increasing in a quarter of them. Nitrate levels are highest in the south and south-east, primarily due to agricultural activities and the use of artificial and organic fertilisers. The east of the country also has higher nitrate levels associated with urban wastewater discharges. Areas of particular concern include the rivers Bandon, Lee, Barrow, Suir and Liffey. These nutrients affect the waterway ecosystem, causing algal blooms that displace other flora and fauna, while high nitrate levels in drinking water supplies pose a risk to human health.

The deterioration in our river waters of highest biological quality has been apparent over the past few decades, with a decline from 31 per cent of sites in 1987–90 to 17 per cent in the latest assessment. Within this grouping, there has also been a dramatic loss in our most pristine river sites, from 13 per cent of sites in 1987–90 to less than 1 per cent of sites in 2016–18. In the 1980s there were more than 500 pristine rivers in the country. The number of remaining high-quality sites is now at an all-time low of under twenty rivers. These rivers are important reservoirs of aquatic biodiversity and their loss is a very significant concern.[37] The number of sampling sites that record the highest quality declined to as low as 0.7 per cent in the period

2016–18. The majority of these high-quality sites are found in clusters near the coast in the west, south-west and south-east.[38] The causes of this decline are less obvious than those which affect the more polluted end of the spectrum, but the majority of recent losses have been in smaller acid rivers and are likely to be caused by land drainage. The pressures that cause the loss of the highest-quality waters include upland forestry on peat soils, one-off housing, overgrazing by sheep, farm intensification, land clearance and drainage activities, peat harvesting and insecticides such as cypermethrin – used for sheep protection and in forestry.[39]

Much research has linked water pollution with application of fertiliser to fields in the dairy industry. In all, 7,000 dairy farmers have an EU-approved derogation that allows them to use up to 250 kilograms of livestock manure nitrogen per hectare. Fertiliser imports have risen by more than a quarter since 2015 and the abolition of milk quotas. The resulting grass production (including silage and hay) has fuelled the huge expansion in the state's dairy herd numbers over the last seven years. Since 2015, dairy output has increased in volume by 60 per cent, significantly ahead of targets set by the government back in 2010.

According to EPA Programme Manager Mary Gurrie, agriculture is 'definitely' the leading cause of the deterioration in water quality. Only twenty of the state's 3,000 rivers are now regarded as 'pristine', with half of all rivers and lakes affected by excessive dairy production. The pollution problem is worst in the south and south-east, where dairy herd numbers are higher than elsewhere. For Gurrie, 1,600 rivers, lakes and streams are in poor condition – with the blame in 1,000 of these cases lying at the door of agriculture.[40]

Citizen science, or the collecting of useful information by enthusiastic amateurs, has gained popularity in recent years. A one-day introductory course led by Dr Ken Whelan is based on the content of the Freshwater Detective series of lectures and field trips run over many years in University College Dublin and the more recent Small Streams Characterisation Programme. Participants gain a basic knowledge of life in a range of aquatic water bodies. They discover how to identify the more common plants and animals, which may act as indicators of the health of the stream. The course also introduces participants to the threats faced by these water courses, not only the widespread impacts of land drainage and pollution but also the impacts invasive fish, invertebrate and plant species can have on the functioning of rivers, streams and lakes. The course includes training on how to carry out a basic river survey, the collection and identification of key indicator invertebrate and plant species, how river and stream catchments work and the importance of removing barriers to fish migration. Rivers may appear to us as unchanging, with their water destined to flow for ever to the sea. But, like all wetland habitats, they are easily damaged and great care is needed to ensure that they remain in good condition.

The Shannon floodlands

The 'hollow lands' and 'long dappled grass' mentioned in the W.B Yeats poem 'The Song of Wandering Aengus' are symbolic of the extensive wet grasslands of the midlands and west of Ireland that were so familiar to the poet. This includes such places as the margins of lowland rivers where the water frequently floods into the grassland. These floodlands are known as callows.

In the midst of a survey of the River Shannon Callows, my colleagues and I had eaten dinner on board a large motor cruiser tied up by a floating pontoon in the small town of Banagher, County Offaly after a day of walking the riverbanks. The sun was starting to go down in a clear, cloudless sky to the west when I set off for an evening walk in the meadows that border the river. It was now several months since the floods had receded and the grass was long, brushing against my boots as I walked. In places I had to jump across deep drains, filled with aquatic vegetation and fringed with reeds and the large yellow flowers of marsh marigold. Swallows and sand martins dipped over the river surface feeding on great swarms of insects above the water. As the light faded, I took from my pocket two large, dried bones into which I had carved a series of notches. Rubbing them together repeatedly, I produced a sound like an electronic signal. And then there was an answer. From the long grass a corncrake was calling back, apparently treating me as a rival. Then a second bird joined in and, before long, the large meadow had several corncrakes calling out their strange territorial sounds. These meadows also resounded to the distinctive calls of several species of breeding waders, such as the snipe, redshank and lapwing, that we had come here to survey.

Known as callows from the Irish word *caladh*, these river meadows were flooded for up to six months each winter. Often the water remained on the fields right into the spring, receding just in time for the returning birds to settle here for a few short summer months. The ground is peaty and too soft for heavy grazing animals so the meadows have traditionally been left to grow long and were used only for hay. The wetness of the soil also prevented farm machinery being used to cut the hay until the late summer, when the birds had finished nesting and the broods with young birds were already mobile.

The flooding of the Shannon Callows has been likened to a 'badly functioning gutter' by ecologist Stephen Heery, who has studied these meadows for at least forty years.[41] The slope or gradient of the river channel is so gradual that the flow in places is barely perceptible. The large lakes of Lough Ree and Lough Derg act as reservoirs, holding back the floodwaters for a while and releasing them slowly downstream. Constrictions in the riverbed and natural dams such as esker ridges left by prehistoric glaciers mean that the channel is frequently unable to contain the large volumes of water coming off the surrounding landscape. As the flow increases the water rises and spills out across the adjacent grasslands at various points along the river between Lough Ree and Lough Derg. At first this is hard to witness, as the regular drains across the land fill to the brim and water creeps around the tussocks of longer vegetation. The raised banks or levees soon become long narrow islands, as the water surrounds them, and then the grass begins to disappear beneath the floods. Some level of flooding occurs here each winter, but in some years, the floods come early in autumn and may also remain late into the spring. April is a key month when ground-nesting birds start to breed and when farmers wish to move their cattle onto the land. If the callows are still flooded at this time, the birds will often desert the breeding grounds or delay their nesting to later in the year when the chances of their chicks surviving are severely reduced.

Flooding in spring also delays the start of growth of the grassland plants, including those that the farmers want for their grazing livestock. Fertilised only by the nutrients in alluvial silt left by the river waters, a stunning array of wildflowers appears as if by magic as the soils dry out. The large yellow flowers of flag irises reach up to the sun, while delicate pink cuckoo flowers and blue water forget-me-nots are everywhere. The ground may appear to have a yellow tinge as the flowers of creeping buttercup emerge among the sedges and rushes. Occasionally, a rare species like the green-winged orchid pokes its delicate flowers out from the grass. Along the riverbank and most of the drainage ditches tall reeds grow in the permanent water and water mint releases its delicious aroma when crushed by a passing foot. Botanists group the wild plants into communities and relate these to habitats such as wet alluvial grasslands, marsh grasslands, fens and dry grasslands. Here is one of the best places to see the natural transition from wet to dry soils and vegetation as one walks away from the river's edge.

In 1987, our survey team found large numbers of breeding waders and corncrakes all along the Shannon Callows between Lough Ree and Lough Derg.[42] Since then, the lapwing has declined drastically in this habitat. In the 1980s we found some 268 pairs on the Shannon Callows but a repeat survey in 2019 revealed just 41 pairs. The reasons are not altogether clear. In the early years, a series of summer flooding events on the callows reduced breeding success. Four consecutive years of April flooding, from 1991 to 1994, hit the population badly. In recent times, it seems that the number of predators, mainly foxes and crows, has

increased and these ground-nesting birds are quite
vulnerable in open grassland. Ian Herbert, also one of
the survey team in 1987, did some experiments using
a camera mounted near a nest and found that foxes
were indeed stealing the eggs. We recorded sixty-one
male corncrakes in 1987, calling loudly from the hay
meadows in summer, but by the early 2000s they had all
but disappeared.[43]

I went back to the callows recently in May to
see the changes for myself. Here I met with Stephen
Heery and together we walked among some of the
hay meadows around Banagher in County Offaly. The
fields where we had done our surveys more than three
decades earlier looked just the same, but the sounds
were different. There were no mewing pairs of lapwing
calling overhead, no snipe chipping from the wet
hollows, no curlews with their haunting whistle and
definitely no corncrakes calling in the evening sun. Just
a few tiny meadow pipits rose up from the grass as we
walked through field after field. It felt like a deserted
place, once so alive and full of life, now silent and
empty. What could possibly have caused this change, I
wondered. The farm management was much the same,
with grass growing long through the summer months.

Just a few horses were the only livestock we saw. We met a callows farmer on his tractor at one of the gates, but he was too young to remember the richness of birdlife here in the 1980s.

Walking down by the banks of the Shannon, Stephen and I stared out across the sluggish river water to an island called Inishee. Here, at last, we saw a pair of redshanks calling loudly from fence posts to warn their chicks in the vegetation on the island. Then a single lapwing rose up to chase off a marauding hooded crow that threatened its young chicks. So there were still some waders on the island, and this suggested that the moving water might be a barrier to some mammalian predators such as fox and badger which would take both eggs and young on the ground. This knowledge had prompted BirdWatch Ireland to erect some further defences here in the form of anti-predator fences around the perimeters of two islands in the river. These were tall wire fences that were electrified to discourage mammals like the introduced American mink, which had increased in numbers in the Shannon valley in the 1990s. In the following years the fences were clearly shown to increase breeding wader productivity and populations. Unfortunately, the anti-predator fence at

Inishee is now fallen in places and in need of extensive
repairs or complete replacement.

Green plover

I cast my mind back to a day on the Shannon Callows
in the 1980s when a distinctive black and white bird
rose across my path and flew about over my head
with a plaintive, mewing call. Then it was joined by
another and another until there was a small flock of
lapwings fluttering around the field calling to their
chicks to stay in the cover of longer vegetation. Once
they hatch from the eggs, the fluffy chicks are led by
their parents into long grass or wetter areas where they
learn by mimicry to feed on the abundance of insects
and soil invertebrates until they are able to fly. I kept
walking, and within a few minutes all the adult birds
had dropped down to resume watch over their growing
broods. This was once a common enough experience
when visiting wet grassland.

Threats to their habitats are not a new phenomenon
for lapwings (or green plovers as they were called in
the past). In 1853, the naturalist John Watters wrote, 'it
has somewhat diminished in numbers, in consequence
of the great advance of drainage and reclaiming of

waste lands in Ireland'.[44] With loss of the 'waste lands' some lapwings adapted to nesting on grassy meadows and ploughed fields, and they are sometimes still found in these habitats today. Many of the birds that nested on the Shannon Callows in the 1980s may have simply moved to a new habitat – abandoned peatland around Lough Boora in Co. Offaly. Here Bord na Móna is helping to create new areas of wilderness, flooding parts of the cutaway bog to make lakes for waterbirds. This project was initiated by the Grey Partridge Trust, which fenced in a former peatland to protect the nests of these threatened game birds. To their surprise, lapwings also benefited from this conservation project, their nests being protected from ground predators. In 2015, BirdWatch Ireland found over 122 lapwing nests in this area, one of the highest surviving concentrations in Ireland of a species that was once widespread and common in Irish wetlands.

Like all of the plover family, lapwings have developed a distinct type of behaviour to distract predators away from their eggs or chicks. Their sad mewing song first attracts the attention of the fox or crow. When walking the adult birds may limp or drag a wing, pretending to be badly injured and thus an easy catch for a predator. When the hunter has started to chase down the adult lapwing, it flies away at the last minute, and the predator is left well off the trail of the nest. The nests of lapwings were sometimes associated with hares in local folk traditions. Egg-laying hares appear sometimes in pagan myths, too, although it is well known that mammals like hares do not lay eggs. This seems to be linked to the shallow depressions in vegetation, known as forms, where hares rest and rear their young. Ground-nesting birds such as lapwings have similar nest-like structures in open grassland. On finding these eggs in what looked to be a hare's form, people believed that the hares themselves were laying eggs in spring. Hearing even one lapwing call is, for me, a refreshing signal that nature is still functioning here and a sign of hope for the future.

Wellbeing in water

I often sit by a pool in the river that flows through our farm to stare for a while into its crystal-clear waters. The music of the water bubbling over stones as it flows into the pool drowns out other sounds, except for louder birdsong in the alder trees overhead. The sounds of the river and an almost hypnotic view of the moving water bring on a kind of peace and serenity that only nature can offer. The pool is not deep enough for swimming, but I sometimes lie down in the water and feel the river flow over me, washing away the cares and perspiration from a hot day in the sun.

The English nature writer Roger Deakin spent a whole summer wild swimming across Britain, in the sea, rock pools, rivers, streams, lakes, ponds, fens, aquaducts, waterfalls, canals and in the moat around his own country house. He explored the importance of immersion in water to the human condition. In his classic book *Waterlog* he wrote:

Natural water has always held the magical power to cure. Somehow or other, it transmits its own self-regenerating powers to the swimmer. I can dive in with a long face and what feels like a terminal case of depression and come out a whistling idiot. There is a feeling of absolute freedom that comes with the sheer liberation of nakedness as well as weightlessness in natural water, and it leads to a deep bond with the bathing place.[45]

Water comprises as much as 60 per cent of our

bodies, making it a critical component of health and wellbeing. While we are often advised to drink six to eight glasses of water a day, we don't often hear about the health benefits of being in or around water. Just spending time around rivers and lakes can have just as significant an effect on your mind and body as increasing your water intake. In addition to helping build physical strength and stamina, swimming has been shown to have an overall positive benefit on mental health. Swimming in a pool, river or the sea can improve mood in both men and women, decreasing the risk of depression.

When I was a child, I would play for hours with my brothers in a local stream. In those days, parents were less concerned about the dangers to children and wild play was a normal activity. To find out if this is something that children still do today, I spoke to my friend Angie Kinsella, who is a forest school leader. She said:

I feel that wild water play is important for positive development in children. The site where I lead all my forest school sessions has a stream running through it. Watching the children build dams, boats or simply splash about was always a pleasure and certainly a highlight for the children themselves. I saw such joy in those moments. It was also a great lesson of cause and effect. A little girl decided one day to sit in the stream and she quickly realised that she was very, very wet.

I also spoke to Amber Godwin, another forest and nature school leader in Wicklow. She told me:

Children learn what they're capable of, where their boundaries are, and where they want to push and extend those boundaries. Specifically for water play, the physical experience of navigating cold water, slime, rocks under their feet, currents and riverbanks helps develop their motor skills, balance and coordination, whilst building resilience through experiencing unpleasant (or pleasant!) feelings. Through trial and error they find out about how water works, what floats, what sinks and learn how everything in the natural world fits together. They are immersed in nature and become familiar with the plants, animals, fish, insects that surround them and they will grow up feeling part of this world.

In a later stage of life, swimming can have a particularly profound effect on aging minds and bodies. Hydrotherapy can be ideal for frail or older adults who want to stay active. Regular swimming is ideal exercise that can help to reduce the risk of chronic illness and disability in older adults and improve mental health, increasing longevity and allowing them to live independently for longer. Using the healing power of water is not a new idea. Both the ancient Egyptians and the Greeks used bathing rituals to help cure physical ailments, while Native American tribes believed in the purifying power of sweat lodges. Today, saunas have taken the place of sweat lodges. People around the world today use hydrotherapy to treat everything from poor posture to anxiety and depression. These are just some of the benefits of embracing the healing power of water.

River coracles

Fishing for salmon and sea trout in the estuary waters of some of Ireland's streams and rivers has been pursued since ancient times. Skin-covered boats have been used for this purpose since the earliest people colonised this country. The design of the lightweight coracle, eminently suited to fast-flowing rivers, was tailored to meet the specific conditions where it was used. The boat was rowed with a short wooden paddle, which allowed the boatman to manoeuvre the boat with one hand while the other arm was free to handle the salmon net. Two coracles worked in tandem, dragging the net stretched across the river downstream until a fish was caught, and then each boatman gathered up the ends of the net and the two coracles were brought close together to secure the fish. The coracles used on the River Boyne were made with hazel rods, willows and cowhide, shaped to form a steep-sided oval bowl. Willow was sourced from the river islands at Oldbridge, a townland at the furthest tidal reach upstream of Drogheda on the River Boyne.

The construction of coracles was a tradition that caught the eye of Irish photographer Frank Stephens, whose collection of over 2,000 lantern slides, now housed in Trinity College Dublin, captures a disappearing lifestyle in Ireland in the opening decades of the twentieth century. In this series of images Stephens recorded the building of a coracle on the River Boyne. This was a specimen coracle built for the National Museum of Ireland by Michael O'Brien, who was born in 1853. The work was photographed, filmed and recorded in 1930 by Stephens and Dr Adolf Mahr, then keeper of antiquities at the museum. When finished, O'Brien's coracle was described as 'a round-shaped curragh', measuring less than a metre in diameter. These glass plate slides are an evocative record of the tradition of building a boat of ancient design by the last of many generations of coracle builders based at Oldbridge, Co. Meath.

Estuary – the river's grave

Ultimately all the water that flows down a river meets saltwater and discharges to the sea in an estuary of some sort. It is not a sudden death but a gradual mixing of freshwater with seawater brought in by pulses of the tide. Salinity, the term used to describe saltiness of water, changes from close to zero in the freshwater to about 35 parts per thousand (ppt) in the sea. The intermediate state of slight saltiness is called brackish water. This gradient is rarely a simple one as each estuary differs in shape, each river differs in the volume of freshwater that it carries and the rotation of the earth exerts major effects on the mixing process. As saltwater is denser, it sinks to the bottom of the estuary and forms a wedge pushing up beneath the lighter freshwater. The mixing may be complicated when two arms of the estuary converge or by breaking waves or turbulence in the water caused by narrow constrictions or deeper areas in the estuary bed.

The largest estuary in Ireland is that of the River Shannon which stretches from above Limerick to the open sea at Loop Head, a distance of about ninety-five kilometres. It is joined halfway down by the Fergus Estuary, and each dries out twice every day, exposing a huge area of soft mudflats stretching away as far as the eye can see. The largest tides, which occur at the time of full moon, have a range of up to five metres between high and low tide. Given its huge size, the estuary has many distinct and interesting habitats including mudflats, saltmarsh, brackish marsh, stony shores and reedbeds. These hold a wide variety of wild plants, such as sea beet, sea lavender and scurvy grass, that are tolerant of different levels of salinity. I once paddled a canoe in the upper reaches of the Shannon Estuary, searching for a rare plant called triangular club-rush that grows only at the lowest edges of extensive reedbeds and is found in Ireland only in the eastern part of the Shannon Estuary. The celebrated

naturalist Robert Lloyd Praeger was the first to report
its presence in 1900, and it still survives in this location
today.[46]

Many thousands of years ago, the waters of the
Shannon Estuary were a lot lower than they are
today. At the mouth of the estuary, at Rinevalla Bay,
are the clear remains of a submerged forest with large
root masses and stumps of oaks and pines embedded
in peat exposed by the low tide. This ancient forest
dates from the New Stone Age (or Neolithic) period.
We might imagine the estuary then as a complex
system of saltmarshes and channels winding through
a coastal forest that stretched right down to the edge
of the tide. Red deer bones of similar age have also
been discovered in tidal sediments in the upper Fergus
Estuary. Human settlers in the earlier Mesolithic
period were hunter-gatherers who would have hunted,
fished and gathered plant foods along the estuary.
The archaeologist Dr Aidan O'Sullivan has excavated
a number of fascinating fish-traps from the mudflats.
These comprise lines of wooden posts laid out in a
V-shape and leading to a trap made from basketwork.
As the tide rose and fell each day fish moving up the
estuary towards land would have been trapped in

the baskets and people could have walked out at low tide to collect them. These coastal communities also gathered dogwhelks, periwinkles and limpets from the shoreline and hunted wild pig, hares and birds in the neighbouring forests.[47]

The variety of estuary birds today is probably much as it would have been in the Stone Age. Most prominent are the wading birds such as curlew, godwit and oystercatcher, while wildfowl like Brent geese and wigeon graze on estuarine plants. Some estuarine species such as common sandpiper, snipe and moorhen are also found in the freshwater sections of rivers. Kingfishers move freely between the river and estuary at different times of year. All of these species were quarry for early hunters, and for sports shooters right up to the early twentieth century. They were pursued in flat boats that could be paddled along the shallow channels or towed across the mudflats. Today estuaries offer exciting birdwatching with vast swirling flocks of geese, golden plovers and tiny waders such as dunlin and sanderlings. There is always the chance of rare species such as American or Siberian waders turning up in the spring and autumn. Many of the birds are quite accustomed to close approaches of people, especially near the major cities such as Dublin, Belfast, Cork, Limerick and Galway.

The waters of all rivers eventually become absorbed and mixed with seawater, often carrying with them a large volume of terrestrial sediments. As the flow is slowed down or halted by a rising tide this material is deposited at the mouth of the river and can result in the build-up of a delta and saltmarshes. The river has run its course and the constantly turning water cycle from rain to the sea is completed.

The future for Irish rivers

Irish rivers today are in the emergency ward. The majority are polluted, with only twenty rivers in the country remaining in pristine condition. For a century, many catchments have been subject to arterial drainage, which straightens and deepens the channels, changing them from diverse wildlife habitats into lifeless canals. Native fish populations including salmon, sea trout and eels have been decimated, and the rare freshwater pearl mussel is on the verge of extinction. Weirs and hydroelectric dams form barriers to migratory fish, and invasive species such as American signal crayfish, African curly waterweed and American mink threaten our native plants and animals. Overarching all of this are the impacts of climate change, already evident in higher water temperatures and reduced river flows. One could be forgiven for thinking that we care little for our beautiful waterways.

Despite this, rivers supply us with most of our drinking water and drive the turbines that provide us with free electricity. They are vital cogs in the water cycle that returns rainfall to the sea. Rivers are the cradle for salmon and trout populations that are so highly valued by anglers and ecologists and were once abundant. Some of our top tourist destinations are centred on rivers – the River Shannon, Ashleagh Falls, Glencar waterfall, the Vale of Avoca and the Bend of the Boyne. Rivers have provided inspiration for artists, poets and photographers down the centuries. The fascination of moving water is good for our mental health and for appreciating the beauty of our landscape. In short, we could not do without our rivers.

It is not too late to rescue some of the damaged waterways. Enthusiasm for rewilding is growing across Europe, and in 2022 the European Commission proposed a new law on nature restoration. We need to limit the damaging impacts that agriculture is having on water quality through the spreading of slurry and the more insidious effects of fertiliser run-off. The havoc that arterial drainage is wreaking on many rivers needs to stop and other solutions to flooding of properties, such as restoration of natural floodplains, pursued. Unnecessary barriers to the migration of fish should be removed or at least bypassed and a sustained effort made to prevent the import of invasive freshwater species. Establishing native woodland on the banks of lowland rivers helps both with improved water quality and erosion prevention. There needs to be support for such measures from the population as a whole so that more sustainable decisions are made in future.

There are some small positive signs of a change in attitudes, for example in the formation across the country of rivers trusts, which are promoting citizen science as a way of monitoring water quality and raising awareness of river conservation. The Local Authority Waters Programme (LAWPRO) is working on behalf of all thirty-one local authorities in the Republic of Ireland coordinating efforts to achieve good or high water quality in rivers, lakes, transitional and coastal waters and groundwater, as required by the EU Water Framework Directive. Other projects, such as the Waters for Life initiative, act as a catchment-scale demonstration project to test and validate the effectiveness of implementing locally tailored 'best practice' measures across a range of landscapes and land uses typically associated with the catchments of high-status rivers. The project will trial and validate the implementation of these measures to improve water quality, mainly in the upland sections of river catchments.

The National Floods Directive does state that it aims to 'focus on managing flood risk rather than rely only on flood protection measures aimed at reducing flooding'. IFI says that this approach could be beneficial to river enhancement programmes, allowing bank erosion to occur in favour of stone bank protection, reinstating or reconnecting meanders, designating specific flood plain areas and providing in-stream channel features that allow rivers to dissipate high energy in a more natural manner.[48] However, we need to see more of these aspirations turned into action.

In river catchment management, the OPW carries out drainage maintenance and dredging in order to permit faster flow. Their approach to riparian management can be described as 'hard' engineering solutions, such as mechanised channel clearance and construction of defensive embankments along rivers. The alternative nature-based approach to flood management includes such measures as 'leaky dams', which are constructed of natural materials like locally sourced timber and act to release the floodwater slowly, thus avoiding flash flooding. This approach appears to mimic the effects of beaver dams in other European countries without acknowledging the animals that evolved the method thousands of years ago. Similar techniques are now widely used in damaged Irish peatlands where multiple peat or wooden dams are inserted into drains that are causing the bogs to dry out and shrink. Another method is to return river water to historic floodplain channels when peak flows occur, thus delaying the release of damaging floods. The restoration of riparian woodland is also now seen as a natural flood retention measure, although there are few examples to date of the practical implementation of this in Ireland. All of these nature-based solutions are being investigated by a team from Trinity College Dublin as part of a project called SloWaters (Natural Water Retention Measures).[49]

The International Union for the Conservation of Nature has issued a helpful report on nature-based solutions for restoring the rivers of the UK and Republic of Ireland.[50] This accepts that reversing the long history of alteration and bringing back the features characteristic of naturally functioning rivers is a considerable challenge, but the arguments for achieving it are compelling. Alongside biodiversity conservation and enhancement, there can be considerable benefits to society, including improved resilience to climate change impacts, improving water storage and attenuating peak flows, reducing river maintenance costs, improved human wellbeing as well as new opportunities for tourism and leisure. Fundamental to any of these measures is the need for a renewed sense of stewardship by communities towards their local river environment leading to a political will to do things better.

Lakes

I will arise and go now, for always
night and day
I hear lake water lapping with low
sounds by the shore;
While I stand on the roadway, or on
the pavements grey,
I hear it in the deep heart's core.

From 'The Lake Isle of Innisfree' (1890) by W.B. YEATS

William Butler Yeats's love of Sligo, the home of his
mother's family, is well known, and much of his poetry
was inspired by the natural beauty of this area. In one
of his best-loved poems, 'The Lake Isle of Innisfree',
the poet remembers one of the islands on Lough Gill,
a large lake on the borders of Sligo and Leitrim. Yeats
spent many childhood summers in this area, and he
was clearly yearning for the solitude of the lake as he

walked the streets of London in 1888. The island is only accessible by boat.

My own boating experience on lakes began with a trip aboard an old wooden cruiser on Lough Derg in the lower Shannon valley in the 1960s. My family had borrowed the boat from a friend for our annual holiday. I felt confident that this would be no problem for my father, who was an experienced sailor and former naval officer. At the little village of Dromineer we packed all our kit on board including several bicycles which were strapped securely on the cabin roof. Things went well, and we docked the boat at several other piers around the lake for overnight stays. Then on the last day of our holiday, crossing back across the lake, the wind blew up, and sizeable waves formed on the surface of the water. Heavy rain made the trip even more miserable. The boat began to rock violently, and we feared that the cabin, which had been added to the former lifeboat, made it too top heavy. The other hazards we faced were the numerous rocks and shallows, many just below the surface and invisible from the boat. However, after an hour of skilful seamanship my father guided the boat to safety by the pier, and we went home thankful that it was only a close shave.

In later years I visited many other lakes across the country, mainly to survey their bird populations. I came to understand that every lake is different. The underlying geology, surrounding habitats, use of land in the area and water quality all combine to make each individual lake unique. In addition, there are some very special types of lake, including limestone waters and turloughs, coastal lagoons and deep mountain lakes. Some have important fish or bird populations, while others have been the sites of important archaeological finds.

Lake facts

By comparison with rivers, lakes have been described as merely a 'hiccup in a drainage basin, caused by natural or human interference in the slope of the land'.[1] In contrast to many other countries, where the majority of lakes were formed by dams, Irish lakes are mostly natural in character. Added together, they cover about 2 per cent of the Irish landscape, about twice the European average.

It is difficult to define when a pond becomes large enough to be called a lake but there are more than 4,000 water bodies over five hectares in area in the island of

Ireland. Countless more are smaller, and seven lakes cover more than 50 square kilometres each. Lough Neagh is by far the largest at 385 square kilometres (about half the size of County Louth). In Ulster alone there are probably more than 2,000 lakes, but this includes everything larger than a small millpond or upland pool.[2] It is certain that there were many more lakes in Ireland immediately after the last Ice Age when meltwater flooded the landscape, but many of these, especially in the flat midland plain, have subsequently turned into bogs.

Most of the lowland lakes of the midlands formed on limestone rocks or glacial deposits containing limestone which influences their chemistry, making them mainly alkaline in character. By contrast, upland lakes are mostly acidic, because they drain off acid rocks such as granite or quartzite. This has a big influence on the type of vegetation that they support and the invertebrates, amphibians and fish that live in their waters. The lowland hard-water lakes have the greatest biodiversity. The water in most Irish lakes is clear enough to be able to see down to between one and four metres. These surface layers are where most of the plant life is found, where there is enough sunlight for photosynthesis. Some lakes show a seasonal variation in transparency due to blooms of phytoplankton or green algae in the warmer weather. Mountain lakes tend to be rather brown in colour due to the peat from which the water flows. Although ice rarely forms on the surface in winter and lake water is mixed during colder periods, layers of warm and cold water may form for short periods during the summer.[3]

The biological life in lakes is quite different from that in rivers, because of their relatively still waters, greater depth and the fact that different water may stratify into distinct layers. As in the sea, lakes have their own plankton, microscopic bacteria, algae and invertebrate animals. First to appear in spring are the diatoms, tiny plant species with intricate silica cases. In summer, the green algae appear. When they multiply this is sometimes described as an algal bloom. Among the most spectacular creatures are the non-biting midges. After a year living on the lake bed they emerge as adults in April or May. Around Lough Neagh great swarms of flies form twisting pillars, like smoke, that are visible from some distance.

Glendalough, the valley of two lakes, is one of the best-known and most heavily used tourist spots in Ireland. Situated within an hour's drive of Dublin city, it is often congested with tourist coaches and cars full of day trippers. This complex of rivers and lakes is part of the upper catchment of the Avonmore River. I walked the banks of both lakes in winter and up along the Glenealo River which flows from a hanging valley high above Glendalough. The Upper Lake in particular is deep and dark, reaching down to a maximum depth of thirty metres.

Microscopic floating plant life, phytoplankton, does occur here but the density is low. Even so, over a hundred different types of plankton have been recorded from this lake. Most of these have a high tolerance of acidity. So too the larger animal life in the water is reduced by high levels of acidity and aluminium, while zooplankton (microscopic animal life) is diverse in acid lakes. Molluscs and crustaceans do not survive where the pH (acidity) is less than 6.0. In the Upper Lake at Glendalough, the shoreline creatures are dominated by midge larvae, stoneflies and mayflies, most of which are acid tolerant. Research by Dr Marinus Otte of UCD showed that the marsh at the Upper Lake has 40 times the level of iron as nearby Lough Dan, 6,000 times the level of zinc, 1,200 times the arsenic and 2,899

times the lead. All of this metal pollution dates from
the nineteenth century when these valuable minerals
were extracted from surrounding hillsides where great
spoil heaps of mine waste dominate the scene today.[4]

Lake legends

In the days before internet, television or radio, and
throughout the millennia when few ordinary people
could read or write, storytelling around the fireplace
was a common form of entertainment and a way of
passing on knowledge from one generation to the next.
Most people have heard the story of how Lough Neagh
was formed when Ireland's legendary giant Fionn mac
Cumhaill scooped up a chunk of earth and tossed it
at a Scottish rival. His aim was poor, and it fell into
the Irish Sea, forming the Isle of Man, while the crater
left behind filled with water to form Lough Neagh.
Manchán Magan retells another story about the origins
of this lake. Eocha, the son of a Munster king, eloped
with his stepmother Eibhliu, and, travelling north,
they borrowed a horse from Aengus at Newgrange to
speed them on their way. However, on reaching Ulster,
Eocha and Eibhliu forgot to return the horse. Furious,
Aengus made the horse urinate, which formed a magic

well. The well overflowed and, after drowning the fleeing couple, eventually formed a giant lake, now known as Lough Neagh.[5]

Many of the best-known monastic settlements, founded by the saints, are associated with lakes. Some examples are Glendalough in County Wicklow, founded by St Kevin in the sixth century; Holy Island on Lough Derg, associated with both St Colum, who founded it in the sixth century, and St Caimin, who was the inspiration behind its fame as a centre of learning and prayer in the following century; and Errew Abbey, on the western shore of Lough Conn, where St Tiernan founded a monastery in the seventh century.

Long ago, it was a regular duty of saints to intervene when locals were visited by some fearsome beast, and the normal practice was to guide it to a lake and restrain it there through the medium of prayer. Unfortunately, prayers were insufficient to confine some water monsters to the depths, and these required more permanent disposal. A large creature was believed to live in the depths of Lough Ree, leaving trails of bloodied carcasses on the lakeshore. However, not all monsters were considered evil. One such creature was said to haunt the larger of the three Coumalocha

corrie lakes on a plateau in the centre of the Comeragh
Mountains of County Waterford. Normally, fishermen
avoided lakes reputed to contain a monster, but here
they were encouraged by the actions of a kindly creature
known as 'the Dark Fisherman of Coumalocha'. When
an angler cast his line without success, the creature
was said to quietly rise from the depths and attach a
trout to the line before returning to its murky lair. As
Lady Gregory once remarked, 'there are queer things
in lakes'.[6]

Stories of a king otter date back to 1684, when
it was named by Roderick O'Faherty in his book *A
Description of West Connacht*. Two centuries later, in the
1896 edition of the *Journal of Royal Society of Antiquaries
of Ireland*, a letter from a Ms Walkington described
her sighting of a creature that was 'half-wolfdog, half-
fish'. Months later, her letter was responded to by
one Mr H. Chinchester Hart who had heard stories
of a creature much like the one Ms Walkington had
described. He believed it to be 'the king of all lakes and
father of all otters' who could 'run his muzzle through
rocks'. Much more recently Manchán Magan was told
about the legend of a giant otter that swam around at
dusk searching for young children to take back to the

Otherworld where they would become part of the fairy tribes.[7] I can imagine any children who were told this story in the kitchen candlelight would grow up with a fear of rivers and lakes and what might live in their waters.

In a cemetery in the Glenade Valley of County Leitrim, the sandstone grave-marker of a local woman bears the image of a savage-looking otter. Though the carving is faded, the creature's gargantuan size is evident, particularly in relation to the disembodied hand driving a sword into its neck. Dated 1722, this marker is the last resting place of Grainne Con (Grace Connolly) whose death is still attributed by many to a terrible monster, the *dobharchú*. On a September morning that year, Grace left her home in a town on the north-western shore of Glenade Lake to bathe in the nearby lake. According to the legend the *dobharchú* emerged from the water, killing Grace in seconds.

Several hours later, her husband Terence set out for the lake in search of his wife and found her dead near the great beast, which had fallen asleep on the shore beside her body. Mad with grief, Terence attacked the *dobharchú* with his blade, and killed it. The water of the lake began to ripple and the creature's enraged mate rose from the depths. Terence ran for his horse, with the second *dobharchú* close on his heels, and rode for miles, the creature relentless in its pursuit. The chase went on for hours until he was forced to stop to rest his faltering horse. When the *dobharchú* caught up with him, it thrust its fearsome head through the body of the horse. At this moment Terence struck, cutting the monster's head off to end the chase and avenge his wife.[8]

Though the legend of the giant otters has its roots in times long past, belief that this fearsome species may still be out there persists in some places. In the year 2000, noted Irish artist Sean Corcoran reported seeing a *dobharchú* in a lake while visiting Omey Island in Connemara with his wife. 'The creature swam the width of the lake from west to east in what seemed like a matter of seconds,' Sean said. After doing so it bounced onto a boulder on the shoreline, gave 'the most haunting screech' they had ever heard and disappeared into the depths. Reminiscent of the famous stories of a monster in Scotland's Loch Ness, this legend underlines the fears that some superstitious people have of what might lie in the dark waters of many lakes.

Jackson's Falls on the Avonmore River, County Wicklow. Tumbling over low rocky outcrops, the river is well oxygenated as it enters its lowland stage.

Upper Lake at Glendalough, County Wicklow. With the water draining off peaty soils in the mountains, this deep, acidic lake is naturally low in nutrients.

The dipper is a bird of fast-flowing rivers, where it often nests beneath bridges or water-falls. It feeds by diving into the water and hunting for insect larvae among the stones. (*Photo by John Fox*)

A female goosander swims downstream with her chicks on the Avonmore River in County Wicklow. These fish-eating ducks breed in riverside trees, and the chicks drop straight into the river below before they can fly. (*Photo by Ann Fitzpatrick*)

Otters are widespread in Ireland and can be found on rivers, lakes and the coast. They are mostly active at night, hunting for fish, frogs and other aquatic creatures like freshwater crayfish. (*Photo by John Fox*)

Annalong Mill, County Down. Water mills were once common in every part of Ireland and were used to grind corn, saw timber and process wool and flax. (*Photo courtesy of Fáilte Ireland*)

Salmon leaping over a weir to reach its spawning area in the headwaters of a river. These fish spend part of their lives in the ocean and have declined steeply in recent decades. (*Photo by Will O'Connor*)

Japanese knotweed is one of the most difficult invasive plants to eradicate from a riverbank.

Kingfishers live on the lower reaches of most large rivers throughout the country. They nest in holes in vertical riverbanks. (*Photo by John Fox*)

Powerscourt Waterfall, County Wicklow, is the second highest waterfall in Ireland. (*Photo courtesy of Fáilte Ireland*)

Freshwater pearl mussels are in danger of extinction in Irish rivers. They depend on clean water and gravel that is free of silt. (*Photo by Will O'Connor*)

Flyfishers on Gougane Barra Lake, County Cork. (*Photo courtesy of Fáilte Ireland*)

Altan Lough, County Donegal, is a typical upland lake that is low in nutrients. Errigal Mountain is in the background.

Bunduff Lough, County Sligo, is a shallow lake close to the coast. Benbulben is in the background.

This grey heron caught an eel that proved to be a beakful to deal with. (*Photo by Karl Partridge*)

A reconstructed crannog. At least 1,200 of these ancient dwelling places were built for defensive reasons in lakes, mainly in the north-west of the country. (*Photo courtesy of the National Heritage Park, Wexford*)

Reeds growing on the edge of a lake. They were extensively harvested in the past for thatching houses.

Water lily leaves and reeds.

Turlough in County Clare. These lakes dry up in the summer, as the water drops into the limestone below.

Fallen trees block the stream, causing flooding in a wet woodland.

Frogspawn in a woodland pond. (*Photo by Brian O'Toole*)

Reedmace growing on the edge of an artificial pond.

Darter dragonfly on a water lily flower. (*Photo by John Fox*)

Pond dipping is a fun activity for all ages. (*Photo by Aoife O'Rourke*)

A barge on the Grand Canal. These waterways were once important routes for the transportation of goods and passengers before the age of railways. (*Photo courtesy of Fáilte Ireland*)

A cutaway bog that has been allowed to flood, forming a new lake.

Flooded land on the lower River Shannon, with wet woodland in the foreground.
(*Photo by Will O'Connor*)

The river drops over a series of rock steps at Ennistymon Falls, County Clare.

Crannogs

I was walking in the hills near Portnoo, County Donegal, when I came upon a beautiful lake surrounded by reeds with a heron stalking its prey in one shallow area. Out in the centre of the lake was a perfectly circular island that looked inviting. Enquiring locally, I found a boatman who was prepared to ferry me out for a closer look. This island is in fact man-made. It is a type of archaeological site known as a *crannóg*, a lake dwelling from the early medieval period. The Irish word *crannóg*, meaning a small island built with young trees, was only used in the native Irish annals from the thirteenth century onwards. The age of these features has been calculated by dating timbers found in crannogs in counties Antrim, Down and Fermanagh. Tree-ring dating studies have shown that crannogs were first constructed in Ireland during an eighty-year period in the late sixth and early seventh centuries.

They were usually built of dumped layers of peat, brushwood, heavier timbers, stone and soil, and many were originally surrounded by a palisade or fence of closely spaced vertical timber and roundwood posts. Sometimes a crannog would have had a stone causeway leading from the mainland. This would have made it easier to defend against raiders unfamiliar with the twists and turns of the path. Some may have been defended farmsteads where men, women and children would have lived and worked in safety. We also know that many crannogs were royal residences, where kings, surrounded by their stewards, warriors, craftsmen, labourers and slaves, would have resided at certain times of the year, such as feast days. Some crannogs may have been used only as places for craftsmen to practise their trades. It is also possible that some were used by whole communities as more easily defended refuges from their enemies. They were used again in the sixteenth and seventeenth centuries by the Irish lords to store gold, silver and ammunition or as dwellings for troops, prisoners or the wounded.

Some crannogs, such as those at Lagore, Ballinderry and Moynagh Lough, were associated with the Irish kings. Archaeological evidence of high-status foods and delicacies at these sites suggests that they were locations for periodic royal feasting. At some crannogs, such as Rathtinaun, County Sligo, submerged wooden boats have been found, underlining the importance of boat-based transport for accessing these structures. Life in a crannog was usually based on the agricultural economy of the surrounding landscape. The people who lived there would have moved out each day to work in the fields, producing food, tending their cattle and collecting materials for such work as basketry, fishing and boat-building. Cattle-herding was particularly important in medieval times, and land values were often measured in terms of cattle ownership, the size of the herd being an indication of a farmer's wealth and status. Other livestock such as chickens, sheep, pigs and goats would also have been kept and some people would have foraged for plant material from the surrounding waters.[9]

Useful lake plants

Some plants that grow in the water were particularly important to early people, who would have taken great care to find them and prepare them as food. I once waded into a lake in Connemara just to collect the roots of a water lily whose leaves were floating on the surface. Apart from the shock of the cold water, I was quite surprised that I had to wade out waist-deep before I could reach down to dislodge the large rhizomes. The beautiful big yellow flowers open out in the summer sun and their seeds then float off to lodge in other parts of the lake. Seeds of both white water lily and yellow water lily have been recorded at a number of Irish Mesolithic sites, sometimes in large quantities, highlighting the importance of lake waters to these people. While water lilies naturally produce large numbers of seeds, their recovery from archaeological deposits, sometimes in a charred state, suggests that they were cooked and eaten. More than 2,000 waterlogged white water lily seeds were found in archaeological deposits at Clowanstown, close to the Hill of Tara in County Meath, while several thousand waterlogged yellow water lily seeds were recorded in a hollow at Lough Kinale on the borders of Cavan, Longford and Westmeath, perhaps representing a processing or storage area.

Charred assemblages of wetland plant food have also been found on estuaries; more than thirty-five possible white water lily seeds were discovered in a hearth pit at Mount Sandel near the mouth of the River Bann in County Derry. Some indigenous peoples of North America still consume water lilies, going through a detailed process to prepare the seeds, which involves gathering capsules, fermenting them in water (perhaps in a lakeside pit), followed by cleaning, dehusking, winnowing, parching, grinding and then roasting the seeds. This takes at least two weeks, highlighting the extensive time involved in processing of these plants.[10] Or, the seeds can be fried in fat to make a kind of popcorn. They can also be used as an insect repellent and in dyeing. The rhizomes may also be edible.[11]

Water mint is a small, pink-flowered herb that grows by the water's edge. When crushed it has a strong aroma and is still used to flavour a sauce eaten with roast lamb. It can also be used to flavour cooked potatoes. In previous centuries it was used to treat a number of ailments such as indigestion, stomach pains, headaches, measles and jaundice, after being first boiled and strained through linen. A thimbleful of the resulting liquid could also be poured into the ear to cure deafness. It was thought that placing mint leaves in your shoes protected you against infection when visiting a sick patient. Many of these treatments relied on the faith of the user, and there is little proof that they worked.

The common reed was widely used for thatching in Ireland but also has some value as a wild food. Its roots can be dried to make a flour or used as a vegetable when boiled. The stems contain a sugar-rich sap which becomes like a brown toffee when cooked. The seeds are also edible and can be ground up to make a gruel. The thick rhizomes of bullrush (or reedmace) are also edible and were probably used as a source of starch by early people. Roasted bullrush seeds can be ground down to make a flour. Both of these tall grasses are commonly found growing in water around the shores of many lakes.[12]

Logboats

On the ground floor of the National Museum in Dublin city centre lies a long, straight dugout canoe carved out of a single oak tree, measuring over fourteen metres long by one metre wide. I often stand for a while to marvel at its size, with the knowledge that this type of boat, powered only by men with paddles, was in use in Ireland for thousands of years before the first motorboat was invented. Estimated to be over 4,000 years old, the Lurgan canoe was discovered in 1901 by Patrick Coen while working in a County Galway bog that had once been a shallow lake. The boat is easily the largest artefact on display at the museum, and it was a major operation to get it there. It took nearly a month for the canoe to be transported by horse and cart from the Lurgan bog to the railway station at Tuam. When it finally arrived in Dublin, the boat was pulled through the streets on specially linked horse-drawn carts, and its eventual arrival at the front gates of the National Museum was greeted with curiosity by the city people.

Transforming a massive oak tree into this sleek canoe, using just stone axes and fire, must have taken the prehistoric craftsmen considerable time and effort. Inside the boat they left a series of raised 'ribs', which appear to separate the vessel into sections, as well as number of small holes, possibly to secure attachments. This has led some archaeologists to suggest that the boat may originally have been joined to a second canoe to form a double-hulled vessel or that an outrigger of some kind was attached.[13] This would have given the canoe much greater stability and allow it to travel safely across large areas of open water, even at sea.

The Lurgan boat is not unique in an Irish context, and two very similar Early Bronze Age canoes have been discovered recently in this part of Connacht. They include part of a boat from Carrowneden in County Mayo and a complete vessel from Annagheen in

County Galway. Fashioned out of oak, the Annagheen canoe measures twelve metres in length, while the Carrowneden vessel was once of similar size. A survey of the age of logboats, using carbon dating and the study of tree rings, was undertaken to establish the date they were first introduced, as it is known that they were in still in use up to the eighteenth century.[14]

Similar vessels are known in other parts of the world, such as New Zealand and the US Pacific Northwest where they were used as war canoes. The Irish boats may also have served a ceremonial role, which could explain their exaggerated size. More mundane activities, such as trading, cannot be ruled out either, especially if the canoes formed part of larger, composite vessels, such as catamarans or outrigger canoes. Such boats would have been capable of carrying heavy loads over long distances, when their stability would have been important.

Mayfly

I was out in a boat on Lower Lough Erne on a warm summer day when I noticed some small insects dancing above the water. They were mayflies and their ancestors had probably been emerging from these waters for thousands of years. The brief lives of mayfly adults have been noted by naturalists and philosophers since Aristotle and Pliny in classical times. The German engraver Albrecht Dürer included a mayfly in his 1495 engraving *The Holy Family with the Mayfly* to suggest a link between heaven and earth. The name 'mayfly' is quite misleading because this group of insects can appear throughout the year. The common name comes from the habit of one species, the green drake mayfly *Ephemera danica*, which emerges as an adult when the hawthorn or 'mayflower' is in bloom. In fact, at one point they were called dayflies, as some species have an adult lifespan of a single day.

Although some species live for only a brief period, even just a few hours as adults, other species can live a bit longer. In fact, most of the life of a mayfly is spent underwater as a nymph. They start life as an egg on the bed of a river or lake, before hatching into a nymph. The nymphs feed on algae and other vegetable matter, for up to two years in some species, before emerging from the surface of the water as an adult. Mayflies are unique as insects in having two winged adult stages. After emerging from the water, they fly to the bank where they shelter on the underside of leaves or in the grass. Then they moult again, leaving behind their drab 'dun' skin to reveal their shiny 'spinner' skin. Following this moult, they fly back to the water to join mating swarms dancing above the surface.

The nature writer Gordon D'Arcy described a spectacular hatching of winged mayflies he witnessed above the waters of Lough Bunny in the Burren. 'What we took at a distance to be a foggy aura materialised into a series of wavering columns around and above the bushes. We stood transfixed, watching the columns grow and grow as though they were stimulated by gaseous pockets in the limestone.' Males and females mate and drop into the water to lay their eggs, as the flights continue and sometimes last for long periods. D'Arcy continued, 'the columns had grown into dense clots high above the lakeside. As I watched they took on a new life, pulsing and moulding into gracefully changing shapes like careening flocks of starlings.'[15] Having completed the essential task of reproduction, the insects die, and their bodies litter the ground and water surface. Here they provide a bonanza for fish like trout.

Mayflies are one of the most ancient insect groups, with fossils dating back over 300 million years – long before the dinosaurs. There are thirty-three species of mayfly known in Ireland today, and they range in size from less than five to over twenty millimetres long. Along with other insects, mayfly are important indicators of the health of a water body, and the presence of certain species is frequently used in monitoring water quality. In running water, mayflies can constitute a high proportion, both numerically and in terms of biomass, of the total macroinvertebrate fauna, except where conditions are highly acidic. Their emergence is important in terms of the energy returned to terrestrial ecosystems. Both mayfly larvae and the mayfly adults emerging from the water are a vital source of food for many other freshwater creatures, especially fish such as trout and salmon. The adults are consumed by a variety of animals from birds and fish to spiders.[16]

The emergence of the mayfly is a signal for specialist flyfishing enthusiasts to take to the water. It is known that mild, dry, sunny weather brings an early 'rise' of mayfly, but it is not known if this is due to rising water temperature or the amount of sunshine, which heats the silt in the shallow waters where the larvae grow. The sunshine may also help the growth of algae, which provide food, and trigger an early hatch. Alternately, the rise may be rain-related, since low rainfall means lower water levels, leaving the water rich in nutrients.

The art of fly-tying is highly skilled and involves the creation of artificial lures that resemble different species of adult mayfly to entice trout and salmon onto the fisherman's hook. Fly-tying is usually done using hand tools and a variety of natural and man-made materials, such as feathers, fur, animal hairs, threads and other synthetic materials, that are attached to the hook. Although the recent history of fly-tying dates from the mid-nineteenth century, skilled craftspeople were engaged in tying flies from at least AD 200.

Water fairies and horses

The dancing of mayflies across the surface of water is the closest that I have seen to the legends of water sprites or fairies. There was widespread belief in fairies up to the early twentieth century in Ireland. It was thought that fairies were neither human nor ghosts but rather natural beings with supernatural powers. They were always small and typically lived underground. They could die, just as they could give birth to children. They could be generous and bring good luck and fortune. But if someone harmed them or their property, they could be extremely vengeful. Mixing Christian dogma with older pre-Christian traditions, country people often saw fairies as fallen angels. Water sprites were said to be able to breath water or air as well as fly. They existed in the mythologies of various countries. Ancient Greeks believed that they were divine entities but differed from gods or earthly creatures in that they were fixed in one place.

Magical horses also feature in lake mythology in Scotland and in Ireland, where an *each uisce* was a steed that lived in the sea or in freshwater loughs. Each of these beings was a shapeshifter, disguising itself as a horse or pony, an enormous bird or a handsome man. If a man mounted one of these horses he was only safe as long as the *each uisce* was ridden on dry land. With the merest smell or glimpse of water, the rider stuck to the skin of the *each uisce*, and it would dive to the deepest part of the lough and drown its victim. Then the animal would devour the entire body of the man, except for his liver, which floated to the surface. Gruesome tales like this underline how early people feared what lived in the deep water of lakes.

Herons or 'cranes'

My attention is sometimes attracted by an unusually large bird flying over our farm as it makes for the lakes near the coast. My neighbours call these birds cranes, although the correct name for them is grey heron. Seen through binoculars, they look very ungainly and could easily be taken for flying dinosaurs or pterodactyls. Long legs stick out behind like rudders, and the long neck is folded back in flight. Herons are frequently seen wading in Irish lakes and rivers and often on the seashore. Their loud squawks as they fly overhead sometimes make me think of a turkey or a goose. I have often watched a stately heron standing still as a statue by the ruined weir on our local river waiting for an unsuspecting fish or frog to swim with reach of its stabbing bill. The birds normally breed in groups of nests, small colonies known as heronries, at the tops of tall trees. Occasionally the adults will stand around on the ground below, while the prehistoric-looking chicks call loudly from above. Herons are widespread and common in Ireland although there has never been a full census of their numbers. In Northern Ireland a survey of the major breeding colonies in the 1970s discovered 630 nests in 57 heronries with an average of 11 nests per site.[17]

My wife Wendy and I spent our honeymoon in a somewhat different way from most newlyweds. Recently graduated students, we had very little spare cash, so instead of going abroad or staying in a hotel, we opted to camp in Connemara for a week. Here we visited our friend Dr Karl Partridge, who is an ornithologist. His attention had been drawn to the high numbers of grey herons feeding around the weedy shorelines here. In most parts of Ireland, herons build substantial stick nests on the crowns of high trees. However, Connemara is known for its absence of trees, largely as a result of exposure to high winds and salt spray. The other factor preventing tree cover is the grazing of sheep, which are unrestrained by fences. But the sheep cannot reach the many islands in the lakes, and these are among the few places where permanent trees survive.

This is the only part of Ireland where I have been able to walk up to a stunted willow, holly or rowan tree and look directly into a heron's nest. However, to get to the islands we had to strip off and swim out across the lakes carrying a waterproof bag with boots and clothing. Karl had started a long-term study here into the breeding biology of herons in Connemara. The total of twenty-nine heronries he surveyed in the 1970s had an average of between nine and ten nests, each one built in a stunted tree. In one case, rhododendron bushes were used in the absence of other more substantial trees. The most unusual nest site, at Ballynakill Lough on Gorumna Island, had seven nests built directly on a huge rock in the middle of the lake. Some other nests were built in ivy on the ground. Surprisingly, given the absence of tall trees, the Connemara population of herons then bred at a higher density than in any other area in Ireland or Britain. The reason may be the abundant food supply to which the birds had easy access along the low rocky shores of Connemara. This is suggested by the fact that almost all colonies were located within five kilometres of the coast. The paucity of fish in the inland lakes where the herons nest makes the coast the most profitable place to feed.[18]

Recently, Karl has resurveyed the Connemara heronries after an interval of nearly fifty years, and it transpires that many of the former lake islands have been abandoned by nesting herons in favour of tall trees nearer the coast. The reasons for this are not clear but copses of tall conifers are now more common in Connemara than hitherto, and they provide nest sites that are more secure and closer to the favoured coastal feeding areas.

Limestone lakes

South of a line from Dundalk to Limerick, natural lakes are relatively rare due to the geology and soils found there. The remaining northern and western parts of Ireland hold the majority of the larger lakes, and this is also related to the high rainfall levels in these areas. County Mayo has a myriad of lakes, 258 of them in the River Moy catchment alone. They range from the peaty acidic waters of the mountain lochans to the shallow limestone lakes of Loughs Conn and Mask, which are rich in plant and animal life.[19]

One of the Mayo lakes, Lough Carra, has been the subject of extensive study by students and staff of the Galway Mayo Institute.[20] It is joined to Lough Mask by the short Keel River. This is the largest marl lake in Ireland, covering 1,560 hectares. The bedrock is limestone, and this has a major influence on the ecology of the lake. The rocks along the lakeshore are covered with a curious, whitish, slippery layer known as marl crust. This forms in a somewhat similar way that dental plaque and tartar form on teeth. Marl is generated by cyanobacteria – ancient organisms which can grow as filaments, clusters of cells or interwoven masses, depending on the species. Also present in the crust are microscopic plants called diatoms, each of which has an outer transparent shell made of silica.[21] A multi-agency organisation, the Lough Carra Catchment Association, has been formed to try to coordinate action for conservation of the lake.

I also went to visit Lough Arrow, which lies between counties Sligo and Roscommon. It is known for its crystal-clear waters and complex biodiversity, including wild brown trout and extraordinary underwater plants. The lake has a small catchment that is fed mainly by springs on the lakebed, making it hydrologically unique. It is famous for the underwater plants, chiefly the stoneworts, which are large algae that grow in dense underwater meadows. They are the temperate freshwater equivalent of coral reefs, providing food and shelter for a wide variety of plants and animals, including invertebrates, waterfowl and many species of fish. These plants cannot tolerate significant levels of nutrients, so their presence is a really useful indicator of healthy ecosystems. Due to its unique status, a team from Collaborative Action for Natura Networks and Atlantic Technological University are working together with local communities to conserve and improve the environmental condition of the lake, including commissioning scientific studies, identifying means to halt the spread of invasive species, delivering educational and outreach programmes and raising awareness of the significance of the habitats and species.

Black lady of the lakes

When I lived in Northern Ireland I used to look far out to sea in Dundrum Bay, County Down, straining my eyes to see flocks of black ducks bobbing up and down in the waves. These were common scoters that had bred in Scotland and Scandinavia and had moved into Irish waters for the winter. A small number of scoters also breed in Ireland, but these are limited to a few lakes in the west of Ulster and Connacht. Here they select areas of trees and shrubs on the shores and islands where their nests are well hidden in the undergrowth in an attempt to avoid ground predators such as fox.

The first Irish group of scoters to be studied in detail nested on Lough Erne in County Fermanagh.

Here they had reached a peak of 150 pairs in the 1960s, but a steep decline in the following decades led Karl Partridge to undertake a study for the Royal Society for the Protection of Birds (RSPB) of the possible causes. He concluded that the enrichment of the lake waters, probably by agricultural run-off, had initially favoured the scoters but eventually led to a serious decline as food resources became unavailable to the birds. He also suggested that competition for food with the introduced fish (roach) and predation by introduced mink were both possible factors.[22] By the early 1990s the birds were no longer breeding on Lough Erne, and it is thought that they may have redistributed to County Mayo lakes including Lough Conn and Lough Cullin. As the decade continued more scoters were found breeding on Lough Corrib in County Galway, Lough Ree in County Roscommon and Lough Arrow in County Leitrim. However, the total Irish population was now much lower, and the continued enrichment of all these lakes may well make their habitat unsuitable.[23]

In 2012, and again in 2020, pre-breeding and brood surveys of scoters were carried out at four known breeding sites in Ireland. These latest surveys revealed a recent increase in the national population, due largely to an increase at Lough Corrib to 38 pairs in 2020.[24] At Loughs Conn and Cullin the major decline in scoter populations between 1995 and 1999 also appeared to coincide with the peak in serious deterioration of water quality at this time. The invasive mink spread into these western lakes in the 1990s, and they are likely to have a significant impact on these ground-nesting birds. At these lakes in the early 2000s, there was also a steep increase of the roach population which may compete with the scoters. It is likely that a combination of factors has been responsible for this slow decline in the number of breeding ducks.[25] It is clear that this species is at the southern edge of its European range in Ireland, and it might be expected that the changing climate and warming of lake waters may also be factors that force it to retreat further northwards.

Lakes of Killarney

There are few more popular natural destinations for visitors to Ireland than the lakes of the Killarney valley in County Kerry. Made famous by a visit by Queen Victoria in 1861, Killarney became a favoured holiday destination for the gentry of the British Empire. During her three-day stay, about 10,000 people flocked to Killarney to witness the queen, and in the evening there was a firework display over the Lower Lake. Next day the royal party went boating on the lakes, accompanied by as many as 800 boats, according to one report. Eight oarsmen propelled the queen's boat. The party stopped for lunch at Glena House and later took a break at Derrycunihy, where a marquee had been set up. Queen Victoria remarked that the beauty of the lakes had surpassed her highest expectations.

My own first visit to Killarney National Park in the 1970s was a much quieter affair. For several hours I walked in the famous old woodlands, where oak trees swept from the summits of the hills down to the lake shores. All around me mosses clothed the tree trunks and branches, boulders on the ground and even old field walls. This is entirely due to the wet Atlantic climate experienced in this part of Kerry, with up to 4,000 millimetres of rain being recorded in one year. The air and the ground here are almost permanently damp, which is not surprising as some form of precipitation is generally recorded on 300 days or more in every year. This is truly a temperate rainforest, and all the water that falls on these hills eventually finds its way into the lakes.

Dr Bill Quirke, who studied these freshwaters, compiled a comprehensive book on Killarney National Park. He wrote:

If you pass by boat from the Middle Lake under Brickeen Bridge into the Lower Lake, you will notice a sudden reduction in water clarity and a dramatic change in the animal life. More boats with anglers, cormorants lined up on the rocks, herons stalking in the shallows, all indicate more fish and bigger fish. Here, if you rummage under the stones in the shallows, you will find tiny animals in amazing abundance – tens of thousands in a square metre. All of this indicates a lake that is rich in nutrients. Even sixty metres down in the dark profundal zone of the lake, the sediments are alive with insect larvae and worms, sustained by the rain of tiny plants and animals, manna from the sunlit surface far above.[26]

The Lakes of Killarney were the main location chosen for the recent reintroduction to Ireland of the white-tailed eagle. The last of these magnificent birds became extinct in the early twentieth century as a result of persecution, poisoning and stealing their eggs. Between 2007 and 2011, a hundred young eagles were collected under licence from nests in Norway and released in Killarney National Park. They can be seen today soaring over the lakes or fishing in the shallower waters for trout and salmon. The population is growing, and they are now colonising lakes in other parts of the country. A new phase of the reintroduction programme started in the 2020s.

Lough Neagh

It was late summer, and the heat had gone from the sun when I left my tent on the shores of Lough Neagh. In fact, it was starting to feel a lot like autumn as the swallows gathered in large flocks to prepare for migration. On the south-east shores of Lough Neagh, the largest freshwater lake in these islands, they were gorging on clouds of tiny flies dancing above the water and flocking around the waterside trees. The flies are a type of midge but, thankfully, they didn't seem to be the biting sort. When the flies hatch from the lake waters they gather in large swarms and spiral upwards like plumes of smoke.

Lough Neagh stretches as far as the eye can see but it averages only nine metres deep. I made a visit to the lakeshore at the appropriately named Lough Neagh Discovery Centre at Oxford Island in County Armagh. While this was once a true island when the lake water level was higher, it is now just a peninsula that sticks out from the mainland near the town of Lurgan. The centre and other facilities such as walking trails, bird hides and the nearby bushcraft centre are all run by the local Armagh, Banbridge and Craigavon Council, while the land is managed as a nature reserve.

As this area was once covered by lake water it is the wetland habitats that are most obvious. Extensive stands of common reed fringe the island shore, with marshy grassland leading into wet woodland. Most of the woodland is relatively young, having been planted in the last forty years. Old photographs show hardly a tree on Oxford Island, and the plantings include many non-native species. There is a waymarked trail with information on at least twenty species of trees native to Ireland. The bird cherry was in fruit as I walked the trail, but the jet-black cherries are bitter to the taste and I decided to leave them to the birds. Among the other less common native trees here are alder buckthorn, foodplant of the brimstone butterfly; aspen, whose rounded poplar-like leaves tremble in the wind; and spindle, whose bright pink fruits are attractive but poisonous to both humans and animals.

Unfortunately, there are many pressures and threats to the future of Lough Neagh and its wildlife. Sand extraction at Lough Neagh was unregulated until 2021, when a handful of firms were licensed by the Northern Ireland government to dredge up to a total of 1.5 million tonnes annually. Sediments have been removed from the shallow lake bed such that the water is now up to 21 metres deep. New research has exposed severe scarring of the lake bed caused by the dredging of sand and these areas are said to be dead areas for fish.[27] Among other threats is water pollution, which has increased over the decades and caused enrichment with nutrients and the decline of key invertebrates and fish species. This in turn has triggered a long-term decline in waterbird numbers, including the huge flocks of wigeon and coot that once fed here throughout winter. Thankfully, the reedbeds around the shoreline still hold sizeable numbers of great crested grebes, and I was pleased to see some of these colourful birds still in breeding plumage in August.

Oxford Island is a very popular amenity with beautiful, wooded lakeside walks, and the Discovery Centre has excellent information on wildlife in the area. When I was there, it housed a very informative exhibition on the history, nature and management of Lough Neagh. The management of the nature reserve is the responsibility of the local council, and this is mainly aimed at maintaining a diversity of habitats and species that are representative of Lough Neagh shores.

Vanishing eels

I sat watching a heron on the shore of Lough Neagh as it struggled with a large eel that it had managed to capture. The wriggling black fish had wrapped itself several times around the long neck of the bird, which was having difficulty getting more than a mouthful of one of its favourite foods. Eels are among the very few species of catadromous fish, spending part of their lives in freshwater but going down to the sea to spawn. The salmon, sea trout and lampreys undertake similar marathon migrations in reverse to find spawning areas in the headwaters of Irish rivers. These are among the few freshwater fish considered to be native to this country, because they were able to make the crossing

by sea after the last Ice Age. Eels also formed part
of the diet of the earliest known settlers in Ireland.
Their remains have been found in a number of early
archaeological sites including the Mesolithic settlement
at Mount Sandel (dated 7900–7600 BC), which overlooks
the River Bann near Coleraine in County Derry.

The huge body of water contained in Lough Neagh
is one of the richest inland fishing areas in Ireland.
Fed by water from six major rivers, it flows to the
sea only via the lower River Bann in its north-west
corner. This is the channel used by migratory eels as
they return to the Atlantic Ocean to spawn. Silver eels
migrating down the River Bann are trapped in nets at
Toomebridge, County Antrim, set within an elaborate
complex of eel weirs constructed over a century ago. Eel
fishing on the river and lake is controlled by the Lough
Neagh Fishermen's Cooperative Society, which issues
licences each year to catch approximately 500 tonnes
between May and January. The eels are exported live
from nearby Belfast Airport to European fish markets
where they are prized for their high fat content. I have
eaten delicious smoked eel sold at a street market in
Amsterdam, and I wondered if it once swam in Lough
Neagh. Although rarely eaten in Ireland today, eel was

also a valuable quarry at one time in the Republic of Ireland with about a hundred tonnes caught annually in the 2000s. But declining stocks prompted a total ban on eel fishing in this country from 2010 onwards. Historically, Lough Neagh had an average run of elvers (young eels) estimated at eleven to twelve million fish annually. According to the fishermen's cooperative this figure has fallen dramatically since 1983, with the present annual recruitment figure around two to three million.

Fishing for eel was once a traditional practice throughout all of Europe and the Mediterranean. For centuries the life cycle of the fish remained a mystery, but it is now known that the smallest larvae originate from a single spawning stock in the Sargasso Sea, located off Bermuda in the western Atlantic Ocean. From here the tiny fish follow the Gulf Stream in a north-east direction, growing progressively larger until they reach European waters. By the time they reach the continental shelf they have adopted a colourless snake-like appearance and are known as glass eels. They enter Irish estuaries from November to February and become darker in colour, migrating into freshwater as juveniles known as elvers.

However, in one catchment at Burrishoole in County Mayo, it is estimated that the current stocks of glass eels are only a fraction of the historical average recorded.[28] The cause of this decline is still unclear, but there are many pressures on eel populations apart from fisheries. Poor recruitment of juveniles to the rivers appears to be the principal cause of the decline, and this has also been observed elsewhere in Europe, with the eel fisheries of countries from Scandinavia to the Mediterranean being seriously affected. According to Dr Kieran McCarthy of the University of Galway, the available evidence suggests that the decline in juvenile eel populations arriving in European coastal zones is due to climatic effects on ocean currents. Declines in eel, Atlantic salmon and other migratory fish may be due to the changes in oceanic circulation patterns caused by global warming.[29]

There is also an invasive nematode worm that first arrived in Ireland in the 1990s and is now present in more than 70 per cent of Irish rivers and lakes. It has an early stage in freshwater copepods, transferred to the eel which feeds on these invertebrates. Here the worm penetrates the eel's gut, ending up in the swim bladder, where it feeds on blood. It can have a significant effect on the health of the fish and may impact on the spawning success of the adult eels, hindering any recovery in the population.

As they are migratory fish, eels must travel upstream from the ocean across multiple barriers such as weirs and waterfalls. They have a unique ability to leave the freshwater for a limited period and wriggle across the land, usually on wet nights, to reach the next stretch of river. Here they are very vulnerable to predation by a wide range of birds such as herons and mammals like otters. The mysterious arrival and disappearance of eels from Ireland led to many legends and stories over past centuries. In the early Irish tale *Táin Bó Cúailnge*, the warrior goddess Morrigan attacked the hero Cúchulainn by turning herself into a slippery eel and wrapping her body around his legs. It was sometimes believed that dead eels could come back to life again. There were also some strange folk cures that involved eels, among them burying an eel in a dung heap for a long time so the resulting oily substance could be rubbed into the scalp as a cure for baldness.[30] Whatever the truth of these beliefs, the chances of catching or even seeing an eel appears to have become very small as populations decline across their full range.

Ice Age fish

Trout come in different forms. There is the common brown trout, in which some of the species take on a silver colour and are called sea trout. Like salmon, these fish spawn in freshwater rivers but swim down to the sea to mature and later return as adults to their natal rivers. Lough Melvin, which straddles the border between counties Fermanagh and Leitrim, hosts a unique trio of trout – the brightly coloured gillaroo, the grey sonaghan and the much larger ferox trout. These probably evolved from three separate invasions of the lake by fish of different genetic stocks at the end of the last Ice Age. In the nineteenth century these fish were so distinct that they were treated as different species but they are now considered to be different varieties of the brown trout. Their separation continues, as they occupy different spawning grounds in the rivers that lead in and out of the lake.[31]

Less well known than the trout is a whitefish called pollan, often misnamed the freshwater herring due to its resemblance to the marine fish of the same name. It is known from Lough Neagh, Upper and Lower Lough Erne and the Shannon lakes, although it was present in other midland lakes in the nineteenth century. Only in

Lough Neagh is it still plentiful, and here it has been the subject of much research by scientists from Queen's University Belfast and elsewhere. In the other lakes the species is critically endangered. The fish is a glacial relict of the last Ice Age and is not found anywhere else in Western Europe. Originally, the species entered Irish rivers as a migratory fish from the sea and spread to the larger lake systems. As the sea temperature and salinity increased after the Ice Age, pollan lost its migratory habit and became restricted to freshwater. The species is now considered to be vulnerable in Ireland and is protected under the EU Habitats Directive.[32]

Ironically, the current threats to this globally important population include climate change, and also the introduction of invasive fish species such the roach and the continued pollution of Lough Neagh. At the start of the twentieth century as much as 400 tonnes of pollan were shipped out by rail every year.[33] The pollan is in season only for a limited time in the months of February and March but, sadly, only a few fishermen catch them now. Most of these beautiful silver-coloured fish are exported to other European countries where they are considered a delicacy. Pollan has been fished in Lough Neagh for thousands of years. In earlier days fishermen would either fry it fresh or scale, gut and dry it, so as to use it at a later date. Ulster chef Paula McIntyre wrote that her mother remembered eating pollan when she was young, in the former Bluebird Café in Antrim. 'They fried it simply in butter and then served it straight off the griddle with hot soda farls. She said that this was one of the most delicious things she had ever eaten.'[34]

The ecology of pollan is linked to the structure of their lake habitats. They mature at two years old and eggs are deposited on rocky or gravelly shallow areas of the lake bed. The fry hatch after about two months at Lough Neagh temperatures. Pollan feed primarily on microscopic zooplankton, although larger items such as midge larvae and freshwater shrimps are consumed, particularly in winter. Pollan spawning in Lough Neagh now occurs at least one month later than in the 1980s, possibly due to delayed winter cooling caused by climate change. A viable commercial fishery still exists for pollan in Lough Neagh, regulated by close season, gill net mesh size and a legal minimum size limit.[35] It seems unlikely that this will continue for much longer.

Portmore Lough

Since 1847 the levels of Lough Neagh have been lowered
by over three metres to reduce seasonal flooding and
increase the area of available farmland. The last such
lowering was in 1959 and, as well as linking Oxford
Island with the mainland, this caused some inlets of
the shoreline to be cut off as separate lakelets. One
of these, at Portmore Lough on the eastern shore, has
now become a nature reserve including wet grassland,
reedbed and willow scrub as well as the lake itself. The
RSPB manages this almost circular lake to replicate the
soft shoreline that once fringed the whole of Lough
Neagh.

I went there when the birds had finished breeding
and were flocking up to depart in the autumn. The
wildflower meadows were humming with bees and
hoverflies and an area specially planted for insects and
seed-eating birds was the main attraction for a flock
of linnets and goldfinches. A wooded walkway leads
down to the former shoreline of Lough Neagh, and
a viewing platform gives a wide vista of the reserve.
Most of it comprises wet grassland and marsh that
forms a wide flat area between the woodland edge and
the lake shore. This is grazed in late summer by cattle

and a herd of konik ponies to create ideal conditions early in the year for nesting lapwing. Now there was a small flock of these delicate wading birds roosting on the shore of one of the shallow scrapes that have been created specially for them. The longer rushy vegetation is the preferred habitat for snipe, and I thought I heard one chipping away from a wet patch near the path. Out in the distance I could see a hare moving across the fields, showing its preference for wide open spaces. A birdwatching hide at the end of a long all-weather boardwalk gives an elevated view across the waters of Lough Neagh itself and, in winter, the sight of greylag geese and whooper swans flying in to roost here at dusk is not to be missed.

Lake islands

The larger lakes and other wetlands of Ireland are of high value for nature and the islands in these lakes are often magical places, as described by W.B. Yeats in 'The Lake Isle of Innisfree'. In the 1980s, Karl Partridge organised a survey of breeding waders across Northern Ireland on behalf of the RSPB, as evidence had emerged of contractions in their range. He found that the islands of Lough Erne were among the best remaining hotspots for breeding waders in the whole of Ireland. Here the atmospheric calls of lapwing, redshank and curlew could be heard echoing across the lake waters in spring and summer. But since then, declines in all these species have been recorded to the point that only a handful of birds remained. Some urgent action was needed.

On first hearing about it, one might be forgiven for thinking that a shooting organisation is not the most likely group to get involved in the conservation of breeding waders. However, the Lough Erne Wildfowling Council began a Wader Recovery Project on Boa Island, County Fermanagh in 2013, which was supported by the Wildlife Habitat Charitable Trust, a grant-making body set up in 1986 by members of the British Association for Shooting and Conservation in the UK. Here the shooting permit fees administered by the wildfowling council are used for evidence-based conservation that benefits the birds. This long-term project aims to increase breeding wader densities and the breeding success of lapwing, redshank, snipe, common sandpiper and curlew on the islands. Of these species, snipe is the only quarry species but, in fact, very few are shot. The project also aims to demonstrate

a successful model for wader recovery, employing both
habitat and predator management, which could be
implemented elsewhere.

The key site is situated on Boa Island and is a
genuine partnership between Lough Erne wildfowlers
and local farmers. Changes in agricultural practices,
the spread of scrub into former grassland and increased
levels of predation, mainly by foxes and crows, have
all contributed to breeding wader population declines
in Fermanagh and across Ireland. The work mainly
involves clearance of scrub that has invaded the open
areas of grassland on the lake shores with the relaxing
of grazing pressure. These areas are then grazed by
cattle to encourage wet grassland and ensure that the
open fields behind the former scrub and woodland
become linked again with the lake shore.

Michael Stinson, a local ecologist involved in
the project, explained to me that the first three years
of the project involved the removal of scrub from
three areas on the shores of Boa Island, formerly an
important area for breeding waders. Michael grew up
in this area, and he took me out in his boat on the
lake on a bright day in May. As we motored along
just off the rocky shoreline, several species of waders

rose from their nesting areas in the grass and rushes which have largely replaced the woody vegetation here. Most exciting was the plaintive calling of a pair of curlew, as this species has declined dramatically throughout its former breeding range and is now seriously threatened in Ireland. Careful monitoring of the birds has been carried out here by Michael with environmental consultant Kerry Leonard. By 2018, the three main areas of the project had a total of twenty-nine pairs of snipe – almost five times the number present when the project started. There was one pair of curlew holding territory and several lapwing pairs have also bred. The opening up of these areas on the lake shore has clearly benefited the snipe but it is not yet clear if the other species can breed successfully here.

A key part of this project is the involvement of local farmers. The older landowners can remember how rich the wildlife of this area used to be but, as Michael says, 'engagement of the next generation of farmers, those under fifty years of age, is a bigger challenge as they are often not so intimately involved with the land. With small changes to the farming practices here, such as delaying rush-cutting to allow chicks to survive, the productivity of the ground-nesting waders can be increased.' Chairman of the Wildfowling Council Tom McGoldrick told me that, 'this project demonstrates the commitment of the shooting community to protecting key breeding wetland bird species in Fermanagh and the wider biodiversity associated with their habitats. It also shows that people who shoot care deeply about wildlife and are prepared to invest their time in protecting it.'

Reedbeds

I love the sound of the wind whistling through the reeds around the edge of a lake or pond. Even in winter, the image of the rays of the setting sun through the dead reed stems is inspiring. Common reed is found in most still waters where there is sufficient depth and even in some estuaries where the water is only slightly salty. It is really just a large grass that is adapted to grow in water and, like most grasses, it can dominate a habitat at the expense of most other plant species. Large stands of reeds, sometimes covering many hectares, are known as reedbeds or reedswamps. Reeds often grow around the edge of a fen where the vegetation is supplied by groundwater emerging from below. Walking through them requires considerable care as there are often deep channels and pools which may be hidden in the vegetation. It is easy to become disoriented as the reeds grow several metres tall, obscuring the surrounding landscape.

I used to help a group of ornithologists who were catching birds in a large reedbed in County Wicklow, fitting the birds with tiny numbered rings in order to study their migration. The vertical mist nets were set on poles in 'rides' cut through the reeds so that the birds would fly into them and become trapped. Then the team would return and carefully extract the birds without harming them, take various measurements and release them, each one bearing a ring with a unique number just like a car registration plate. Reedbeds are important stopover locations for migrating birds that feed on the abundant insect life within them. Some hold huge night-time roosts of swallows, house martins and sand martins in the autumn months as they move south to their wintering grounds.

Typical breeding birds in reedbeds include the sedge warbler and reed bunting. The water rail is rarely seen but can be easily identified by its loud squealing call in the breeding season. Great crested grebes often build their nests on floating vegetation among large stands of reeds. Scarcer breeding species include the reed warbler and the rare bearded reedling. Historically, the bittern and the marsh harrier were once widespread in Irish reedbeds, but both species became extinct in the nineteenth century. Drainage of wetland habitats and persecution by shooting brought about their demise.[36]

Reed was traditionally the main natural material used for thatching roofs in Ireland, its widespread availability being a key factor. It offers excellent insulation value, is more durable and water-resistant than straw and is relatively easy to repair. A roof thatched with reed can last thirty-five to forty years in Ireland, with very little maintenance. When a thatch is in need of repair a new layer is often placed over the old. On some older buildings, over a metre thickness of thatch can accumulate. In a natural reedbed the old material of previous years builds up as a layer of litter through which the new growth emerges. In order to produce good material for thatching a reedbed needs to be harvested every year. If it is left any longer the new growth will come up among the older reeds and stems will be crooked. Straight reeds are required for the best thatching material.

Harvesting of reed is done in winter when birds are finished nesting and the frost has removed a lot of the flower heads, which are not required. The reed has to be cut, bundled and stored once dry. Traditionally the reed was cut by hand, but this is slow and labour-intensive. Commercial thatchers today use specially designed reed harvesting machines with large wide wheels for the soft ground. Once the reeds are cut, they are bundled and stacked like tepees until they are dry. They are then cleaned out, by machine or by hand, and bundled ready for thatching use. The reeds can be sorted by length and fineness. An average roof on a modern house can use around 1,500 to 2,000 bundles of reed. Once on the roof, the bundles are positioned and the strings or bindings cut so the material can be fixed and dressed into place by the thatcher.

As with many traditional crafts, thatchers developed different styles in various parts of the country. In the mid-twentieth century, Kevin Danaher mapped out the various methods he found in Ireland. On his travels in the east of Ireland, he noted the thrusting or stobbing method, in which overlapping, bent handfuls of thatching material are thrust into a underlayer using a forked hand tool known as a stobstick. In the midlands and west, he found thatchers employing scallops (traditionally made from willow or hazel) to fix the thatch on a base of turf scraws. In the western and northern coastal areas the thatch was roped into place, as this part of the country is subject to high winds, so firm anchoring was vital. In Donegal, the thatch was traditionally rounded at the ridge of the house to throw off the wind. In some districts the ropes, formerly made of twisted straw or heather, ran in both directions to make a complete network and were secured on stone pegs left sticking out below the eaves.[37]

Disappearing lakes

Thatched houses were common in the west of Ireland when the poet William Butler Yeats made his regular visits to the home of Lady Augusta Gregory at Coole Park near Gort in County Galway. The poem 'Wild Swans at Coole' is about the poet's search for a lasting beauty in a changing world where beauty is mortal and temporary. To get inspiration, he would have walked around the woodland paths on this picturesque estate and looked out across the waters of Coole Lough, where he saw the flock of swans. I walked around there recently in early winter and was delighted to hear the trumpeting calls of a flock of whooper swans echoing across a very flooded lake. However, this is no ordinary lake. It simply disappears in the summer months, and the 'brimming water among the stones' is replaced by grassland enlivened with colourful wildflowers and limestone rocks. This is a turlough (from the Irish words *tuar loch* meaning a dry lake), a feature that is rare in north-west Europe.

Large parts of central Ireland, including some entire counties like Roscommon and Clare, are underlain by lime-rich rock, which was deposited millions of years ago in a tropical sea. On the bed of this sea, great deposits of dead shells accumulated over a very long time, and the pressure of multiple layers of sediment above eventually converted these to rock. Calcium was the main ingredient of these shells and, as this mineral is alkaline in nature, it is easily dissolved in water, especially where the rain is slightly acidic. Cracks and fissures develop underground and the flowing water eventually carves out tunnels and caves in the rock. The classic stalactites in the caves of the Burren, County Clare are an extreme example of crystallising lime that has been dissolved in water flowing through the rock.

Because the rock has so many cavities, the water table moves up and down with the seasons, high during wet periods and low when there is little rainfall. The floodwater generally drains away into the groundwater through a swallow hole, like a bath emptying through the plughole. When the winter rains resume the water bubbles up from the ground and a shallow lake is formed again. When I visited, the water was already lapping around the base of the trees. In fact, Coole Lough, which inspired Yeats to write his famous poem, is part of a complex of turloughs known as Coole-Garryland. These turloughs are fed by springs and a partly submerged river, surrounded by woodland, pasture and limestone heath. The turlough vegetation includes such species as shoreweed, common spike-rush, water-purslane, fen violet and a species of water-starwort that was first recorded here but has since been found at several other turlough sites. When the waters rise, a variety of pondweeds and rigid hornwort grow here. The area is also home to one of the most important and unique assemblages of insects in the country, including several notable species of beetles and flies. I took a walk around the nature reserve, where the rich complex of water and native woodland made me feel like I was in a wilderness area, similar to one which prehistoric people first encountered.

In his book *The Way That I Went*, Ireland's most celebrated naturalist, Robert Lloyd Praeger, wrote:

> Within the area stretching from Tuam down to Corofin we are in the turlough region, of which Gort is the centre. One turlough, Caherglassaun Lough lies at so low a level that it is influenced by the tide in Galway Bay, three and a half miles away, rising and falling synchronously to an extent of several feet. Another marked feature of the turloughs is the presence of a distinctive black moss on the stones and rocks. This plant can flourish under a frequency of flooding much less than that which inhibits the growth of bushes. The presence of the moss, followed a few feet down by the cessation of bushes, is a sure sign of turlough conditions.[38]

Praeger went on to make a detailed study of turlough vegetation, measuring the distance from the floodline that different plants could reach where regular submergence in the water did not restrict them.

He concluded that, 'for the student of plant-life the turloughs form a fascinating feature and they well deserve study'.[39] Zoologist Dr Julian Reynolds recently told me, 'when I visited Caherglassaun, I noticed the bottom of the shallows, forming small pools which were flooded twice a day by the tide. These tiny ecosystems had algae and zooplankton and I envisaged competition and predation playing out here every six-hour period.'

Turloughs are strongly associated with the limestone rocks of central Ireland, with a broad belt of sites occurring to the east of Loughs Corrib and Mask, more in County Roscommon and a cluster in south Galway stretching south-westwards into North Clare. There are a few isolated turloughs in south Clare, Limerick, Tipperary, Kilkenny, Sligo and Donegal. Most are found in low-lying landscapes close to the water table with two or three on the coast that are actually below sea level.[40] Dr Catherine Coxon found ninety large turloughs in her doctoral research, but she considered that only sixty of these were still functioning in a natural way, most having been damaged by drainage. There are likely to be many hundreds more turloughs, each less than ten hectares in area, scattered across the limestone regions but as yet uncatalogued.

Turlough life

Relatively few wild plants are adapted to the fluctuating water conditions of turloughs, and some of these are specialists that are rarely found elsewhere. Botanist Roger Goodwillie wrote that 'it is useful to think of turloughs as ecotones or boundary zones: they are the shores of underground lakes or the callows of underground rivers and each year they experience different hydrological conditions. The plant community is constantly adjusting to the previous flood event.'[41] The assemblage includes mostly plants that are adapted to regular submergence and those that can colonise quickly when the floods recede. Trees are rare, but hardy shrubs like juniper, gorse, blackthorn and buckthorn will grow here. They appear to die off when covered with water but can quickly regrow from the ground up when drier conditions appear. Although it is normally an evergreen shrub, holly will often lose its leaves when flooded but regrow when the water retreats.

Even when the turlough is dry, the plants can give an indication of the maximum height of the floodwater in winter. The black moss on limestone boulders marks the upper limit, although it can also grow within the zone of splashing from waves. The beautiful yellow flowers of shrubby cinquefoil are also a marker for the higher levels of flooding. Lower down, the area that is often flooded for a limited number of weeks or only occasionally is colonised by bulbous buttercup. In this way, certain key plant species mark out the zones of flooding that surround the turlough. At the lowest zone, where flooding is frequent and prolonged, annual plants can tolerate short bursts of flooding or grow quickly from seed when the water finally recedes. A few perennials such as shoreweed are found in the wetter zones of turloughs in the west and north-west but rarely elsewhere. This has long rooting runners and sometimes forms a dense sward beneath the shallow water. Praeger wrote:

the contrast between the areas subject to flooding and those free from it is enhanced by the fact that intermittent inundation, and the very light deposit of limy sediment that the water leaves behind, produce a sward particularly loved by herbivorous animals, large and small. The vegetation of turloughs is usually nibbled to the last leaf – often more closely shorn than could be done by a lawn-mower. Some species are no doubt excluded by this, and all are much dwarfed. The most successful, and consequently most abundant plants of the turloughs are those which can best withstand submergence or grazing or most commonly both. There is a complete absence of rushes, willows, alder and many other plants which one associates with marshes or with ground liable to inundation.[42]

Local landowners often have grazing rights on their neighbouring turloughs where they put out cattle, sheep and horses when ground conditions allow. The absence of fences and walls means that these animals are free-ranging, with different herds mixing freely. Herds of livestock wandering across some of the larger turloughs, like Rahasane in east Galway, which are often surrounded by woodland, provide a hint of the type of landscape that might have existed thousands of years ago when early farmers used these natural clearings for their animals. In the twentieth century, grazing pressures were relatively low, with less than one animal per hectare, but today the stocking rates have more than doubled. This must be putting greater pressure on the vegetation and invertebrate communities of the turloughs.[43]

The temporary nature of turloughs makes them unsuitable for fish, so invertebrate populations are largely free from predation. This has allowed several rare insects to persist in these habitats including several water beetles and the scarce emerald and ruddy darter dragonflies. These species are well adapted to the fluctuating conditions, as they can complete their life cycle in a single season. The females lay their eggs at the edge of pools, where they will be covered by rising water in the autumn.[44]

Vanishing lake legends

Every twenty or thirty years, Loch na Súl, 'the lake of the eyes', near the village of Geevagh, County Sligo, disappears completely. Local people believe that when the lake water goes a disaster is not far away. Records show that the lake disappeared completely six times between 1833 and 2012. In 1933, the disappearance was associated by local people with the Spanish Civil War and the imminent World War II. In 1965 it is said to have foretold the troubles in Northern Ireland. According to legend, Loch na Súl formed when Balor of the Evil Eye was killed in battle here. He is often described as a giant with a large eye that wreaks destruction when opened. Local legend says the lake has three eyes like Balor, and when they open without warning the lake is swallowed up within days or weeks. The lake supposedly marks the spot where, more than 3,000 years ago, the Battle of Moytura between the Tuatha Dé Danann and the Fomorians occurred. Legend says that the eye of Balor, the Fomorian leader, fell on the ground here after it was popped out of his eye socket with a shot from a sling.

The irregular nature of the lake's disappearance makes it different from other turloughs which disappear annually. Dr Richard Thorn, a hydrology expert at Atlantic Technological University, believes the recurring case of this disappearing lake may have more to do with the effect of rain on the limestone rock underground. He believes there is a complex warren of channels and caves in the limestone under the lake, and when blocked outlets or cavities suddenly give way, the water drains away. In 1933, James McDonagh, who lived on the shores of the lake, reported that enormous piles of trout, perch and eels were wedged on to the bottom of the lake when it disappeared and that these were divided among local people.[45]

Chalk, like limestone, is also dissolved by water, and there can be cavities below ground that hold flowing streams. The remote upland lake of Loughareema, near Ballycastle in County Antrim, is known to most people in Northern Ireland as the vanishing lake. There is a local legend that tells of the drowning of a coach and horses in the nineteenth century as they tried to cross the lake when it was full. Bizarrely, a road had been built through the lake when it was empty, so in darkness it was impossible to tell if water levels were high or low. It is said that on nights when the lake is full, a phantom ghost haunts the shoreline, and together with the prospect of the sight of a kelpie, or water-ghoul, Loughareema is associated with many legends and stories.

To scientists, Loughareema is regarded as one of Northern Ireland's most enigmatic geological sites. The lake has three streams flowing into it, but no water flows out on the surface. Although surrounded by blanket bog and basalt rock, there is chalk not far below the surface. A sink at the base of the lake drains all of the water out of the lake into an underground drainage system. This water reappears from a large spring into the Carey River a short distance away. Its drainage system is not yet well understood. The sink is likely to be through chalk, which is also known in Ulster as white limestone.

Turlough birds

In winter, the shallow waters of the turloughs attract a variety of waterbirds, including the flock of swans at Coole Lough made famous by Yeats. The evocative calls of whooper swans trumpet out across the water, as these migratory birds arrive from the Arctic in about October to spend the winter here. Their numbers have been increasing steadily since organised surveys began in the 1970s. In 2020 the total population of these large birds reached over 19,000, representing several years of good breeding success in Iceland and an increasing trend to use improved pasture for grazing while returning to the safety of open water at night. The open unimpeded views across the turloughs allow them to see approaching predators or other forms of disturbance in time to take diversionary action. Ducks like mallard, wigeon, teal and pochard can also be seen on the lake water, and there are smaller flocks of waders like lapwing, curlew and dunlin.

In spring, sedge warblers call from the longer vegetation around the turloughs, and pairs of reed buntings flit about searching for their insect prey. At one turlough in County Roscommon, the water body in the centre never fully disappears, and an extensive reedbed occupies this area. This site at Lough Funshinagh was the location of an exciting discovery over a century ago. A pair of rare black-necked grebes in full breeding plumage, together with three downy young, were presented as specimens to the National Museum in Dublin by an ornithologist called J. Ffolliot Darling in 1918. Shooting and mounting specimens was a normal way to record rare birds in those days in the absence of good quality telescopes and it allowed the plumage and other distinguishing characters to be closely examined. The exact site of this discovery was kept secret and the finder died in 1926, taking knowledge of the location with him to the grave.

This enigma attracted another leading ornithologist of the time, George Humphreys, who searched for the location and finally found it in 1929. In a series of visits he recorded large numbers of nests of the black-necked grebes among other waterbirds such as great crested grebe, grey heron, mute swans and several duck species. He wrote:

> After watching the grebes for some time I visited the islands and, following a hard day's rowing, got back to Gortfree about 5.00pm. Refreshed somewhat after a cup of tea, and having time to spare, I took a stroll along the shore. Black-necks in pairs and odd numbers were to be seen out in the open water. I reckoned upwards of fifty of these grebes were seen by me.

Later the same year he concluded that at least 250 pairs of black-necked grebes were nesting among the reeds, although how he found these carefully concealed nests remains a mystery. Humphreys also kept the location a secret for half a century, but meanwhile the population declined until the 1960s when there were no grebes left here. It was not until 1978 that Humphreys felt it safe to disclose the location of this remarkable former colony.[46]

Lough Funshinagh used to drain through a swallow hole, as if someone had pulled the plug in a bath, but for an unknown reason, nature's plumbing has broken down, flooding an area thought to be twice the lake's usual size and threatening homes and livelihoods. A plan to drain the lake artificially with a four-kilometre pipeline to the nearby River Shannon was halted in 2022 after the campaign group Friends of the Irish Environment took the local authority to the high court on the grounds that no environmental impact assessment had been carried out, breaching EU rules. A high court order halting the flood relief set off a bitter row, with some local residents arguing that nature was being given greater priority than people's homes. In a 2018 report, the International Association of Hydrogeologists reported that the water level rose by two metres above normal levels in 2016, causing extensive and prolonged flooding. Based on the slow outflow, it was calculated that it would take 600 days or two years for the floodwaters to drain, assuming there were no further flood events.

During my walk around Lough Funshinagh, I heard an unusual whistling sound and recognised a small party of whimbrel, similar in appearance to the curlew. These were migrant birds that had stopped here briefly to refuel on their long annual trip from wintering grounds in West Africa to breed in the cold landscapes of Iceland. On the return trip in autumn, most of these birds make a remarkable non-stop flight down the west coast of Europe, a distance of some 5,000 kilometres, completed in five days. A sample of ten individual whimbrels were tracked with geolocators, attached to their legs, which allowed the calculation of seasonal migration duration and speed of the birds.[47]

Little goat

As I walked across fields of wet, rushy grassland on the edge of nearby Lough Ree one May morning, a strange noise came to my ears. It sounded like the bleating of a young goat calling repeatedly for its parent. But there were no goats in sight, so I listened again. The sound was in the sky above me, and before long I spotted a small bird diving to the ground and rising again to perform this extraordinary display. This was a snipe advertising its territory to the neighbours. The loud noise is made not from the vocal cords of the birds but with the outer tail feathers, which vibrate as they are extended perpendicular to the body. In his poem 'The Backward Look', the poet Seamus Heaney described the snipe as the 'little goat of the air, of the evening

… his tail feathers/drumming elegies in the slipstream'. This likeness to the goat has given the bird other local names such as 'flying goat', and 'heaven's ram'.

A snipe has a very long beak, about one-third the length of its body. It uses this to probe deep into the soil, feeling with the sensitive tip for the tiny soil invertebrates on which it feeds. So the birds are completely dependent on soft ground. When there is a drought or winter ice that hardens the soil, snipe quickly run out of food and can die in large numbers. The other threat to their survival is the complete loss of their wetland habitats due to drainage or agricultural improvement. For nesting, they need longer vegetation with tussocks that can hide their vulnerable eggs from predators like fox and crow. The journalist John Healy, who was born in County Mayo, wrote of his admiration for the self-sufficiency of his beloved western way of life in the poor fields of Connacht which he described as 'snipe grass'.

The snipe is a resident breeding species in Ireland and breeds widely across Europe in habitats such as bogs, marshes, tundra and wet meadows. The breeding range of snipe in Ireland has undergone a decline in recent decades, but the birds are notoriously difficult to survey in long vegetation as they often remain quietly hidden until the last minute, when they can escape explosively from beneath the feet of a surveyor. In Northern Ireland, where a sample of potential sites has been revisited at intervals, snipe numbers have declined by 71 per cent since the 1980s. Snipe generally avoid improved grassland, being more typically associated with marshy and tussocky areas.[48] This population decline, as with many of the breeding waders, is undoubtedly due to habitat loss through drainage and afforestation of wet grasslands, heathlands and bogs and may also be linked with increasing predation from foxes and crows.

As autumn turns to winter, the resident snipe here are joined by migrants from northern continental Europe and Iceland to become our most widespread winter wader species. These winter migrants begin their arrival in August and disperse to a broad range of lowland and upland habitat where they remain throughout the winter period. Population size is very hard to estimate, as the birds are widely dispersed and very secretive.[49] They can be found in almost any part of Ireland in winter but favour wet ground in marshes, drains and bogs. They return to their breeding grounds in spring.

Given the threatened nature of the snipe population, it may come as a surprise to know that they can still be legally shot each winter between September and January. A traditional quarry for hunters, snipe are notoriously difficult to shoot because of their speed and erratic flight when driven from cover, hence the term 'sniper' given to a highly skilled shooter. The snipe is small and very fast in flight with the ability to change direction in a second. Considered by many as the ultimate game shot, they are a severe test of the hunter.

Lagoons

The lake along 'the Flaggy Shore' that Seamus Heaney described in his famous poem is at the exit of Lough Murree, a coastal lagoon on the south side of Galway Bay, some twelve kilometres west of Kinvara. A road now runs parallel to the shore between the lake and the sea and it was from this road that Heaney saw 'the ocean on one side' and 'inland among stones .... a slate-grey lake'. Some other coastal lagoons in Ireland are quite well-known features – Lady's Island Lake in Wexford, Shannon Airport Lagoon in Clare, Rosscarbery Lake in Cork, Broadmeadow in Dublin,

Lough Furnace in Mayo and Lough Atalia in Galway. Some lagoons are entirely natural, where the sea has created a shingle or sand barrier between the beach and a lake by normal coastal processes. Many are artificial in origin, former inlets of the sea that were cut off from tidal movements by the building of a causeway, road or railway embankment. I recently stood on the road near Clifden, County Galway, watching the water below me pouring like a waterfall through a stone archway out of another lagoon called the Salt Lake and onto the shoreline several metres below.

At Lough Murree in County Clare, the lake has formed in limestone bedrock (known as karst) on which a narrow cobble barrier has been deposited along the coastal side. I walked along the shore marvelling at the abundance of fossil corals in the rocks. There is no direct link with the sea, although seawater may enter the lake occasionally by overtopping of the barrier. However, the main routes are percolation through the cobbles and possibly through subterranean fissures in the bedrock. This is the best example of all karstic lagoons in Ireland, and the only one on the mainland. The flora of the habitat is rich and diverse, reflecting the range of salinities in the lake. It has two species of tasselweed and two threatened stonewort species, which are all submerged plants. Some specialised creatures also live below the waters of the lagoon. At least ten rare animal species were recorded here in the 1990s, including crustaceans, molluscs and water beetles.

Places where freshwater and seawater mix are usually described as brackish. Natural lagoons such as Lough Murree are relatively rare on Irish and European coasts, as a consequence of which they have been given special legal protection under the EU Habitats Directive. A major national survey in the 1990s found over a hundred such habitats in the Republic of Ireland, ranging from natural saline lakes to artificial lagoons, but each with a unique collection of plants and animals. The commonest threat to lagoons is nutrient enrichment from agricultural or domestic sources, even though many of these are protected on paper by special EU designations. Fortunately, no Irish lagoons have so far been exploited for leisure purposes in a manner likely to cause their deterioration. Maintaining the integrity of the barriers is more problematic.[50]

The future for Irish lakes

As with rivers, the number of lakes in Ireland that can be described as 'pristine' has declined to a handful. EPA reports show a serious and steady decline in lake water quality over the last fifty years. Agriculture is the main source of pollutants, including run-off of fertiliser and slurry now occurring with increasing frequency. In the 1970s, several lakes in the north midlands, including Lough Sheelin in County Cavan, were polluted by dumping of manure from industrial-scale pig farms. Invasive plant species can occupy the water column from bed to surface with serious consequences for native biodiversity. Some species, such as Nuttall's waterweed, curly leaved waterweed and the water fern, can form exceptionally dense monocultures once established, excluding native species. So too, invasive invertebrate animals such as the zebra mussel, introduced game fish such as the dace and chub, as well as mammals such as American mink are a serious threat to the biodiversity in lakes. Most of our turloughs have suffered damage from drainage, and some have been completely destroyed. Coastal lagoons are often damaged by rock armoury or drainage interfering with the natural exchange of water from the sea. Overall, our lakes are under serious pressure to survive.

Lakes are an important source of drinking water. Think of the Vartry and Blessington reservoirs in County Wicklow, which together supply a large proportion of Dublin's drinking water. Consider the value of Lough Gill to Sligo or Lough Corrib to Galway. In 2007, the bacterium *Cryptosporidium* was confirmed to be present in the drinking water of Galway city, Moycullen, Oughterard and Headford. The water, taken from Lough Corrib, was very likely to have been contaminated by input of animal and human faeces. Lakes are also a valuable resource for angling tourism. According to Fáilte Ireland, over 107,000 overseas visitors engaged in angling while in Ireland in 2011 and spent €90 million while here. In 2014, the total value of angling tourism expenditure in Ireland was estimated to have reached €315 million and sustained over 3,000 jobs.

How to ensure the future survival of these valuable freshwater resources has exercised fisheries managers, water supply agencies and conservationists for decades. Improved provision of proper wastewater treatment works, including the use of constructed wetlands, at least holds out the promise of reducing this load on our lakes and rivers. The problem of agricultural run-off is more intractable as it is not confined to point sources but is more widespread and diffuse across the country. The threat from invasive species is also likely to continue as many are introduced accidentally on the hulls of boats or by escapes from garden ponds. Reduced water levels in many lakes are highly likely as they form a major source of drinking water for towns and cities where the demand is constantly growing. Climate change will also have inevitable consequences, with annual rainfall likely to decline, especially in the east of the country. Perhaps the creation of artificial lakes by reflooding the cutaway bogs offers the best hope for increasing the number of wetlands in the country and recreating something of the ancient landscape that once dominated the midlands of Ireland.

Wet Woodlands

Down by the salley gardens
my love and I did meet;
She passed the salley gardens
with little snow-white feet.
She bid me take love easy,
as the leaves grow on the tree;
But I, being young and foolish,
with her would not agree.

From 'Down by the Salley Gardens' (1889) by W.B. YEATS

The 'salley gardens', where Yeats imagined meeting his lover, were cultivated beds of willows or osiers that were grown specifically for basket-making. In a note on the poem, the poet said that he was trying to reconstruct an old song he had heard being sung by a woman in the village of Ballisodare in County Sligo. Up to the early twentieth century, sally gardens or osier beds were

widely cultivated in Ireland, especially in the south
of the country. The willows were easily established
by pushing cuttings from a tree into wet ground, and
these quickly grew to large bushes. The mature plants
were coppiced to produce withies, which were used for
basket-making, fish-traps, and many other purposes,
as the timber is lightweight, flexible and grows rapidly
as multiple narrow stems. As well as the common
osier, other possibly introduced species include white,
purple, almond and crack willows. There are at least
five native species of willow, commonest of which
are the grey and goat willows, and a host of hybrids
between native and introduced. The marshy fringes of
rivers, lakes and bogs are the most common locations
for willow woods. The term osier is an ancient one
from Old French, probably originating from medieval
Latin. It shows that basket-making has been around
for a long time.

In 1915, the Chief Secretary for Ireland delivered a
report to the Westminster Parliament. He said:

[The] Department of Agriculture had an experienced
osier grower who was available for visiting sites
of proposed osier beds, and advising as to their

suitability, and as to methods of planting, as well as in regard to the maintenance and development of existing osier beds with a view to supplying the raw material in the future for the basket-making industry. The Department also issued a leaflet on the subject, in which are indicated the varieties of osier most suitable for planting in Ireland, and the proper methods of cultivation.[1]

There are a growing number of professional basketmakers in Ireland today, and the crafts using willow are increasing in popularity. One such craftsperson is Diane Carton of Saille Baskets (*saileach* is the Irish name for the willow). She grows her own willows in osier beds in the heart of the Boggeragh Mountains of Cork. The osier grows very tall and straight in its first year of growth, before setting branches or side shoots in its second year. This enables it to be harvested at the end of this first season to provide long supple rods for weaving. In previous centuries baskets were vital containers used in many aspects of rural life from potato-picking to turf-harvesting to fish-traps. The rods of the willow grow straight and fast – several metres a year in the right conditions – and can be harvested from the tree only to regrow a year later. The wood is light and flexible – ideal for bending into all kinds of shapes and structures.

The variously coloured willow used by Diane are all natural varieties, with wonderful names such as Flanders Red, Dicky Meadows, Green Dicks, Black Maul, Britney Blue, Vitalina, Daphnoids and Welsh White. Each variety responds and grows differently according to the local climate. Some willows will not grow well on Diane's osier bed, which is at 240 metres above sea level and north facing. Willow really prefers a wet ground and is happy enough in poor soil, which suits her land close to blanket bogland. The willow twigs are pushed about twenty centimetres into the soil in rows, being careful to ensure each slip is the right way up. The action of the bark grating against stones and soil as it is pushed down activates the growth of roots, and planting early in the winter allows plenty of root growth before the sap rises, to establish and support the new young rods. A fully functioning osier bed will take three years to establish, and cutting of the rods should be expanded every year to encourage more growth.

As the winter sets in, the leaves fall and the sap returns to the roots, effectively putting the plant to sleep and protecting it from the harsh winter cold and winds. This is the time to harvest. When the rods are completely bare, Diane cuts each rod as close to the ground as possible, making a clean cut to allow it to heal and seal over. The rods are then collected and bundled and left to start the drying process, usually under a cover but still outside. The bundles are turned inside out weekly to allow those inside to dry and prevent mould or rot from developing. After about six to eight weeks, if the bark has become tough and a little wrinkled, the willow bundles can be brought into a shed to continue drying out. The whole drying process can take up to three months to complete, although at around eight weeks willow can used 'green', without resoaking, as shrinkage will be minimal at this stage. At this point, Diane usually grades the bundles into lengths to make it easier to choose the appropriate material for each basket she makes.

The harvested material, once it is completely dry, needs to be resoaked to become supple once again for weaving. The rods are totally submerged in water and weighted to keep them under. The rule of soaking time is generally one day for each thirty centimetres of growth, followed by one day out of the water, during which time the rod is stood to allow it to mellow and soften. The rods are tested by bending the butt end to see if the willow kinks without snapping. If it is soft and bends without resistance, then it is usually ready to be woven into a basket.

Wet woodland facts

As baskets became less important in daily life, many osier beds were abandoned in modern times and have developed into mature wet woodland. This is a very distinctive type of woodland in nutrient-rich alluvial soils along the banks of slow-flowing rivers such as the Shannon and the Suir. Woodland expert Dr John Cross wrote about the structure of such woodland:

> This includes the native grey willow but the most prominent species are white willow, crack willow and common osier. As they age the trees often crack in the centre and fall over but continue to grow side branches to fill the space left behind. Combined with the wet ground conditions, this tangle of branches makes such woods very difficult to walk through.[2]

This is a type of wet woodland that I have seen on islands

in the centre of the wide River Shannon as it winds its way slowly into Limerick city. A footbridge through the University of Limerick campus gives excellent views at canopy level of the towering willow trees.

More often I have encountered wet woodlands dominated by alder trees. According to the standard *Management Guidelines for Ireland's Native Woodlands*:

Alder woodlands are species-rich woodlands characteristic of poorly drained gley soils, flushes, stream and river margins, lakeshores and water-logged hollows. The canopy is dominated by alder, sometimes with ash and sally, both of which may often occur in the understorey. The herb layer is very rich in species, with an abundance of moisture-loving herbs, such as meadowsweet, remote sedge, marsh bedstraw, angelica, creeping buttercup, water mint and yellow flag. This woodland type is distributed throughout the country but is particularly associated with drumlins and river valleys.[3]

This classification is very familiar to me as it almost perfectly describes a small patch of old woodland on our farm in County Wicklow. Here, giant alder trees hang over both banks of a small river that powers down from the hills to join the Vartry River. At times in the winter, the river channel cannot hold the volume of water that rushes off the mountainside, and the woodland floods with brown, silt-laden water, filling side channels and pools to the brim. Then the paths through the wood become impassable, and some of the footbridges are lifted by the floodwater. Most winters some tall alder trees are likely to topple over, their root masses dislodged from the wet soil and hoisted into the air. Others rot at the base and break off, leaving a rotting stump in place. These trees I leave to become part of the natural woodland habitat, because I know that a high proportion of all the biodiversity associated with native woodlands depends on dead and decaying wood.

Today, of all the native woodland types in Ireland, wet woods cover the smallest area and are probably the most fragmented. Many stands are tiny, only a few hectares in area, and all have been damaged by people, either through tree felling, grazing of domestic animals or drainage to create more agricultural land.[4] A survey to monitor the condition of wet alluvial woods in

Ireland reported in 2013 that less than a quarter of the forty alluvial woodland sites surveyed received a green assessment (favourable prospects), while over 77 per cent received an amber or red assessment (unfavourable to bad prospects). In the table of negative impacts recorded for these wet sites, invasive non-native species topped the list, with thirty-five occurrences, followed closely by dumping of rubbish and solid waste, overgrazing by deer and livestock and multiple paths and tracks.[5] In simple terms, over one-third of the remaining alluvial woods are in a pretty bad condition, neglected or even abandoned and treated as wastelands. Due to wet ground conditions, these woods are often unsuitable for amenity use and are generally ignored by farmers or, worse, treated as dumping grounds for farm waste.

Ancient wet woods

One of the best surviving examples of wet alluvial woodlands in Ireland is at the Gearagh, near Macroom in County Cork. This was previously an extensive wilderness, reaching almost thirty kilometres along the River Lee, which divided into multiple channels with small islands between, each one wooded and difficult to reach. One day in early summer, I walked through this woodland on a raised embankment surrounded by flowing water on all sides. It still felt very wild although the area of surviving woodland is much smaller than it would have been. Originally, this area of alluvial woodland extended as far as the Lee Bridge, but two-thirds of the former woodland was lost in the creation of a reservoir during the construction of a hydroelectric dam here in the 1950s. In the remaining portion, the canopy consists of oak, ash and birch with an understorey of hazel, holly and hawthorn. Willows and alders dominate the channel margins and waterlogged areas. The difference between this and other alluvial woodlands is that the river is naturally divided into many deep channels even when the water level falls, with multiple free-draining islands that are largely inaccessible. It is reminiscent of some of the major braided (multi-channel) rivers in remote parts of the world such as New Zealand. Multi-channel rivers with large islands are now very rare in Europe, but they were common in prehistoric times, especially in the period immediately after the last Ice Age. The whole area still has a remarkably wild character, with many fallen trees blocking the channels, so that access both by foot and boat is difficult.

The Gearagh woodlands are not only long-lived, they once harboured a unique group of people, probably the last forest-dwelling community that survived in Ireland into the twentieth century. A descendant of this community, Kevin Corcoran, has written a detailed account of the site and its people. Most of the first-hand information came from his grandmother, who lived on the margins of the forest. He relates how the people lived in temporary dwellings and moved to the extensive interior using flat-bottomed boats when the worst of the winter floods had passed. Here they built temporary shelters deep within the forest. They coppiced trees for firewood and construction material, prepared timbers for boat-building and household implements, collected herbs, fished for salmon and trout and hunted duck. The remote and concealed nature of their summer homes also allowed them to make *poitín*, an illicit type of alcohol, and sell this in the local area. Corcoran's book begins with the sad image of some descendants of this unique community watching their forest habitat and homes in the surrounding farmland being permanently flooded in 1956.[6]

Today, what remains of the original alluvial forest is gradually restoring itself through a process of rewilding, whereby trees have returned to many of the islands where they were clear-felled in the 1950s. Protected from interference and grazing by the deep channels, the coppiced stumps have regrown to create a new canopy and a diverse understorey. A study of the remaining area, carried out by scientists from Leicester University in the 1990s, showed that the physical structure of the river channels and islands is highly influenced by biological processes such as trees falling across the river and debris dams caused by timber washing downstream.[7] The whole area was mapped by the Ordnance Survey in the nineteenth century and again in 1939, shortly before flooding by the reservoir took place, so we can calculate how large this wilderness once was.

The Gearagh first came to the attention of botanists in 1907 when it was visited by the naturalist Robert Lloyd Praeger. He was followed by a procession of well-known international scientists from Ireland, Britain and the rest of Europe. Lists of the flora were published in learned journals, most recently by James White.[8] In this survey it became clear that the woodland was rich in flowering plants, fungi and lichens. One significant change was the absence of yew trees, which disappeared with the flooding in the 1950s. Fourteen species of grass and thirteen ferns and horsetails were recorded with twenty-four species of lichens, many growing on the branches and trunks of the trees. An earlier visitor in the 1940s described it as 'an almost impenetrable jungle, certainly one in which the most knowledgeable man might lose his way'.

On another day, I went to visit Abbey Leix estate, in County Laois, at the invitation of the then owner, Sir David Davies. As I arrived the heavens opened, and I had to shelter from a torrential downpour. Then, as quickly as it arrived, the rain disappeared, and a bright summer sun broke through the woodland canopy, lighting up vast swathes of wet bluebells glistening below. Around me were some of the most magnificent oak trees that I have ever seen in Ireland. For centuries they have stood here undisturbed on the banks of the River Nore, aging gracefully and representing the ancient wildwood that has all but disappeared from modern Ireland. Each winter, the river breaks its banks and floods across neighbouring fields, bathing the roots of the trees with a rich deposit of alluvial silt.

The woodlands here are dominated by pedunculate oak, although there are also some sizeable areas of ash and beech, while sycamores occasionally make an appearance. Where the woodland is regularly flooded, alder and willow comprise the main canopy, and the ground flora is quite limited as it is frequently underwater. I walked through a tangle of branches, dodging around wet muddy pools and clambering over dead limbs that lay decaying on the ground. Suddenly a clearing opened up and a huge, spreading oak filled the gap, its substantial trunk hollowed out by age and decay. I half expected Robin Hood and his merry men to emerge from the trees and rob me of anything valuable. One old oak on the estate has been reliably aged at up to 640 years old. There is a good record of these woodlands in a series of old estate maps dating back to 1563. The wettest parts of the woodlands are in the area marked 'Lowlands', which clearly describes the topography and its tendency to flood.[9]

The willow musician

It is late April when the summer migrant birds start arriving in Ireland in force. At this time of year I love to be in my own small patch of wet woodland in County Wicklow to welcome the new arrivals. Among the first sounds of summer are the songs of numerous willow warblers, a beautiful melodious series of notes descending the scale. Willow warblers are very common in summer in suitable wet areas where scrub and trees provide them with prominent song posts. They feed exclusively on insects, which they can catch on the wing or on the leaves of the trees. They are one of a group of birds known as the leaf warblers, partly due to their soft green colour which gives them plenty of camouflage in the foliage. Slimline and weighing no more than a pencil, the birds have a delicate bill for picking up insects. The association of the warbler with willows in its breeding habitat was well known to earlier generations of Irish people who gave them the name *ceolaire sailí* – the willow musician.

Willow warblers breed widely in Ireland, being found in almost every part of the country. Since the 1980s the number of Irish breeding pairs has increased significantly by almost two-thirds, but this has been largely at the expense of the species in England. It seems that the population is shifting to the north-west in response to a warming climate and the decrease in suitable habitat in our neighbouring island. Environmental changes in Africa are also considered to be driving the changes in abundance at a regional scale.[10]

Willow warblers that breed in Ireland leave the country immediately after the young birds fledge and become independent. They fly straight through Western Europe, aiming for wintering grounds in Africa where they are guaranteed a steady supply of their insect food. Willow warblers can travel as far as South Africa, but the main wintering areas of the Irish and British birds are in Ivory Coast and Ghana. Flying across open sea at night, flocks of willow warblers are frequently attracted by the bright beams of lighthouses and drop down to the light. Richard Barrington, a nineteenth-century naturalist from County Wicklow, undertook a twenty-year survey of bird migration at Irish lighthouses and lightships which became the standard work on the subject well into the twentieth century. He described 'falls' of birds, that he called willow wrens, from reports he received from lightkeepers. This is just one of hundreds of examples: '16th April 1881: Blackwater Bank Lightship – flock of "wrens" about the light at 10pm. Four birds killed striking.' The lightkeepers often called the birds 'sallypickers' as country people were well aware of their association with willow or sally trees.[11]

Rewilding with trees

The first light of dawn was breaking in the eastern sky as I left the cabin where I was staying on the edge of the Murrough wetlands in east Wicklow. A cock pheasant crowed to announce the end of the night, and jackdaws chatted in the hollow tree where they were nesting. As I walked across the rushy fields the grass crunched beneath my boots, and a hard frost still glistened white on the vegetation all around. A kestrel launched itself from the branches of a dead alder tree where it had probably roosted for the night and sheared off into the woodland, a dark scimitar shape silhouetted against a reddening sky. I picked my way carefully across narrow planks that spanned the many ditches through the marsh and headed for the reedbeds that fringe the seaward side of this wild land. A solitary snipe rose from the grass and, with a loud drumming noise, shot downwards like an arrow, the sound emanating from its stiff tail feathers.

All around me old hedges filled with willow and alder trees grew unrestricted by any machinery, and in the wettest places, they swelled out to form patches of wet woodland. Here in the muddy ground were the tracks of many deer, keeping to the cover to avoid people. I walked across several rushy fields that have not been grazed for at least five years. As the farmer had told me the previous week, 'there's no money in cattle any more. I don't keep any livestock although I miss the animals.' Rusting electric fences still bounded some of the fields, but there was no power in them, and they were unlikely ever to be connected again. Occasional birches grew on the drier banks of the drains where spoil had been spread in earlier years. Among the rushes, spreading out into the fields, young saplings of willow and alder were bursting into leaf in the spring light. It struck me that this marsh is changing rapidly to become a wet woodland through natural regeneration. If left ungrazed for a few more years, it will become a woodland habitat instead of a grass-dominated one. Natural succession was taking place before my eyes.

This is rewilding in a form that could work in Ireland. All we need to do is to put the brake on farming in the marginal areas of land, and nature will do the rest. Of course, there can be difficulties that need to be resolved. Invasive species like rhododendron or Himalayan balsam may take over the wet ground and need to be removed. Burgeoning populations of Japanese sika deer may threaten to damage the young trees, and these may also need to be controlled. Hopefully, the overwhelming numbers of young trees will be more than the deer can handle, and most will survive. If we want to speed up the rate of wet woodland development, constructing a simple sluice on the main outlet channel would allow controlled flooding to create patches of open water and reedbed for wintering birds, while willow would colonise the area faster. It is clear from this example that a combination of rewilding and some targeted intervention may work in a country like Ireland where the land holdings are small and there is much marginal land that is gradually being abandoned. Many farming enterprises have become uneconomic, but farmers in marginal land need to be compensated for sharing their land with nature. This is not just a technical challenge but an economic and cultural one too.

As a big red sun broke over the eastern horizon, I found myself wondering whether, if I returned in a decade or two, this would have become an extensive mosaic of wet woodland, lake and marsh, rich in wildlife such as dragonflies, egrets, otters and even such exciting birds as the white-tailed eagle, which is now spreading from the reintroduced population in south-west Ireland. It is a vision that I hope will be realised someday.

The future for wet woodlands

Flooded areas with trees are often overlooked by agriculture due to the saturated nature of the soils. Livestock are sometimes fenced out, as animals can become trapped in the wet conditions. These alluvial woods frequently occur around the edges of lakes, bogs and fens and sometimes on the margins of rivers whose floodplains are still intact. Often this is just a narrow fringe of willow or alder trees, but in valley bottoms, where drainage is poor, there may be more substantial patches. The term 'carr' was once given to wet woods, but this is poorly defined. The largest area of wet woodland so far recorded is in Killarney National Park where some 170 hectares of this habitat occurs, mainly on the low-lying ground to the east and south of Lough Leane. In the 1990s, a detailed study of wet woodlands across Ireland suggested that the richness and diversity of this habitat had been underestimated.[12]

Drainage is often impossible due to the absence

of any gradient to the nearest watercourse, lake or peatland. Forestry practice also has largely been excluded, as such areas are considered unsuitable for growing commercial conifer crops. Nevertheless, a survey in the last decade found that over one-third of the remaining alluvial woods are in a pretty bad condition, neglected or even abandoned and treated as wastelands.[13] There is a need to protect and manage what remains of a once extensive habitat that early settlers found when they came to Ireland. A good example has been set by the new entity Coillte Nature in the area known as Hazelwood on the shores of Lough Gill, County Sligo. This project has seen the removal of dense thickets of invasive species, such as rhododendron, enabling the natural regeneration of the alluvial habitat. Biodiversity in the wider woodland is being enhanced by thinning areas of existing trees to encourage the natural regeneration of native species and to improve structural diversity. Following harvesting, some areas of non-native conifers have been replaced with a native woodland mix.

Abandonment of marginal farmland that is less productive for livestock or crops offers the best hope for expanding the area of wet woodland, but this will need to be paid for as a contribution to climate action. If fenced off from grazing, willow and alder trees will naturally colonise the saturated soils, regenerating from seed sources in the surrounding landscape. Drier patches may become colonised by other tree species such as ash, birch and holly. Riverbanks need willow and alder trees to establish their root systems, binding the loose soil and trapping nutrients that drain from surrounding intensive farmland. Recreating these damp corridors along river valleys establishes links in the landscape between other semi-natural areas, allowing sensitive wildlife species to move under cover and recolonise the newly developing habitats. This form of 'rewilding' will have little impact on other land uses but is highly valuable for nature.

Artificial Waters: Ponds, Canals and Constructed Wetlands

Four ducks on a pond,
   A grass-bank beyond,
   A blue sky of spring,
   White clouds on the wing;
   What a little thing
   To remember for years—
   To remember with tears!

'Four Ducks on a Pond' (1860) by WILLIAM ALLINGHAM

One of the joys of childhood is dipping a net in a pond and getting close-up views of such fascinating creatures as tadpoles, water beetles and pond skaters. As well as natural rivers, streams, ponds and lakes, Ireland has quite a few artificial waterways, constructed for a variety of purposes over the centuries – canals for waterborne transport, ponds for watering livestock, flooded quarries, constructed wetlands for nature-based treatment of polluted water and containment of run-off from major roads. Some of these can be quite rich in biodiversity, alongside their main functions. Unfortunately, there has been a major reduction in ponds over the centuries, as these are drained and infilled to provide more land for farming, forestry or urban development. Increasing awareness about the value of such water bodies has led to various conservation measures to restore them to the landscape.

Pond life

In the nineteenth and early twentieth century, ponds were a common feature on farms and in villages. They were important for watering farm animals, as drinking places for work horses and even as a source for water used in houses. There were also fish ponds, duck decoy ponds, moats, millponds, hemp and flax ponds, liming ponds, clay ponds (brick pits and marl pits), peat ponds, gravel pits and decorative ponds in gardens of the landed gentry. As a result, freshwater plants and animals were much more widespread in the country then.

On our own farm, I have started to create a new pond in the grassland at the bottom of one of our fields. The area has always supported more rushes than grass, which suggested that the soil was permanently saturated. With my spade I dug a hole and, sure enough, just below the brown earth of the topsoil was a thick layer of fine sticky mud. Rolling a handful of this soil between my palms produced a sausage-shaped lump not unlike modelling clay. Technically known as gley, this type of soil is made of fine-grained material that has been laid down in saturated or anoxic conditions. Any microorganisms left in the soil extract the oxygen they need to survive from the iron compounds and the soil gradually turns grey, blue or green as the oxygen is depleted.

The pond I had in mind was much larger than one person with a spade could dig, so I hired a mechanical digger for a day to do the work. Even as this dug down, the bottom of the gradually enlarging hole began to fill with groundwater. At the foot of a steep slope made of glacial sand and gravel, the water was filtering down and flowing out where it met the impermeable gleys. I wanted to make both deep and shallow water areas within the one pond so that we get as wide a variety of wetland plants and animals as possible. On one side we created a shallow shelf where I hoped the water would settle with a depth of just enough for a variety of emergent plants such as yellow iris, arrowhead and water mint. Even in the first year, it has been a joy to watch as swallows dip into the water to drink without missing a wingbeat and water boatmen row across the bed of the pond with their spoon-shaped forelegs.

Ponds support an extraordinary two-thirds to three-quarters of all freshwater species. Studies in lowland landscapes across Europe have shown that ponds have more plant and animal species than rivers, streams, lakes or ditches. They also support significantly more unusual species.[1] Ponds are among the least-studied habitats in the mosaic of semi-natural or man-made ecosystems in the Irish agricultural landscape. To address this issue, a study for the EPA investigated the ecological quality and potential conservation value of a range of ponds in two regions in Ireland. Water beetles and wetland plants were used as indicators of pond biodiversity, and a number of local environmental and management variables were measured. The results show that farmland ponds contribute substantially to the maintenance of freshwater biodiversity in Ireland. The seventy-six beetle species collected from the study ponds represented over 30 per cent of the Irish water beetle fauna. There were also rarer species, with four of those found included in the Red List of Irish Water Beetles.[2]

The author of the report noted that grazing intensity and nutrient enrichment have a detrimental effect on the diversity of plant and beetle assemblages and that a buffer zone of marginal vegetation as well as a fence system improved the overall ecological quality of ponds. Temporary ponds were significantly less diverse than permanent ponds, but they may contribute to maintaining water beetle diversity at the landscape level by improving connectivity between freshwater systems. The diversity of the study ponds had little to do with the pond surface area, indicating that the maintenance or creation of small ponds characterised by a shallow zone may play a central role in the conservation of biodiversity. A general decrease in the number of farmland ponds was observed as a consequence of the intensification of agricultural practices and housing developments.[3] Temporary or ephemeral wetlands can also help retain diversity as fish-free microhabitats where some of our rarer plants such as stoneworts can live.

The highlight of the first year in my own pond came

in early August when I was admiring the water plants such as brooklime that I had transplanted from other ponds over the previous weeks. I noticed two insects, linked together as one, performing what looked like a dance above the water surface. These were large red damselflies, a common species in Ireland. With delicate movements they dipped a tail repeatedly in the water engaged in what I guessed was egg-laying. I was thinking about the joys of searching for other species next summer when, suddenly, another larger, bright blue insect appeared, hawking backwards and forwards across the water about half a metre above the surface. It was an emperor, one of the largest dragonfly species in Ireland, and this one was flying in a very determined way, obviously establishing a territory. It aggressively chased off the red damselflies and claimed the pond for itself. I was full of wonder for the speed at which nature can colonise a habitat when the right conditions are there.

Dragons and damsels

The first time I saw an emperor dragonfly was many years ago as I sat on the banks of the Royal Canal in Dublin city, not far from Mountjoy Prison where Brendan

Behan wrote his famous song, 'The Auld Triangle'. It was a place where reeds and other water plants had been allowed to grow in the channel in recent years. A large insect was buzzing backwards and forwards above the water surface searching among the vegetation. Occasionally it hovered like a helicopter then resumed its search, impressive in its speed of flight. It dipped into the water momentarily, touching a suitable plant with its tail. It was laying its eggs, which adhered to the leaves and were left to develop. Out of sight, the newly hatched larvae drop to the bottom and move around for a while feeding on other animals such as tadpoles. These are the raptors of still water, fierce predators that will lie in wait to ambush any passing small creature, even other dragonflies. Some dragonflies and damselflies have an extensive larval stage, typically one or two years, but the range is from two or three months to more than five years. Eventually, the larvae climb out of the water and, after a period of miraculous reorganisation of their internal organs, transform into beautiful adult dragonflies whose sole purpose is to reproduce and start the cycle of life again. Unlike butterflies and moths, there is no pupal stage in dragonflies and damselflies. Instead, the adult insect emerges directly from the larval skin.

Dragonflies have been referred to as 'birdwatchers' insects' because they are large and colourful, fly in daylight and are relatively easily identified in their adult stages. Indeed, I often use a pair of binoculars to watch these insects from a safe distance as they rest on water plants. Thirty-three species of dragonflies and damselflies are known from Ireland, five of these being occasional migrants here. Dragonfly larvae are larger and more robust than damselfly larvae, but otherwise they look quite similar and all are part of the family called Odonata. Dragonflies are the descendants of giant insects that flew in the prehistoric forests of the Carboniferous era. They have attractive names – the beautiful demoiselle, the golden-ringed dragonfly, the variable damselfly and the emerald dragonfly. Dragonfly names often reflect their hunting behaviour, with skimmers flying low over water, hawkers chasing down their prey, and darters zooming in from a perch. They require good water quality to survive to adulthood and can react quickly to changes in environmental conditions. Dragonflies and damselflies can thus be used as bio-indicators of water quality and freshwater habitat quality. Some species, such as the emperor dragonfly, are also good indicators of climate

change as they have expanded their range to the north
in response to increasing average temperatures.

There is one species, known as the Irish damselfly,
which is restricted to Ireland and has not so far been
found in the neighbouring island of Britain, although it
has a patchy distribution across Western Europe. It was
first discovered here in 1981 by zoologist Dr Don Cotton
and is now known from widely scattered colonies
on numerous lakeshores, mainly west of a line from
County Down to County Limerick. Since it was first
found in Sligo, it has been recorded at approximately
forty sites in thirteen counties. The majority of sites
have been in counties Fermanagh, Tyrone, Armagh
and Monaghan. A few colonies have been found on
cutover bogs, where they breed in the shallow pools
left after peat extraction. They catch small gnats and
other flying insects, pursued with dazzling aerobatics.
Their strike rate is around 95 per cent once they set
their huge compound eyes on a prey animal.

Dragonfly spotting suits fair-weather naturalists.
An ideal day for them is sunny and warm, with at least
a 60 per cent clear sky and a minimum temperature
of fifteen degrees Celsius. Strong wind and rain
will usually ground them. 'If the sun doesn't shine,

dragonflies are hard to see,' says Dr Brian Nelson, entomologist at NPWS and a leading dragonfly expert in Ireland. With the photographer Robert Thompson, he published a wonderful account of Ireland's dragonflies, which includes a gazetteer of the best locations for these insects throughout the island.[4]

Dragonflies are regarded by many as the jewels of the insect world. For centuries, they have been revered by humans and celebrated in art, poetry and religion. In country areas, some people once believed that dragonflies were used as horses by the 'little people' to travel to other places in the blink of an eye. Some stories imply that the dragonfly is actually a fairy in disguise that only can be seen from the right angle. As they flit over the water one could easily imagine them morphing into a tiny human form with delicate wings. The name 'nymphs', often used for the larvae of these insects, reinforces the connection with the fairies. The Celts connected dragonflies with the ability to see truth; with the sight of the ancient, powerful dragons who were guardians of the sacred stones and magical wells. It was believed that a dragonfly was a lucky spirit, thought to have the power to restore health.

Seeing a dragonfly or dreaming of a dragonfly could signal that a change was coming, perhaps a rebirth to a new life. Dragonflies were also believed to warn that a person or situation is only hovering on the surface and one should look more deeply to find authenticity.

Little dragons

A newt is the nearest thing I have seen in the animal world to a dragon. This impression might have been influenced by the fact that my first close encounter with the species was in total darkness. I was doing an ecological survey of a railway line due for upgrading, and there were some shallow pools along the sides of the tracks. As I shone my torch on the water surface I could see some tiny creatures swimming away down among the water weeds. Each animal had four legs and a long powerful tail resembling that of a lizard, although the species is unrelated to reptiles. The smooth (or common) newt is one of only three amphibians in Ireland, the others being the common frog and the natterjack toad. Like all members of this group, they spend part of their life cycle in water and part on land.

In winter, adult newts leave the water and hibernate

in damp shady places under stones or in moss or rotting wood. As temperatures rise, they awake from their winter slumber and make their way back to the water to breed. This occurs mostly in February and March, but it is thought that the timing of breeding is shifting to earlier months as winter temperatures increase with climate change. In the water, the male conducts a complicated courtship display in which he moves backwards and forwards vibrating his tail. The pair will then mate and the female lays hundreds of eggs which are attached to aquatic vegetation. Female newts wrap each egg individually with their back feet, which have more toes than the front feet for greater dexterity. Newt tadpoles are carnivorous, and frog tadpoles are among their favoured prey. They have feathery external gills that are used for obtaining oxygen underwater. Over the summer, the newt tadpoles develop into adult form by growing legs and losing the external gills, replacing them gradually with lungs. Around September, the juveniles leave the water and will spend two to three years on land until they become sexually mature and return once more to the water to breed. Smooth newts have an average life span of seven years in the wild.

Between 2010 and 2013 the IWT organised a national survey of the smooth newt in conjunction with the National Biodiversity Data Centre. This involved training ordinary citizens to undertake the survey work in their own areas using simple techniques. The results confirmed that newts are widespread in Ireland with positive records throughout the country. Newts are only found in still or slow-moving water, so ponds, ditches and wetlands are essential to their survival. Although newts were scarce in farmland, the IWT survey revealed that man-made habitats, particularly garden ponds and quarries, are significant components of their natural habitat.[5]

Sometimes newts are affected by new development in the countryside. In 2009, Cavan County Council was proposing to build a new access road to Cavan town in an area of mixed habitat that included a wetland complex centred on Killymooney Lough. During the ecological impact assessment, carried out by their consultants, smooth newts were found in one of a series of three eutrophic ponds located along the southern arm of the route. As part of site clearance works, both newts and frogs were moved to a suitable habitat creation area away from the new road, and by

2012 they were breeding in their new home. However, Dr Rob Gandola of the Herpetological Society of Ireland warns, 'initial population booms can then be followed by subsequent declines in both numbers and habitat quality'. Dr Ferdia Marnell of the NPWS told me that 'translocation is very labour intensive and is not without its challenges. Adult newts generally try to return to the pond where they were born. The terrestrial habitat around the water bodies is also very important for the newts.'

Canals

In early history, rivers and lakes were the highways of their time, carrying people and goods from coastal settlements into the heart of the country. When boats met obstacles such as shallows or rapids, they had to be unloaded and carried across to the next piece of navigable water. Early solutions were found with the creation of weirs built of stones across a river to hold the water upstream at a constant level. However, some means had to be found to allow boats to pass safely through a weir. The most famous of all inventors, Leonardo da Vinci, was the first to design the swinging lock gates that are still in use on most canals today.

This allowed engineers to construct canals that climbed from low levels to a watershed and down again, making it possible to connect adjacent river catchments.[6]

The heyday of the Irish canals was the early nineteenth century, before the advent of widespread rail and road transport. Heavy goods such as coal, turf and potatoes could be transported over long distances on wooden barges drawn by a single horse. A barge could carry thirty tons on a river or fifty tons on a canal where there was no resistance from the flow, compared with a horse-drawn wagon that could carry only two tons on the rough roads of the time. The Newry Canal was the first to be built, linking the Newry River to the Upper Bann and thence to Lough Neagh and the coast at Portstewart. Other canals linked the midlands of Ireland to the major cities of Dublin, Limerick and Waterford via the River Shannon, the Grand and Royal canals and the Barrow Navigation. The main line of the Royal Canal is 145 kilometres in length, stretching from the River Liffey in Dublin Docks all the way to the Shannon in County Longford. It was built in stages during the years 1790 to 1830 but was superseded in the mid-nineteenth century when the Dublin to Mullingar railway was built almost parallel to the canal. During the 1950s the canal became disused, and it was closed to navigation in 1961.

Dense vegetation, including willow trees, grew in the channel, insect life multiplied and wetland birds such as moorhen, mallard and swans returned to breed by the water's edge. Restoration of navigation began in 1986, and a complete channel was open to boats by the early 2000s. By then most of the traffic was tourist motor cruisers and traditional barges used as houseboats. As part of planning for restoration, a full ecological evaluation of the canal was undertaken in the early 1990s, and I was lucky enough to collaborate in this work, surveying breeding birds and dragonflies as indicators of biodiversity value. For ease of access, I used a mountain bike to ride along the grassy towpaths, stopping at intervals to observe the birds and insects. Nesting birds were present in quite low numbers, possibly due to the narrow fringe of vegetation that existed as cover. I found moorhen nests in the low branches of some willow trees where they dipped into the water. I often found grey wagtails close to bridges and locks, where the combination of fast-moving water, insect food and crevices in the old stonework provided the habitat requirements that they would normally find in rivers. Mute swans, in contrast, are entirely vegetarian, feeding mainly on the leaves and stems of submerged aquatic plants. They usually build their nests in dense reeds on the canal margins, but here they can be reached by ground predators such as foxes and mink, so breeding success is limited in some years.

Many of the old stone bridges are named after various developers and patrons of the canal. John Binns, one of the principal supporters of the Royal Canal, is commemorated in a carved stone plaque on each face of Binns Bridge in Dublin. Walking under the bridge I could see the marks left on the stonework where the cables attaching draught horses to the heavy barges had rubbed on the masonry, year after year. The mortar between the masonry blocks of some of these bridges has been eroded over the two centuries since their construction. Some of these crevices provide suitable habitats for roosting bats to slip into during the day, emerging in the evenings to feed on the abundant insects flying over the water.

The water bat

One evening I was cycling along the towpath of the

Royal Canal on the northern fringes of Dublin city. After a long day of surveys, I was tired and anxious to get home, but the light was fading and a low red sun followed me from the west. Suddenly, a small bat appeared from under a canal bridge and flitted across the still water surface hunting insects. Silent except for a series of high-pitched clicks, it swept along the canal like a low-flying aircraft.

The Daubenton's bat is often called the 'water bat' and is easily recognised by its low-level flight a few centimetres above the surface of canals, ponds, lakes and slow-moving rivers. It skims like a hovercraft above the water in search of caddisflies, mayflies and midges, and may even scoop prey from the water surface using its big feet. Daubenton's bats have been recorded following canals for as much as ten kilometres at speeds of up to twenty-five kph. Many other bats feed over lakes and rivers, but none of the other species has such a close association with water. Daubenton's bats can even swim, if they make a mistake and end up in the water. Their preference is for feeding is areas with open water, but they can also be found in low-density urban areas. They prefer to feed over still or slow-moving waters, especially where these are lined with trees.

Daubenton's bats may hibernate overwinter in caves, mines and other underground sites. They enter these winter sites (known as hibernaculae) in October, and individuals often remain here until the end of March or even early April. Then they emerge for the summer and move to breeding colonies, which may be in tunnels or in bridges over canals and rivers.

Daubenton's bats are only occasionally found in buildings, usually old stone structures such as moated castles and waterworks. Individuals are often lodged in tight crevices and may be vulnerable to getting trapped when stonework is repointed and restored. They may also hide among rocks and scree on the floor of caves and tunnels, making them very difficult to find. There are often just a few bats present in a roost. Only two very large roosts, of over 200 Daubenton's bats, have been discovered, one in a cave in County Mayo and another in a church in County Galway.[7]

Constructed wetlands

Designed to improve water quality in a predominantly farmed landscape as well as provide wildlife habitat, integrated constructed wetlands (ICW) represent an innovative approach to wastewater treatment. These combine many aspects of water management with habitat and landscape restoration. In its most basic form, a river or stream can be channelled through a chain of shallow artificial ponds, the water flowing from one to the next in sequence. Each pond contains natural wetland vegetation, which absorbs nutrients, such as nitrogen and phosphorus, from wastewater and water that has run off farmland. Thus, the water becomes cleaner and the ponds become progressively more natural further down the system.

Féidhlim Harty has developed expertise in the use of constructed wetlands for the treatment of wastewater. His books offer the landowner advice on designing, building and planting a constructed wetland to treat septic tank effluent or grey water (from sinks, baths and washing machines) before it soaks into the ground.[8] I met him on his own property near Ennistymon, County Clare, where he grows wetland plants and sells them to landowners building their own reedbed treatment systems. Harty told me:

Constructed wetlands and reedbeds are sewage treatment systems that use the natural filtering capability of wetland plants to clean up effluent in a way that can use zero energy, are low-cost and wildlife-friendly. Willow filters take this a step further and can not only mop up nutrients from the water and convert them to usable biomass but can also be designed to evaporate the effluent into the air, further protecting local groundwater and waterways. These natural systems are a wonderful example of working with nature to achieve desired outcomes with multiple benefits for people, water quality and wildlife.

One of the most exciting applications of this concept has been in the Anne Valley near Tramore in County Waterford. This river catchment is approximately twenty-five square kilometres in area and farming is the main land use activity. Throughout Ireland's farming landscape a proportion of the water pollution comes from the washings of slurry tanks and silage pits. In this area, three-quarters of all dirty water from farmyards, generated within the watershed, is treated by constructed wetlands, which were all built around the year 2000 and are generally not shaded by terrestrial vegetation.

Dr Rory Harrington, formerly a scientist with the NPWS, has been the driving force behind this landscape-scale experiment. He pioneered the ICW concept on a river catchment scale with a group of landowners in the Anne Valley. He especially acknowledges his neighbouring fellow farmers and Dunhill residents. All of them took a considerable risk, he says, whether in funding the project or in giving over precious agricultural hectares to zones of 'unproductive' rushes, sedges and water. Harrington based the design for his constructed wetlands on hard science, but they were quite experimental at first. Much of the Anne River catchment area thus became an open-air ecological laboratory. The value of such artificial wetlands in improving water quality is well known now, but do they help to increase freshwater biodiversity?

To explore the invertebrates of these wetland systems in the Anne Valley, a group of scientists from University College Dublin, led by Dr Gustavo Becerra Jurado, selected five ponds on the basis of size, nutrient loading and habitat type. These were considered to represent the variety of constructed wetlands present in the Anne Valley. No large fish species are known to inhabit the constructed wetlands. For comparison they also studied five relatively natural wetlands in the south-east of the country. They found that the last ponds in the chain of these ICW systems are capable of supporting a similar number of species of invertebrates to natural ponds. The greatest diversity of animal groups in the artificial ponds were among the beetles and bugs, which also tend to dominate in natural ponds. The high connectivity of ponds within ICW systems provides a virtually continuous habitat for invertebrates that disperse by flying from one wetland to another.[9] As Harrington told me:

Local soils, embankments and vegetation reflect the needs of each individual site ranging from those heavily contaminated by pollutants such as animal/farmyard effluents, industrial and mine drainage, to lightly soiled run-off. This interconnectivity is best achieved when clients, landowners, experienced scientists and engineers, state agencies and local communities collaborate by exploring and manifesting what can be done with land, water resources and a diversity of vegetation types.

There are now functioning ICWs adjoining Castle Leslie at Glaslough, County Monaghan, and Clonaslee in

County Laois. Both are owned and managed by Irish Water and are great examples of a functioning nature-based solution with significant benefits for wildlife.

Motorway ponds

Attenuation ponds, constructed along many motorways in Ireland, are designed to drain road run-off, including stormwater, before it is filtered and allowed to enter natural water courses. These new aquatic habitats can potentially make a significant contribution to biodiversity, as farmland ponds have declined significantly. A study in Sweden found that larger ponds are better for supporting aquatic biodiversity as they have a greater variety of habitats and greater ability to dilute pollutants. Also, the presence of a number of ponds in the same area can facilitate the movement of invertebrates between them through increased connectivity. The retention of polluted water in these stormwater ponds creates a unique environment which is more suitable for animals that are tolerant of pollutants and that may not be found in natural ponds.

These constructed wetlands tend to dry out occasionally and are often seeded with different wild plants. The ponds range in water depth and vegetation composition, presenting a particularly suitable habitat for highly mobile insect groups. A study by Irish ecologists sampled five attenuation ponds along the M7/M8 motorway to find out what beetles, bugs and dragonflies were using these aquatic habitats and the environmental factors affecting the animals. They found that the ponds supported a diverse aquatic invertebrate community, dominated by mobile insect groups. Just over forty species of beetles were recorded in these five ponds. Some rare species and new arrivals to Ireland were also recorded. The type of vegetation strongly influenced the beetle species, with bottle sedge and branched bur-reed supporting the greatest diversity. The authors have made recommendations to motorway authorities on the value and management of attenuation ponds as new aquatic habitats in the Irish landscape.[10] Some follow-up studies found that frogs were also very likely to be present in these stormwater ponds, with smooth newts a good deal less likely. Bats were also very often seen foraging over the attenuation ponds, and dragonflies were present in good numbers. Clearly such ponds are useful substitutes for older ponds that have disappeared due to modern land use.

Restoring artificial wetlands

Some artificial wetlands have their origins in industrial development. When the Irish Sugar Company opened its factory in Thurles, County Tipperary in 1934, it brought enormous changes for the people of the town and the farmers living around it. Poverty and unemployment were common in Ireland then, due to a worldwide depression and a trade war with Britain. The factory had over 300 well-paid employees and many more seasonal workers during the 'campaign' – the time of year when sugar beet was harvested. However, in the early twentieth century, environmental controls were virtually non-existent. Sugar beet was washed before processing, and the sludgy effluent was released directly into the River Suir, causing serious pollution.

This river was renowned for angling, but there were frequent fish kills downstream of the factory. During the 1960s, local anglers led a campaign to clean up the effluent from the factory. As a result, lagoons were built to allow the sludge to settle before the wastewater was discharged. These 'settling ponds' had the desired result of reducing the fish kills, but they were built in an area of former wetland and probably destroyed some very rich habitats. Still, migrant

waders and ducks discovered that the lagoons were a
safe place when many other wetlands were regularly
shot over. The late Chris Wilson was an enthusiastic
naturalist who later became the warden at Wexford
Wildfowl Reserve. He explored the lagoons at Thurles
many times in the 1980s, and he noted that they were
drained each year after the sugar beet season, leaving
'superb feeding areas for waders and passerines in
the autumn and winter'. He found roosting flocks of
over 500 curlews, with up to 1,000 lapwing and golden
plover. The numbers of wildfowl were also impressive,
with hundreds of swans and over 1,500 ducks of at least
nine species. Rare migrant waders such as ruff and
green sandpiper were frequent autumn visitors in
significant numbers.

In 1989 the Thurles factory closed, and the sugar
company filled in several of the lagoons. So, I
wondered, what became of the migratory birds that
had found refuge in the settling lagoons? Visiting the
site, I drove past the remains of the old sugar factory to
reach the impressive new visitor centre that Cabragh
Wetlands Trust has built here. A group of local people
set up the trust in 1993 to save the remaining habitats
and interpret these for visitors. They bought over five

hectares from the sugar company and some natural wetlands adjacent to the lagoons. Since then, they have negotiated management agreements covering another forty hectares. Further funding from the Leader Programme and North Tipperary County Council allowed the excavation of new ponds, the creation of bird hides and the purchase of additional wetlands.

The centre is run by a group of committed volunteers who provide field trips for children and adults of all ages. The wetlands now have no less than fifteen different habitats including ponds, reedbeds, willow carr and wet grassland. The largest area is covered by reeds, but these are difficult to access because there is surface water throughout the year. Footpaths and raised walkways with illustrated information boards as well as a large bird hide make it an ideal place for school children to discover the sights and sounds of nature in a safe and child-friendly environment. A nest box erected on a tall pole in the centre of the wetland was readily occupied by a pair of barn owls which has bred here for more than a decade. The visitor centre, which has panoramic views of the wetlands, includes education and research facilities that promote environmental awareness. Jimmy Duggan, a retired school principal who is a long-time supporter of the trust, told me that 'ecological education is a huge growth area and we see it as the primary way ahead for the project.'

Walking through the extensive reedbeds in early summer I was impressed by the loud songs of well-hidden sedge warblers and grasshopper warblers and more gentle calls of prominent reed buntings. From deep within the reeds came some loud squealing like that of a piglet. This turned out to be the normal territorial 'song' of the water rail, which rarely emerges from cover. The permanent water is also a perfect habitat for dragonflies and damselflies, and I managed to see the beautiful demoiselle and a large hawker quartering a pool for food. A brimstone butterfly flew past, and I was told that its larval food plant, the alder buckthorn, is also present here. In winter, the wetlands are a magnet for flocks of migratory waterbirds such as wigeon, teal, shoveler and pochard with occasional flocks of whooper swan. As the site is in the floodplain of the River Suir, some of the surrounding fields flood in winter, attracting thousands of golden plover, lapwing and curlew that swirl above the site if disturbed. It is also a good place to see hunting hen harriers and the occasional migrant marsh harrier.

Kevin Collins, a long-time member of BirdWatch Ireland's Tipperary Branch, was my guide at the site. He believes that if water levels could be controlled over the fields in the northern part of the wetlands they would be readily colonised by breeding waders such as lapwing. With the help of professional ecologists, the trust has agreed to prepare a management plan for the site that would guide this process. Some simple sluices will be built on the streams that drain the site to the river, thus allowing the retention of water at critical times and giving this managed site a crucial role to play as a stepping-stone for wetland species.

Why build more waterways?

Artificial waterways offer multiple benefits for biodiversity and improving water quality. As the water quality in rivers and lakes declines, ponds, canals and constructed wetlands can provide refuges for many sensitive wetland species. The original uses of canals and ponds may be largely finished, but they have taken on new functions in the modern, intensively used landscape. Most of all, ponds and canals are often in easily accessible places, sometimes in towns and cities, where they offer great opportunities for education about freshwater life. Children love the excitement of pond-dipping with a net. Even common creatures like water boatmen and tadpoles are a thrill and a great way of learning about ecology.

Over half of Ireland's wetlands that once supported amphibians have been lost to drainage, industrial peat extraction, pollution and natural senescence in the past century. Of the 12,200 small, enclosed water bodies across Ireland, 8,000 are less than a hectare in extent. Yet ponds have been shown to host more biodiversity than rivers and lakes, particularly macroinvertebrates and less common species. Permanent and naturally vegetated ponds can also sequester twenty to thirty times the amount of carbon compared with woodlands, grasslands and other habitats. Constructed wetlands such as reedbeds offer a nature-based solution for improving the quality of wastewater and can serve anything from a single house to a small town.

An Taisce, the National Trust for Ireland, has recently launched a new national project on ponds with support from the European Commission. The aim of this project is to improve the role that ponds can play in biodiversity, providing expertise in pond creation, management and conservation. The project works to enhance public awareness and mobilise community consciousness regarding the amenity value that these small wetland habitats possess for biodiversity, water quality and climate adaptation. Project ecologists Rob Gandola and Aoife O'Rourke encourage landowners and local communities to develop new ponds through workshops and pond visits. They told me:

> If we could ask you to do one thing for wildlife and the climate it would be to build a pond. These habitats act as refuges for a wide range of wildlife including invertebrates, birds, bats and amphibians, and are excellent for storing carbon and other greenhouse gases. By creating a network of ponds throughout the landscape we can help make nature more resilient to the challenges it faces due to biodiversity loss and climate change and in turn we can help make our own communities more resilient too.

Artificial waterways have a significant role to play in the effort to reverse the biodiversity emergency that has been declared in Ireland. They also have a part to play in actions to mitigate climate change and improve water quality. They can enrich the countryside and go

some way to taking the place of the natural wetlands
that have been damaged over the centuries.

Rewilding the Waters

What would the world be, once bereft
Of wet and wildness? Let them be
   left,
O let them be left, wildness and wet
Long live the weeds and the
   wilderness yet.

From 'Inversnaid' (1881) by GERARD MANLEY HOPKINS

All the scientific evidence indicates that, in the period immediately after the last Ice Age about 10,000 years ago, the centre of Ireland was largely dominated by wild rivers, lakes and wet forests. The flat landscape and high rainfall resulted in meandering rivers and hundreds of lakes and fens surrounded by ancient wet woodlands. Gradually, over the millennia, much of this disappeared, the woodlands cleared by a growing human population and the lakes transformed into raised bogs as the climate changed and vegetation accumulated.

Today, once again, we see a changed landscape, with many of the rivers drained and straightened, lakes trapped behind dams and most of the peatlands damaged beyond repair by peat harvesting. But nature has a way of restoring damaged landscapes, given half a chance and a little assistance from us. In the twenty-first century there is a new interest in the topic of rewilding – letting nature take control and change habitats by natural succession. There has also been a cascade of new projects aimed at restoring some damaged bogs with the potential to become active again and rehabilitating others to create different habitats such as shallow lakes and woodlands. Rivers too have received the attention of restoration ecologists, but unfortunately the continued dredging of damaged rivers to ameliorate flooding persists. Rewilding can also include restoring lost species, provided the habitats that they need still exist and the factors that caused their extinction from the country are no longer operating. Perhaps a combination of rewilding and intervention is the best solution for Ireland where the need for essential services for a dispersed human population would prevent a wholesale transformation to wilderness conditions.

Impacts of a changing climate

Climate change is no longer just a future threat. It is happening here and now. In the next decade it is expected that average temperatures in Ireland will have increased significantly and rainfall amounts will have changed dramatically. But how will this affect our valuable rivers and lakes? A recent study undertaken at Maynooth University has investigated the implications of these changes in temperature and rainfall patterns. Dr Conor Murphy explained that the study simulated changes in precipitation and evapotranspiration for thirty-seven rivers across Ireland using twelve state-of-the-art global climate models, developed by the Intergovernmental Panel on Climate Change. These models give an insight into how key inputs to the hydrological cycle may change under different levels of greenhouse gas emissions in the future. He writes:

We looked at three scenarios, including a sustainable future where the world manages to cooperate and achieve deep cuts in greenhouse gases, a rocky road marked by regional rivalry and medium to high greenhouse gas emissions, and a fossil-fuel-intensive future where little is done to limit greenhouse gas emissions. Next, we produced estimates of flows from 1976 to the end of this century. We evaluated changes in seasonal and low flows for different future time periods; early century (2020s); mid-century (2050s) and late century (2080s).[1]

The results of the study indicate that substantial changes in river flows are likely to occur that would challenge water management without concerted efforts to both reduce greenhouse gas emissions and adapt water management practices to changing conditions. Increases in winter flows and decreases in summer flows are likely as the century progresses, with changes being more severe for higher greenhouse gas emissions. In the worst-case emissions scenario, by the end of the century winter flows are likely to increase on average by about 13 per cent, but up to 30 per cent for some rivers. Reductions in summer flows of about 20 per cent on average are simulated, dropping more than one-third for some rivers.[2] The EPA also predicts that there will be significant reductions in average levels of annual, spring and summer rainfall overall but a substantial increase in the frequency of heavy precipitation events in winter and autumn.

A complicated picture emerges with regional differences across the country. The Maynooth study found that most river catchments located along the wetter, western seaboard and uplands have poor natural storage capacity and are most sensitive to changes in the seasonality of rainfall due to climate change. River catchments in the midlands and east are drier and low-lying, with greater natural storage, and so will be better able to withstand reduced summer rainfall than rivers in other parts of the country.

With these predictions in mind, I found myself wondering: what are the implications of such dramatic changes in such a short time and what are the most practical ways of avoiding the worst impacts? In Ireland, the majority of our drinking water (over 80 per cent) originates from rivers and lakes, while the remainder comes from groundwater and springs. Irish Water, the state agency responsible for managing our water services, predicts that extreme weather such as drought or heavy rainfall events will have a significant impact on water services as they become more frequent, intense and prolonged. With a growing population and expanding economy, reduced rainfall will put increased pressure on Ireland's water supplies during drought events. More intense and prolonged rainfall events may also damage infrastructure due to flooding, increase the variability of source water quality and reduce the quality of treated drinking water supplies.[3]

Even today there are frequent water shortages in Dublin and other urban areas in some summers, such as during the prolonged drought of 2018. At present about 85 per cent of Dublin's water supply comes from the River Liffey. Irish Water says that this is the 'maximum sustainable abstraction' from the river and is at risk from climate change. The agency also says that fixing leaks alone is not enough to meet future demand and ensure resilience.

But what about the wild inhabitants of Ireland's rivers and lakes? How will they survive in such dramatically altered habitats? Overall, climate change is likely to have the most profound long-term disturbance effects on freshwater creatures due to changes in water temperature and patterns of flow. Indirect consequences will include increases in water pollution, acidification in low flow conditions and silt released into the water in big floods. Most invertebrates, especially in headwater streams, need cold water, so temperature rises are likely to lead to the loss of species. Even common species such as caddisflies and stoneflies are likely to become scarcer in some areas. Catastrophic flooding events, which are predicted to increase in frequency, can severely reduce the diversity and abundance of invertebrates in rivers and streams. The recovery of such populations will also be slower with climate change.[4] Large floods caused by damage to peatlands and afforestation in the headwaters have also been shown to adversely affect the endangered freshwater pearl mussel. Although these sudden events were rare historically, they are now occurring more often as a result of climate change. Populations of the mussels may also be affected by a number of other climatic factors, including predicted changes in temperature, sea level, habitat availability, host fish populations and human interference with rivers.[5]

IFI has produced guidance for river restoration in the era of climate change.[6] Without giving any precise prescriptions, they recommend that restoration projects should be planned at a catchment scale. The guidance advises a fully integrated approach to river restoration, tackling all the causes, the underlying drivers of river degradation, climate change associated impacts and also important biological aspects. Proposals are centred on addressing the root cause of perceived river system problems rather than observed symptoms. Passive restoration that allows the natural recovery process to take place in a river is suggested as a way forward.

When the rivers run dry

Veteran environmental journalist Fred Pearce travelled to more than thirty countries around the world in his examination of the global water crisis. In the western world we are mega consumers. Although we drink on average no more than seven litres of water per day, if water for washing clothes and flushing the toilet is included, each person uses about 180 litres per day. He writes, 'in some countries, suburban lawn sprinklers, swimming pools and sundry outdoor uses can double this figure. Typical daily water use in suburban Australia is about 1,864 litres while in the United States it is around 2,068 litres per person.' However, these figures are left in the shade when it comes to our food in western countries. Pearce reports that 'it takes an average of 1,330 litres to grow a kilogram of wheat and a staggering 14,000 litres to grow the feed for enough cow to make a single quarter pounder hamburger.'[7]

An average Irish person uses 213,000 litres of water per year. That is 583 litres per day per household. During medieval times a single person used an average of only twenty-three litres per day. Despite our traditionally wet climate, Ireland is no stranger to water shortages. In summer 2022, after the second hottest temperatures ever recorded here, water supplies were under pressure in fifteen areas of the country, and this number was expected to increase during the rest of the year. Outdoor use such as watering gardens and washing vehicles increases during hot weather. Restrictions on use are typically introduced to deal with the problem but there is very little chance of increasing supply.

The greater Dublin area faces particularly acute water shortages. Dr John Sweeney, Emeritus Professor at Maynooth University, has said that, as the city's population grows close to two million, there will be a demand for an extra 300 million litres of water per day. Rivers and lakes, which are the sources for much of the Irish water supply, are just not able to keep up with the demand. In 2007 it was predicted that in forty or fifty years, water levels in the River Liffey could be just half of what they are today. As the usual freshwater sources of rivers and lakes become depleted, alternative water supplies will have to be found to offset the problem. Possible solutions include the desalination of sea water from Dublin Bay as well as finding a groundwater source or an alternative surface water supply for the capital.[8] The main proposal by Irish Water is to construct a major pipeline to abstract water from the lower River Shannon in County Tipperary, with water treatment nearby. The treated water would then be pumped 170 kilometres to a large reservoir near Dublin. Treated water would also be available for connection to midlands communities along the route. However, despite being suggested in a 2006 report, not a single kilometre of pipeline has yet been laid, and the crisis is deepening year by year.

The obvious solution, of course, lies in reducing consumption, but there is little chance of this in the short term, as consumer culture becomes embedded in our lifestyles. Another solution is rainwater harvesting by individual households and businesses. Every garden, factory and farm should have at least one water tank that stores rainwater from the roofs for watering plants, industrial use, drinking by livestock and even for use in toilets. Toilet flushing, with water already purified for drinking, for example, accounts for up to a third of the average household's water use. Rainwater harvesting is widespread in Germany, with more than 1.8 million households using this 'free' resource. Rainwater harvesting clearly helps to take the pressure off water supplies, but it also helps prevent big downpours overwhelming drains and leading to floods and sewage overflows into rivers. The incentive in Germany is that, based on the amount of water that goes down their drains, householders collecting rainwater do not pay a drainage charge. However, with no water charges for the majority of the urban population in Ireland, there is no financial incentive to change from 'business as usual' here.

We could go further and make it easier for Irish households to install composting toilets instead of flushing scarce water down the drain at all. Incorporating a modern design, these are efficient, odourless and easily managed with the finished 'product' becoming a useful resource for gardening, agriculture or forestry. I built a composting toilet on my own farm for use when working in the fields. The challenge is to get decision-makers to 'think outside the box'. As with other impacts of the climate crisis, it will probably take some major catastrophes to change the current trends. In the meantime, we must expect that the levels of exploitation of rivers and lakes will be pushed to the limit, with predictable consequences for the natural life in these essential arteries.

Restoring the waterways

From the mid-twentieth century on, the arterial drainage programme funded by the Irish government caused significant damage to lowland rivers and wetlands so that their value for populations of fish such as salmon and trout was reduced. Since then, the emphasis has been on 'maintenance', which generally involves the removal of blockages that cause flooding of surrounding land. This is undertaken by the OPW, while IFI tries to ensure that the measures do not cause further damage to fisheries. However, the priority is still to speed up the discharge of water from the land, and biodiversity recovery is treated with much less urgency. Not only are Atlantic salmon under pressure but a whole range of other aquatic lifeforms are threatened by these policies. Barriers such as old weirs and culverts need to be removed from some rivers to allow the migratory fish to reach the headwaters where they spawn.

Rather than piecemeal maintenance measures river restoration needs to take a 'whole catchment' approach so that large volumes of water are released slowly rather than in massive flood events. This means restoring peatlands in the headwaters and re-establishing native woodland corridors in lowland valleys to slow the run-off. The Native Woodland Scheme supports the planting of riparian woods which have a wide range of benefits for freshwater ecosystems. The recent projects of KerryLIFE and DuhallowLIFE+ are focused mainly on improving water quality for the seriously endangered freshwater pearl mussel and Atlantic salmon. The key issues that need to be addressed are intensive agriculture, run-off from peat-cutting and short-rotation forestry. The long-term problems of silt release and pollution from fertilisers can be tackled by using constructed wetlands such as those piloted in the Anne Valley of County Waterford. The establishment of voluntary river trusts on many big catchments north and south of the country is a welcome development and should lead to better involvement of local communities and anglers' groups in the future of 'their rivers'.

Such projects have so far been focused on quite small areas and will thus have a limited impact on the overall loss of wetland habitats and species. A bigger opportunity for wetland conservation lies in the large cutaway peatlands of the midlands, which could be reflooded and converted to habitats such as lakes, reedswamps and fens. Such work has been pioneered by Bord na Móna with some success and there are ambitious proposals for bigger 'wilderness' areas in the upper catchment of the River Shannon. If extensive wetlands could be restored here these would be ideal places for the reintroduction of extinct wetland species such as osprey, crane and bittern. Large, flooded areas of former peatland with extensive reedbeds would make the perfect habitat for the marsh harrier, which is already making a comeback and has bred in Ireland in recent years.

Bogs to lakes

After the last Ice Age, in the midlands of Ireland most rainfall ended up in large lakes and the vegetation that filled these wetlands, where it lay in the water, accumulated in a partially decomposed state as great mounds of peat. Thousands of years later the peat had built up to form domes of living material. Today intact raised bogs are among the rarest habitats in the country and special conservation measures are required to protect and restore them.

Just a few kilometres east of the River Shannon lies Turraun Bog in County Offaly. This was once a mechanically worked bog but the northern section is now zoned entirely for biodiversity and has not had any peat removed from it for over twenty years. Part of this area was rewetted by Bord na Móna in the 1990s, mainly by blocking the drainage outflows and creating an embankment along the northern boundary. A lake then formed in a natural depression in the cutaway. Around this lake, extensive and diverse marginal wetland communities have developed. Already it is a site of high biodiversity value, but the wetland habitats, birds and flora here are different from those of the original raised bog.

I walked around the former bog with Dr Mark McCorry, an ecologist with Bord na Móna. The birch woodland at Turraun is still somewhat immature relative to other native woodlands in Ireland. Interestingly, patches of sphagnum moss have appeared in the woodland where conditions are wet and more acidic. Sphagnum moss is the main bog-building plant, and its appearance suggests that water levels are returning to those that formed the bog in the first place. The bog woodland extends towards higher ground around Cocta Hill. Some glacial sub-soil and bedrock are exposed along this ridge, and other sections are covered with a much shallower layer of peat. Consequently, other habitats such as dry heath dominated by heather, dense bracken, dry grassland with purple moor-grass and more typical dry calcareous grassland communities appear on and around this ridge in association with pockets of emerging and more developed downy birch scrub. A Native Woodland Scheme has been recently established by Bord na Móna to the east of the ridge.

Bord na Móna does not intend to actively intervene in the ecological development of this site once it has been rehabilitated, and it will be interesting to watch how it continues to develop and change in the future. McCorry told me that 'one of the future challenges for cutaway peatland sites is to consider whether they should be allowed to continue to naturally develop by allowing ecological succession, as at Turraun. The alternative is to intervene and manage some sites for particular conservation objectives, for example, improving the habitat for breeding waders.'

Deep in the heart of County Offaly at Ballycon lies another large area of flat peat that was once a raised bog. This bog was industrially harvested by Bord na Móna until 2001, when industrial peat production ceased. There are no plans to recommence industrial production at this site, as the peat has been commercially exhausted, and this has changed the environmental conditions of this site radically. While the original raised bog is acidic, the cutaway environment is strongly influenced by an alkaline water chemistry. A key Bord na Móna rehabilitation strategy is rewetting peat, where possible, and the rehabilitation at Ballycon is an excellent example of this strategy; the footprint of the rewetted area has been increased. While the raised bog is gone and cannot be restored, here the new cutaway habitats have significant biodiversity value.

In time, habitats of conservation value like alkaline fen and fen carr woodland will develop at sites like Ballycon, as part of a wet peatland habitat mosaic. My walk here with Mark McCorry was in June, when the fluffy white heads of bog cotton appeared like snow on the ground. Rehabilitation works carried out in

2006 involved blocking drains and constructing an embankment through the centre of the site in order to hold more water in the northern half and to increase the extent of wetland habitats. Rewetting has been successful, and the majority of the site is vegetating and developing a mosaic of wetland and other habitats. While the site has a multi-purpose function with part of it planted with conifer forestry and a large wind farm on the adjacent Mount Lucas bog, most has been zoned for biodiversity by Bord na Móna.

The wetlands are attracting a wide range of wildlife including wintering waterfowl such as whooper swans and breeding waders such as lapwing and ringed plover in the summer. Hen harriers are also occasionally spotted using the site, and there are kingfishers and otters here too. Several rare vagrant birds, such as marsh harrier and crane, have been recorded on the site in the past.

As we walked along, McCorry suddenly flicked his butterfly net onto the ground and showed me a marsh fritillary that he had caught. This was the first record of this species at this site. Its intricate orange and black pattern was distinctive, and this confirmed the continuing increase in scarce species at the wetland. A nationally rare plant, blue saw sedge, has recently been recorded on the site. This tall sedge is an indicator of possible rich fen or fen swamp development here in the future. For McCorry, this shows the potential for rehabilitated cutaway to provide new wetland habitat for many plants and animals, including rare species, not typically associated with the former raised bog areas.

Peatlands cover around a million square kilometres in Europe. In many countries, peatlands have been artificially drained over centuries, leading not only to enormous emissions of carbon dioxide (CO_2) but also soil subsidence, mobilisation of nutrients, higher flood risks, and loss of biodiversity. These problems can largely be solved by stopping drainage and rewetting the land. Wet peatlands do not release CO_2, can potentially sequester carbon, help to improve water quality, provide habitat for rare and threatened wildlife, and can still be used for production of biomass. Wisely adjusted land use on peatlands can substantially contribute to low-emission goals and further benefits for the environment, farmers, the economy and society.[9]

Cranes return

A flock of cranes flying over a wild wetland in the evening sun is a stirring experience. These are sizeable birds with very long legs, familiar to people in parts of America and continental Europe. They are very graceful, both in flight and on the ground, with a long neck and drooping, curved tail feathers. Today the breeding grounds of the Eurasian crane are mainly in Scandinavia, the Baltic and northern Russia but, with improved protective measures, these elegant birds have increasingly been breeding in north and east Germany and are spreading even further to the south. In Britain, there is a small breeding population in Norfolk, a reintroduced population in Somerset and small numbers pass through in spring and autumn.

There is ample evidence of the presence of cranes in Ireland from ancient times, with bones found during excavations at Neolithic/Bronze Age sites at Lough Gur, County Limerick, Roscrea, County Tipperary and in the cities of Dublin and Wexford. The twelfth-century naturalist Giraldus Cambrensis wrote in his *History and Topography of Ireland* that 'cranes are so numerous that in one flock alone you will often see a hundred or about that number'.[10] The exact date of extinction in Ireland is unclear but it may have been linked with over-hunting for food in Norman times.[11]

Numbers in Europe have declined over the last 300 years because of disturbance, shooting and drainage. In 2011, the Golden Eagle Trust invited members of the Swedish Crane Working Group to visit Ireland to look at the potential for a crane release programme here, and they visited a number of possible breeding sites in midland counties. In Sweden, cranes build their nests where they are surrounded by water to make them less accessible to mammal predators, mainly foxes and badgers. If the water level drops during egg incubation, breeding often fails. Although cranes may breed relatively close to human settlements, they are often extremely secretive when incubating, so relatively undisturbed habitat is essential. During their visit, the Swedish experts identified many places that fulfil these requirements, especially on cutaway Bord na Móna bogs that are being rehabilitated as wetlands. In Sweden, several crane pairs have readily accepted newly constructed ponds on farmland as nesting sites, which shows their great adaptability and ability to respond to and take advantage of man-made habitats.

In May 2021, Bord na Móna announced that a pair of cranes was nesting on a rewetted bog in the midlands. If they bred successfully, it was believed they would be the first common cranes to do so in Ireland for 300 years. There had been two previous breeding attempts at the same location, which were ultimately unsuccessful. Though cranes have been extinct in Ireland since at least the 1700s, there have been increased sightings of them in Irish skies in recent years during migration and overwintering. This has been largely due to conservation work in the UK, which has seen their numbers there rise from zero in the 1970s to more than 200 now. While two chicks did hatch from this first Irish nest they disappeared shortly afterwards, and it is thought that they may have been predated. Then, in 2022, came exciting news that the same pair had produced two more chicks and that a further adult bird, probably one of the first brood, was seen on a nearby site. 'Common cranes usually take several years to successfully fledge young,' said Bord na Móna's lead ecologist Mark McCorry. 'This is why these sightings are particularly significant.'

The crane is deeply connected to the culture and history of Ireland and central to folklore tales such as those about Fionn mac Cumhaill, the druids, St Colmcille and the Book of Kells. 'Unfortunately, they were also a popular food item for people in earlier times. Their vulnerability to predation by foxes and the historical draining of wetlands resulted in their demise sometime between 1600 and 1700,' said McCorry. He continued: 'Crane nests float amongst emergent wetland vegetation such as reeds. It is obvious, then, as wetlands disappeared, then so would they. But thanks to the ongoing work by Bord na Móna in rewetting bogs, we are in with a chance once again of seeing these majestic birds breed and thrive in Ireland.' In 2020 the company announced that 33,000 hectares is to be rehabilitated as part of its Peatlands Climate Action Scheme that will operate with significant government funding.

Woodlands for water

When I walk between the old alder trees that line the banks of the river on our own land, I imagine how the landscape might have looked before farming came to this valley some 6,000 years ago. The lower land would have been filled with trees, some forest giants like oak, ash and alder and some more open glades where the boggy ground supported only small willow bushes. Today, in our neighbours' lands, just patches of trees remain along the river's entire length, and there are large gaps between them where pasture and cereal crops reach right down to the water's edge. The corridor of wooded land that once stretched from the mountain slopes right down to the sea is gone and has been largely replaced by intensively managed farmland.

Without its cloak of trees the river is naked, exposed to the worst side-effects of modern farming. Increasing loads of artificial fertiliser and slurry spread on the land find their way eventually to the water. Fungicides, insecticides and all manner of chemical treatments for modern crops run off the soil with no buffer between the field and the river. Where cattle drink in the river, they create muddy pools, stirring up sediment that is then washed downstream to blanket the gravel beds where salmon and trout need to lay their eggs.

A corridor of trees or, better still, a band of woodland along a lowland river valley has huge benefits for biodiversity both on the land and in the water. The roots of the trees intercept nutrients draining off agricultural land in the catchment, trapping these in the woodland soil. Studies have found that streamside forests are very effective at removing excess nitrogen and potassium as well as excess sediment from surface run-off. Up to 90 per cent reductions in nitrate concentrations in shallow groundwater discharging from farmland through riverside trees have been measured in the USA.[12] Studies of a coastal plain agricultural watershed in eastern USA showed that riparian forest ecosystems are excellent nutrient sinks and buffer the nutrient discharge from surrounding farmland. Nutrient uptake and removal by soil and vegetation in the riparian forest ecosystem prevented outputs from agricultural uplands reaching the stream channel.[13] Riparian woods can also ameliorate the effects of many pesticides used on surrounding land. They also support life in the water. Leaves and small branches of trees fall into the river providing dissolved organic matter and food for the myriads of tiny animals and fish in the water.[14]

In 2018, the Irish Forest Service launched a new measure, Woodland for Water, which supported the establishment of new native woodland and undisturbed water setbacks along river corridors. It showed how these can be used in combination to deliver meaningful benefits that protect and enhance water quality and aquatic ecosystems. New woodland within floodplains is encouraged in recognition of the rarity of riparian and alluvial woodlands and their role in protecting water. Riverside vegetation is well known to be a rich habitat for all types of wildlife from mosses to mammals. The diversity of habitats, from canopy forest, scrub, marsh and open water to old stream channels, isolated pools and reedswamps, make this a rich hunting ground for many species. Some creatures such as dragonflies and frogs require both aquatic and terrestrial habitats to complete their full life cycle.

Look at any satellite picture of Ireland and you will see that we now live in a highly fragmented landscape with small pockets of semi-natural woodland isolated in a sea of intensive farmland and forestry. There is enormous value for biodiversity in reconnecting pockets of habitat in the landscape, such as along a river valley, allowing species that have difficulty dispersing to expand into other suitable habitats.[15]

I have a long-term vision for the valley that links our east Wicklow landscape. Under a revised Common Agricultural Policy, farmers and other landowners would be grant-aided to fence out livestock and deer from agricultural land along the river, creating a corridor at least fifty metres wide on both riverbanks from the source to the sea. This would allow linkage between the present areas of forest through natural regeneration of trees and shrubs from the existing seed sources in the valley. It might take some decades for it to resemble a fully wooded valley again, but allowing nature itself to select the right trees for the right soils would be much better and cheaper than a huge planting programme. I envisage a valley somewhat like the one that existed before 1600 and the great forest clearances of later centuries.[16] Weirs and other barriers could be removed from the river, which might then be inhabited by healthy populations of salmon, otters and kingfishers. People would be encouraged to use the river valley for passive recreation, such as kayaking or hiking on long-distance trails, and rural communities would benefit from the increased number of visitors coming to appreciate the beauty and tranquillity of water and woods.

Eagles have landed

In the 1980s I was fortunate to visit the Isle of Rhum nature reserve in the Inner Hebrides of west Scotland. My host was the ornithologist John Love, who was in charge of an exciting new project to reintroduce the long-extinct white-tailed eagle to Britain. Like other large predators, this species had disappeared altogether from the skies of Britain and Ireland in the early years of the twentieth century due to decades of persecution, poisoning and egg-collecting. Rhum had been chosen as the release site in 1975, because it was believed to resemble most closely the mountainous coastline of Norway where the birds were still common.[17] After decades of dedicated work and releases in other locations, the white-tailed eagle became well established in Britain by the 1990s.

Things took a bit longer in Ireland where the use of poison in some farming areas was still widespread at that time. Led by the Golden Eagle Trust, and with support from the NPWS, Dr Allan Mee was employed to manage a similar reintroduction project for white-tailed eagle in Ireland. Between 2007 and 2011, a hundred young eagles were collected under licence from nests in Norway and released in Killarney National Park in County Kerry. The eagles are simply magnificent birds. With a massive yellow hooked bill and wide wings well over two metres in span, they are often likened to a 'barn door' when in flight. To see even one eagle soaring over the iconic mountains or hunting fish in the Lakes of Killarney was inspiring. After release, some of the young birds hung around County Kerry, but within a few months, they were travelling further afield, exploring their new country and frequently moving from county to county.

The first nesting pairs were recorded in 2012, and the first Irish-born white-tailed eagle chicks fledged successfully in 2013. Two successful pairs nested on wooded islands on Lough Derg, where they spent long periods perched on trees occasionally swooping down to pluck a fish from the waters. The rich fishing here has clearly been a key factor in the success of the birds. The local community here has rowed in behind the project. At Mountshannon, a local group set up and staffed a viewing facility in a lakeside carpark, where visitors could learn about the project. This facility was funded and built by Clare County Council, and a total of nearly 6,000 visitors were recorded in the first year. After some untimely losses due to avian influenza the two pairs of eagles on Lough Derg have been the most productive in the country, suggesting that the fish resource here is more than adequate to support them.

Local farmers also seem to have accepted the eagles as part of the scenery. On his suckler and sheep farm on

the shores of Lough Derg, Joss Hogan has taken up a
new hobby – birdwatching. He said, 'It didn't dawn on
me when I read about the reintroduction project first
that I'd ever see eagles here but since I've got to know
them and seen them over my own flock of sheep they
never bothered me at all.' Writing in a recent report on
the eagles, the project manager Allan Mee said, 'The
positive influence of farmers like Joss on the wider
farming community should not be underestimated.'

As the reintroduced birds reached maturity, the
number of territorial pairs across the country grew
steadily. By 2018, with at least twelve pairs holding
territories in Ireland, the eagles were breeding across
four counties (Kerry, Cork, Clare and Galway) and
were showing signs of expanding their range again, into
the north-west and midlands.[18] In 2020, a new phase of
the reintroduction programme began with the release of
young eagles at several sites, including Lough Derg, the
lower Shannon Estuary and the Lakes of Killarney. The
juvenile white-tailed eagles were flown into Kerry Airport
and were held in specially built aviaries in Munster
before being released by the NPWS. All of the birds were
fitted with wing-tags and satellite transmitters. By 2021,
the satellite tracks showed they had spread out across

Munster and northwards up the Shannon River.

The elimination of illegal poisoning, which is a threat to the survival of all large bird and mammal scavengers, remains a priority for conservation of the species in Ireland. Poisoning accounted for almost half of all mortalities of sea eagles recovered dead in the reintroduction programme to date. This is one of the highest rates of loss to poisoning in any wild raptor population in Europe, compared to 31 per cent in Spanish imperial eagles and 38 per cent in bearded vultures across the EU. Additional but important causes of some eagle deaths have been wind-turbine collision and avian influenza, the first confirmed cases of this virus in white-tailed eagles in Ireland or Britain.

All the major lakes in the country are now used extensively but especially Loughs Derg, Corrib, Mask and Ree, the midland lakes Ennell and Owel, Upper and Lower Lough Erne and the Killarney lakes, with a few smaller lakes also used by breeding pairs. It seems that lowland lakes may now be the eagle's preferred habitat and the most likely places from which they were first driven by persecution, forcing them to retreat to remote coastal cliffs, shortly before their complete extinction in the country.

Draining the Shannon

With over 10,000 kilometres of channels and several of the biggest lakes in the country, the Shannon is by far the largest river system in Ireland. Surviving river–lake systems are rare in Europe, making the Shannon more important in an international context. Despite its value to the country, the river system has not always been treated with the respect it deserves. Éamon de Valera, when he was Taoiseach some eighty years ago, is famously said to have promised, 'we will drain the Shannon'. This was not the first time this idea had been floated. Mr George Stephenson, Civil Engineer, reported in 1831 to the Committee Appointed to *Inquire into the Practicability of Improving the Navigation of the Shannon, and for Draining the Lands in the Vicinity* that:

> It has appeared to me that it may be found of advantage to prevent the waters of Lough Allen from flowing into the Shannon, and to cut a channel in a north-westerly direction, along which they may run into Sligo Bay. By this disposition of the waters of Lough Allen, not only will the channel of the Shannon be relieved from the superabundant water

which now flows along during the rainy season, but they will act very beneficially in scouring out the harbour of Sligo. The Shannon might likewise be made available to the supply of power to several valuable mills to be erected on its course.

Despite this recommendation, there was no drainage scheme for the river, which continued to flood and caused significant damage in Limerick city during major events in the 1850s and 1950s. Since then, the Shannon has flooded over its banks every few years, isolating houses and farms for months in some winters, with occasional summer flooding submerging the grasslands on its margins. After each major flooding event, calls to 'drain the Shannon' are made repeatedly by politicians and farming lobbies. In reality, the only effective drainage has been on tributaries such as the Inny, Maigue and Mulcair. Flooding is also partly due to exploitation of the midland raised bogs that once functioned as a sponge, soaking up excess rainfall and releasing this slowly to the river catchment.

The recently formed Shannon Flood Risk Group concluded that 'room must be made for the river'. This was immediately represented by government as involving extensive dredging, but it should have been interpreted as allowing the river to expand onto natural flood plains. This technique, used throughout Europe, involves holding back rather than speeding up the water flow, so that downstream towns are not flooded. It means providing for seepage, rather than drainage, in upland areas in order to limit run-off. Instead of canalising rivers and erecting barriers in anticipation of torrential weather events, the authorities should work *with* nature. In the context of rapid climate change, this is a much cheaper and more effective approach.

Flooding can be made worse by bad planning. Rezoning of floodplains for housing, the construction of industrial projects at pinch points and excessive carbon emissions have all played their part. Scientists warn of wetter winters to come because of climate change. In such circumstances, dredging a barely moving river and piling spoil along its banks simply repeats the misguided hard-engineering responses of the past. If towns are to be protected and room made for the river, the use of natural floodplains is necessary and environmentally less damaging.

The construction of the Ardnacrusha dam and

power station just upstream of Limerick in the 1920s also had negative impacts on the river ecosystem. It caused a major barrier to migrating fish, largely destroying important salmon and eel fisheries and impounding water in the Parteen reservoir. Its construction took about one-fifth of the new state's annual budget, but it was seen at the time as a symbol of independence and modernisation of the country and contributed to widespread rural electrification. When it was built, Ardnacrusha had the capacity to supply power for the entire country. With demand now increased to a huge extent, it currently accounts for only 2–3 per cent of overall power generation in Ireland. Given the small overall amount of power produced per cubic metre of water passing through the now antiquated turbines, there is a strong case for phasing out this unnecessary infrastructure and restoring water flow to the natural channel.

Restoring river flows

The Vartry River flows through the centre of my local village of Ashford in County Wicklow. Some days the clear water flows gently through the boulders and water plants under the bridge. At other times it is a roaring torrent, heavy with sediment and coloured brown with mountain peat. For most of the time I have known it there was a steep concrete weir just upstream of the village, a place where a familiar heron often stood, still as a statue, waiting for passing fish or frogs to appear at the edge of the pool. Then, during one major flood, the weight of water building up behind it caused a serious crack to develop in the face of the weir. Within a few days the structure had broken up and floodwater poured through the weir as if released from captivity. In effect, the river was returning to its natural bed.

River fragmentation is the breaking up of a river's continual flow from source to the sea. It is one of the greatest global threats to freshwater ecosystems, because it interrupts fish migration, blocks the movement of fish and other animals within the channel, alters the flow of sediment throughout the channel, affects habitat diversity and impacts overall biodiversity. Irish rivers are heavily fragmented by weirs, dams, sluices, culverts, bridges and other artificial barriers. These structures cause the loss of many natural features and add to the other pressures on biodiversity such as water pollution, channel alteration and water abstraction.

IFI, the government agency that aims to protect our fishery waters, has been monitoring the barriers on Irish rivers. They have been joined by colleagues in local authorities, a number of whom have been trained to help and have identified over 73,000 potential barriers on the Irish river network. To date, they have surveyed almost 22,600 of these structures, recording their construction and dimensions and their potential to prevent fish movement and migration.

Internationally, there is mounting evidence that the removal of barriers in rivers can make a major contribution to restoring nature in the freshwater environment. The EU 2030 Biodiversity Strategy calls for greater efforts to restore freshwater ecosystems and the natural functions of rivers. It sets a target to make at least 25,000 kilometres of rivers across Europe free-flowing again by 2030, primarily by removing obsolete barriers and restoring floodplains and wetlands. The EU interprets 'free-flowing rivers' to mean rivers or other surface water bodies such as lakes that are not impaired by artificial barriers and not disconnected from their floodplain.

Globally, removal of obsolete barriers on rivers is accepted as a key objective for conservation. One of the latest examples of such flow restoration is on the Sélune River in Normandy, France. With two obsolete dams – the Vezins and La Roche Qui Boit – currently being removed, 90 kilometres of waterway will soon be opened up, allowing Atlantic salmon to migrate once again to their ancient spawning grounds. With barrier removal increasing juvenile salmon habitat threefold, it is hoped that the number of adult salmon returning annually to the river will increase by more than 1,400. In Yorkshire, England, five weeks of work in 2022 at Scotton Weir on the River Nidd has resulted in the full removal of that barrier, reconnecting thirty-five kilometres of river and tributaries. The River Nidd is a major tributary of the Humber basin, the largest catchment within Britain. The weir removal project, the largest in the UK to date, will restore fish migration for salmon. Eel populations have been boosted by weir removal or fish passage projects on other Humber tributaries.

In Ireland, the migration of salmon, sea trout and lamprey from the ocean to their spawning grounds in the headwaters of many rivers has been interrupted by barriers such as weirs, culverts and hydroelectric stations. While fish passes and ladders of shallow pools can make a difference, these are expensive to construct and only allow a fraction of the fish to pass. The removal of these significant barriers would open up a huge number of tributaries to migratory fish and many other species and would cause little impact on the national electricity grid.

Ecosystem engineers?

While removal of artificial barriers in rivers can lead to restoration of migratory fish populations, the waterways would also benefit from slowing down the rate of flow, especially in rivers that have been subject to severe drainage works. On a visit to the west of Scotland I decided to have a look at the beautiful Knapdale Forest near Tarbert on the Mull of Kintyre. The sun was sinking fast as I walked along the forest tracks until I reached a lake surrounded by woodland where I sat for a while to enjoy the peaceful surroundings. I noticed that there were many dead trees as well as living ones, lying at all angles in and out of the water. I got a surprise when I saw a round head paddling slowly through the water. At first I thought it was an otter, but then it climbed out of the water and sat grooming on a semi-submerged log. I recognised it immediately as a beaver – similar to the animals I had seen previously in North American lakes.

In 2009, Knapdale had been chosen for a very special project. The Scottish Beaver Trial was the first carefully planned reintroduction of European beavers into the wild in Scotland, where they had become extinct centuries earlier. The animals were confined within fences so that they could be scientifically monitored, with special emphasis on their impact on the environment. The original beavers were brought in from Norway to Knapdale where they bred and expanded their territory, establishing a small colony around Loch Coille-Bharr. Since then, there have been many unauthorised introductions of beavers, especially in the Tay valley in eastern Scotland, where a 2017–18 survey estimated that this population had grown to several hundred animals occupying up to 114 territories. In England and Wales there are also a number of small groups of beavers, some in enclosed trial projects, with a free-living population of around thirteen territories on the River Otter in Devon.[19]

About 400 years after being hunted to extinction, these hardy river-dwellers are back in Britain, making good use of local woodland for building their dams and lodges. Apart from the excitement of re-establishing a native mammal that was driven to extinction, there is huge interest among ecologists and conservationists in the wider effects that these animals can have on rivers and other wetlands. On their reintroduction to Scotland, they immediately began to fell trees and create dams, thus raising the water levels to flood large areas, creating ponds and wetlands. This is entirely natural, and the trees mainly grow back from the roots, which remain undisturbed. Studies in southern Sweden have shown that, in areas where beavers are found, the plant species richness is up to one-third higher than in wetlands unoccupied by these animals. The effect of these ecosystem engineers is to increase the complexity or 'patchiness' of the habitat, radically transforming uniform rivers and lakes and the species that they support. A UK study found that the abundance of freshwater invertebrates – dragonflies, damselflies, diving beetles, water boatmen and backswimmers – was three times higher in beaver ponds than in unmodified agricultural streams. In reshaping rivers and wetlands, their dams have been shown to improve downstream water quality and reduce peaks of flooding and drought.[20] In his inspirational book *Bringing Back the Beaver*, the author Derek Gow described the campaign to return this keystone species to Britain in an astonishing tale of determination to overcome any bureaucratic obstacles that got in the way.[21]

So far, however, there is no evidence that beavers were native in Ireland after the last Ice Age. This is thought to be because Ireland was cut off from the European continent by rising sea levels much earlier than Britain, and thus far fewer species managed to migrate here in time. This is surprising as post-glacial Ireland must have been a very wet place, and it could be expected that an aquatic animal might have managed to colonise by itself, just as the otter did. It is equally surprising that beavers were not introduced here in the past by early colonists, as their skins were very valuable for fur, their flesh is quite palatable, and they were widely trapped across Europe and North America in past centuries. But the twelfth-century Welsh author Giraldus Cambrensis wrote, 'Ireland has badgers but not beavers'.[22]

Had they been present in Ireland, beavers would almost certainly have been hunted as they were elsewhere in their range, and some bones would have turned up in archaeological excavations. But, so far, none have been found. One other notable feature is the absence of beaver-chewed wood on any archaeological or other wetland sites. Whatever the reason, any attempt to bring beavers to Ireland today would be considered a new introduction rather than reintroduction. There are strict international rules governing such introductions in nature, given the havoc that invasive species such as grey squirrels, American mink and rhododendron have caused, and it is unlikely that such a proposal would be accepted here. It is much more likely that unauthorised introductions of beavers will take place at some time, in much the same way that wild boar and muntjac deer have been secretly released in Ireland in recent years.

Rewiggling rivers

Where beavers have been reintroduced to river systems, their leaky dams re-establish floodplains. These are the wide, flat banks of a river that are covered with water during long periods of heavy rainfall. Floodplains are like sponges – they hold on to water during floods and slow it down. They act just like a reservoir or a dam, except that they do not form barriers to fish movement. Floodplains bring the damaging peak flow height down by spreading it out over a longer time. This means floodplains help to prevent property damage downstream.

Engineers in the past tried to improve river navigation, prevent farmland flooding and reduce the unpredictability of river erosion by artificially straightening and deepening rivers. However, a meandering river can contain more floodwater and a slower river has flattened flood peaks, so channelised rivers caused even worse flooding in urban areas than their natural, winding counterparts. 'Rewiggling' is a new term that involves adding natural bends and meanders back into a river or stream if the watercourse has been straightened artificially in the past. This is usually done by digging out a new course that winds across the original floodplain, though it may also be achieved by removing levees and letting the river rewild itself. The aim is to reduce flooding downstream and improve local water quality and biodiversity.

River restoration in Poland has shown that rewiggling is likely to reduce flooding downstream, the flow is slower, and over time floodplains begin to recover their original capacity. Biodiversity should also increase, as bendy rivers are safer places for fish and invertebrates, with slow-flowing refuges and a variety of depths.[23] The number of river restoration projects is also growing in the UK. At Goldrill Beck in the Lake District, nearly two kilometres of new channel were dug to reconnect this river with its historic floodplain and move it away from an older straightened channel.

The River Waal in the Netherlands was experiencing very high peaks flows and needed more space to hold back floods. The rewilding solution was to remove the summer dykes, reintroduce some extinct herbivores and restore the old river morphology. Once the old river meanders were excavated, the black poplar, a very rare tree, began to reappear with a flush of young seedlings. By restoring the river braids, warm lapping water conditions returned, the conditions that poplar seeds, carried down from Germany, needed to germinate. The same principle applied for other plant and insect species that had become extinct in the Netherlands but were still present in the upper catchment. They suddenly found a habitat to settle and re-establish. With a little help in the removal of past damage, the freshwater ecosystem can largely restore itself. We can learn from such experience in many other countries as we strive to rewild Irish rivers.

A midlands wilderness

The upper catchment of the mighty River Shannon drains a large area of peatlands that first appeared as large shallow lakes after the retreat of the last Ice Age. These lakes filled with water plants such as reeds and the decomposition of this vegetation over thousands of years led to the classic raised bogs of the Irish midlands. Today, most of the bogs in the area between Lough Ree and the little village of Tarmonbarry have been worked out and lie idle now that the turf-cutting and milling machinery of Bord na Móna has been withdrawn. They appear like brown deserts, left behind after a huge industrial-scale exploitation of the last seventy years. But when the pumps are turned off, the bogs begin to rewet again and start to return to lakes, resembling how they might have looked after the last Ice Age. As I walked around this area, I could see that some of the cutaway bogs have already started to transition back to lakes and woodlands. Natural regeneration was happening by default.

This form of rewilding is just a side effect of the end of peat mining here, which has been responsible for destroying the majority of the midland bogs. Now the area has the potential to once again become a wonderful mosaic of wetland, woodland and grassland, much like the first human settlers must have found when they entered this wilderness in the Mesolithic period some 10,000 years ago. Dr John Feehan, a celebrated scientist, writer and historian, has written eloquently of the possibilities for creating a Peatlands Park in this area. His book *A Long-lived Wilderness* tells of the long and interesting history of the area and outlines a new approach to produce a unique natural area of great benefit to tourism in the area, focused on the Mountdillon Bog Group found on both sides of the winding Shannon River.[24]

Feehan, a prolific author, has now retired from his academic post in UCD and concentrates on writing from his home in Birr, County Offaly, in the centre of another network of bogs. Two decades after producing his proposal for the Peatlands Park, he says, 'Bord na Móna was supportive of the idea and of the many community groups that were enthusiastic about it but not in any proactive sort of way. There was no sense of urgency about it at the time. But that has changed over the last very few years.' Feehan continued:

In the longer term, I see some such scenario as

that spelled out in my book as inevitable, relying on natural succession mainly rather than through intervention. The long-term cost of maintenance is something that is easily lost sight of in proposing such initiatives. Although ecologically informed intervention with a light touch is often of considerable value at an early stage (or indeed at any time), the ecological vitality of the bog should be the driving force, even though we don't know enough about this to predict the precise direction or outcome.

Local activist Niall Dennigan told me, 'Too much time and too many jobs have already been lost since the closure of these bogs and progressing with full scale rehabilitation works is part of a true just transition. With the scientific evidence growing every day around the importance of rewetting peatlands and improving our biodiversity, immediate action is necessary on these bogs.'

The future for wild waters

Despite the important benefits that rivers, lakes and bogs have brought to people down through the millennia, we have often treated them as 'problems' to be exploited, tamed and controlled. Widespread pollution, water abstraction, drainage, dams and canalisation have all taken their toll, to the extent that we now have just twenty rivers in the country that are regarded as 'pristine'. Lakes have similarly been abused or exploited for water supply, waste disposal and by the introduction of invasive species. However, there are a few signs that attitudes are changing. Rewetting of some cutaway bogs is already producing diverse complexes of wetland habitats. The removal of barriers to fish migration on rivers is beginning to be treated as an important contribution to waterway restoration.

We hear a lot these days about 'rewilding' land-scapes. While this term can mean many different things to different people, it may include active intervention with the objective of restoring some of the natural processes that will maintain the water habitats in good condition indefinitely. While the focus of much rewilding has been on farmland, woodland and upland habitats, the concept is equally viable for wetland habitats such as rivers, lakes, marshes and peatlands. There are already some exciting examples of river restoration in Europe, and these could readily be repeated here. The focus should be on restoration of the natural habitats, and lost species will eventually find them.

In 2022, the European Commission proposed a new nature restoration law with binding targets. The new initiative aims to bring nature back across the continent for the benefit of biodiversity, climate and people. This could be a gamechanger if fully implemented. The overarching objective of the law is to achieve continuous, long-term and sustained recovery of biodiverse land and sea areas and increase climate mitigation and adaptation through restoration. Nature-based solutions should be a cornerstone of these efforts, and international agencies can provide expert advice for all stakeholders on the design and implementation of restoration projects. The commission has set an overall target to restore 20 per cent of the EU's land and sea area by 2030 and *all ecosystems* in need of restoration by 2050. Within that total, 25,000 kilometres of free-flowing rivers across Europe are to be restored by 2030. This proposal will add a new level of legal support to conservation and restoration efforts across Europe. Previous attempts to increase restoration have failed, in both the EU Biodiversity Strategy and the global strategic plan for biodiversity to 2020. Let us hope that changed attitudes will lead to full implementation of the new law, which will be binding on all member states, including Ireland.

Before any of this can take place there is a need for Irish people to rediscover the beauty of their rivers, lakes and other wetlands and to understand the important roles that they play in our landscape. I love to walk along the banks of a free-flowing river such as the Avonmore, gazing at the power of the water sweeping around and over the boulders where dippers dive, plunging over small waterfalls and swirling in pools where trout hide beneath the shady banks. I love to paddle a canoe through shallow lake waters, past reedbeds and overhanging willows, watching for kingfishers and marvelling at the light reflected off the water surface. To love a river or a lake is the first prerequisite for protecting and defending it against damaging developments. I will take my grandchildren with me to explore our rivers and lakes, to learn from a young age the value of these wild waters so that, when they are influential in society, they will make the right decisions to protect these valuable assets into the future.

References

Introduction

1   Ó Dónaill, N. (1877). *Foclóir Gaeilge-Béarla.*

2   Giraldus Cambrensis (*c.*1200). *The History and Topography of Ireland.* Translated from the Latin by John J. O'Meara. 1982 edition. Portlaoise. Dolmen Press.

3   O'Sullivan, A. (2007). Exploring past people's interactions with wetland environments in Ireland. *Proceedings of the Royal Irish Academy* 107C: pp. 147–203.

4   Otte, M.L. (ed.) (2003). *Wetlands of Ireland: Distribution, ecology, uses and economic value.* Dublin. University College Dublin Press.

Chapter 1: Meeting of the Waters

1   Crowe, O., Smiddy, P., Whelan, R., & Copland, A. (2020). Birds of Irish Rivers. In: *Ireland's Rivers* (eds M. Kelly-Quinn & J. Reynolds). Dublin. University College Dublin Press.

2   Padulli, L., (2021). Luggala: The magic, history and environment of a pristine Wicklow valley. *Roundwood & District Historical, Folklore & Archaeological Society Journal* 30: pp. 6–10.

3   Corlett, C. (2010). The ruined farmhouses of the Clohogue and Inchavore valleys. *Roundwood & District Historical & Folklore Journal* 21: pp. 55–63.

4   Igoe, F., & Kelly Quinn, M. (2002). The char *Salvelinus alpinus* L. of Lough Dan: Extinct? *Irish Naturalists' Journal* 27: pp. 2–9.

5   Davies, M. (2016). Glendalough House. Gems of architecture. *History Ireland* 2: p. 24.

6   Boorman, J. (2020). *Boorman's Nature Diary: One eye, one finger.* Dublin. Lilliput Press.

7   Murphy, D. (2021). *The Spirit of the River: A quest for the kingfisher.* Dublin. Lilliput Press.

8   Mitchell, G.F. (1976). *The Irish Landscape.* London. Collins.

9   Sheppard, J.R. (1978). The breeding of the Goosander in Ireland. *Irish Birds* 1: pp. 224–228.

10   Murphy, D. (2021). *op. cit.*

11   Hayes, S. (1974). *Treatise on Planting and the Management of Woods and Coppices.* Facsimile edition. Dublin: New Island Press.

12   Copland, A. (2012). *Avifauna of Bridges in Co. Wicklow.* Report to Wicklow County Council by Birdwatch Ireland.

13   O'Keeffe, P., Simington, P., & Goodbody, R. (2016). *Irish Stone Bridges: History and heritage.* Revised edition. Newbridge, Co. Kildare. Irish Academic Press.

14   O'Sullivan, O. (2019). *Riparian Bird Survey of Avonmore, Avonbeg and Avoca Rivers, County Wicklow, 2019.* Unpublished report to Wicklow County Council, Heritage Office.

15 O'Toole, C. (2015). *Glenmalure: The Wild Heart of the Mountains*. Privately published.

16 Fewer, M. (2007). *The Wicklow Military Road: History and topography*. Dublin. Ashfield Press.

17 Connell, J. (2022). *The Stream of Everything*. Dublin. Gill Books.

18 D'Arcy, G. (1999). *Ireland's Lost Birds*. Dublin. Four Courts Press.

19 Carey, M. (2009). *If Trees Could Talk: Wicklow's trees and woodlands over four centuries*. Dublin. Coford.

20 Burke, J. (1991). Arklow in the 1930s and 1940s. *Arklow Historical Society Journal* 1990–91: pp. 32–34.

Chapter 2: Rivers

1   Kelly-Quinn, M., O'Grady, M., Delanty, K., & Bradley, C. (2020). Ireland's Rich and Varied River Resource. In: *Ireland's Rivers* (eds M. Kelly-Quinn & J. Reynolds). Dublin. University College Dublin Press.

2   Quirke, B. (ed.) (2001). *Killarney National Park: A place to treasure*. Cork. Collins Press.

3   Feely, H.B., Giller, P.S., Baars, J.R., and Kelly-Quinn, M. (2020). Benthic Macroinvertebrates. In: *Ireland's Rivers* (eds M. Kelly-Quinn & J. Reynolds). Dublin. University College Dublin Press.

4   Macalister, R.A.S. (1935). *Ancient Ireland: A study in the lessons of archaeology and history*. London: Methuen.

5   Warren, G. & Westley, K. (2020). 'They made no effort to explore the interior of the country'. Coastal landscapes, hunter-gatherers and the islands of Ireland. In: *Coastal Landscapes of the Mesolithic* (ed. A. Schulke). Oxford and New York. Routledge. pp. 73–98.

6   Warren, G. (2022). *Hunter-gatherer Ireland: Making connections in an island world*. Oxford. Oxbow Books.

7   McQuade, M. (2008). 'Gone Fishin': an update on the discovery of evidence for 3,000 years of prehistoric trap fishing along the Liffey estuary. *Archaeology Ireland*. 22 (83): pp. 8–11.

8   O'Sullivan, A. (2001). *Foragers, Farmers and Fishers in a Coastal Landscape: An intertidal archaeological survey of the Shannon Estuary*. Discovery Programme Monograph No. 5. Dublin. Royal Irish Academy.

9   Corcoran. K. (2021). *Saving Eden: The Gearagh and Irish nature*. Cork. Gearagh Press.

10   Carlsson, J., Cross, T.F., McGinnity, P., Prodohl, P.A., & McDevitt, A.D. (2014). The use of genetics to infer the origins of the terrestrial and freshwater elements of the Irish fauna. In: *Mind the Gap II*. Belfast. Irish Naturalists' Journal.

11   Marnell, F. (2020). Riparian Mammals and Amphibians. In: *Ireland's Rivers* (eds M. Kelly-Quinn & J. Reynolds). Dublin. University College Dublin Press.

12   Williamson, H.W. (1927). *Tarka the Otter: His joyful water-life and death in the country of the two rivers*. London. Putnam & Sons.

13 Reid, N., Hayden, B., Lundy, M.G., Pietravalle, S., McDonald, R.A., & Montgomery, W.I. (2013). *National Otter Survey of Ireland 2010/12*. Irish Wildlife Manuals No. 76. Dublin. National Parks and Wildlife Service, Department of Arts, Heritage and the Gaeltacht.

14 Hamilton-Dyer, S. (2007). Exploitation of birds and fish in historic Ireland: A brief review of the evidence. In: *Environmental Archaeology in Ireland* (eds E.M. Murphy & N.J. Whitehouse). Oxford. Oxbow.

15 Kelly, F., King, J., Gargan, P., & Roche, W. (2020). Fish in Irish Rivers. In: *Ireland's Rivers* (eds M. Kelly-Quinn & J. Reynolds). Dublin. University College Dublin Press.

16 Gibson, C. (2011). Jewels in the Landscape. In: *The Natural History of Ulster* (eds J. Faulkner & R. Thompson). Holywood. National Museums Northern Ireland.

17 *Ibid.*

18 Whelan, K.F. (2014). Sea-trout populations in small coastal streams. *Biology and Environment: Proceedings of the Royal Irish Academy* 114B: pp. 199–204.

19 Reimchen, T. (2001). Salmon nutrients, nitrogen isotopes and coastal forests. *Ecoforestry* Fall 2001: pp. 13–16.

20 De Buitléar, E. (ed.) (1985). *Irish Rivers*. Dublin. Country House.

21 O'Reilly, P. (2009). *Rivers of Ireland: A flyfisher's guide*. 7th edition. Ludlow, Shropshire. Merlin Unwin Books.

22 Reynolds, J. (2020). Crayfish in Irish Rivers. In: *Ireland's Rivers* (eds M. Kelly-Quinn & J. Reynolds). Dublin. University College Dublin Press.

23 Viney, M. (2018). Crayfish plague: no wonder the Irish species is white-clawed. *The Irish Times*, 6 October 2018.

24 Caffrey, J., Gallagher, K., Broughan, D., and Dick, J.T.A. (2018). Rapid response achieves eradication – chub in Ireland. *Management of Biological Invasions* 9: pp. 475–482.

25 Smal, C. (1991). *Feral Mink in Ireland: A guide to the biology, ecology, pest status and control of feral American mink* Mustela vison *in Ireland*. Dublin. Office of Public Works.

26 Roy, S., Reid, N., and McDonald, R.A. (2009). A review of mink predation and control in Ireland. *Irish Wildlife Manuals*, No. 40. Dublin. National Parks and Wildlife Service.

27 Smal, C.M. (1991). Population studies on feral American mink *Mustela vison* in Ireland. *Journal of Zoology* 224: pp. 233–249.

28 Hamond, F. (2009). *Mills of Co. Offaly: An industrial heritage survey*. Tullamore. Offaly County Council.

29 O'Connor, P. (2001). *Atlas of Irish Place-names*. Newcastle West, Co. Limerick. Oireacht na Mumhan Books.

30   Greenwood, J.G. (2016). The legacy of Christopher W. Bailey: his Belfast contribution to the Common Bird Census and Waterways Bird Survey (1964–1999). *Irish Birds* 10: pp. 315–328.

31   Connell, J. (2022). *The Stream of Everything*. Dublin. Gill Books.

32   Crowe, O., Cummins, S., Gilligan, N., Smiddy, P., & Tierney, T.D. (2010). An assessment of the current distribution and status of the Kingfisher *Alcedo atthis* in Ireland. *Irish Birds* 9: pp. 41–54.

33   O'Grady, M.F. (2006). *Channels and challenges: Enhancing salmonid rivers*. Irish Freshwater Fisheries Ecology and Management Series No. 4. Dublin. Central Fisheries Board.

34   Lucey, J. (2005). *The Irish Pearl: A cultural, social and economic history*. Bray. Wordwell.

35   Kuemmerlen, M., Moorkens, E.A., & Piggott, J.J. (2022). Assessing remote sensing as a tool to monitor hydrological stress in Irish catchments with freshwater pearl mussel populations. *Science of the Total Environment* 806: pp. 1–16.

36   Moorkens, E. (2020). The Freshwater Pearl Mussel. In: *Ireland's Rivers* (eds M. Kelly-Quinn & J. Reynolds). Dublin. University College Dublin Press.

37   O'Boyle, S., et al. (2019). *Water Quality in Ireland 2013–2018*. Wexford. Environmental Protection Agency.

38   Trodd, W., & O'Boyle, S. (2021). *Water Quality in 2020: An indicators report.* Wexford. Environmental Protection Agency.

39   McGarrigle, M. (2020). River Monitoring in the Republic of Ireland. In: *Ireland's Rivers* (eds M. Kelly-Quinn & J. Reynolds). Dublin. University College Dublin Press.

40   Mulligan, H. Q. (2022). Keeping rivers and lakes safe may burst Ireland's dairy farming bubble. *The Irish Times*, 9 July, 2022.

41   Heery, S. (1993). *The Shannon Floodlands: A natural history.* Kinvara, Co. Galway. Tír Eolas.

42   Nairn, R.G.W., Herbert, I., & Heery, S. (1988). Breeding waders and other wet grassland birds of the River Shannon Callows, Ireland. *Irish Birds* 3: 521–537.

43   National Parks and Wildlife Service (2015). *A Framework for Corncrake Conservation to 2022.* Dublin. Department of Arts, Heritage and the Gaeltacht.

44   Watters, J. (1853). *The Natural History of the Birds of Ireland, Indigenous and Migratory.* Dublin. J. McGlashan.

45   Deakin, R. (1999). *Waterlog: A swimmer's journey through Britain.* London. Chatto & Windus.

46   Reynolds, S.C.P. (2013). *Flora of County Limerick.* Dublin. National Botanic Gardens.

47   O'Sullivan, A. (2001). *Foragers, Farmers and Fishers in a Coastal Landscape: An intertidal archaeological survey of the Shannon Estuary.* Dublin. Royal Irish Academy.

48   Delanty, K. (2013) *An Irish Strategy for River Restoration: How it works on the ground.* Inland Fisheries Ireland presentation. Dublin. River Restoration Centre workshop.

49   Collier, M., & Bourke, M.C. (2020). The case for mainstreaming nature-based solutions into integrated catchment management in Ireland. *Biology and Environment: Proceedings of the Royal Irish Academy*: 120: pp. 107–113.

50   Addy, S., Cooksley, S., Dodd, N., Waylen, K., Stockan, J., Byg, A., and Holstead, K. (2016). *River Restoration and Biodiversity: Nature-based solutions for restoring rivers in the UK and Republic of Ireland.* International Union for the Conservation of Nature. CREW Reference: CRW2014/10.

Chapter 3: Lakes

1   Reynolds, J.D. (1998). *Ireland's Freshwaters*. Dublin. The Marine Institute.

2   Gibson, C. (2011). Jewels in the Landscape. In: *The Natural History of Ulster* (eds J. Faulkner & R. Thompson). Holywood: National Museums Northern Ireland.

3   Reynolds, J.D. (1998). *op. cit.*

4   Otte, M.L. (ed.) (2003). *Wetlands of Ireland: Distribution, ecology, uses and economic value.* Dublin. University College Dublin Press.

5   Magan, M. (2022). *Listen to the Land Speak*. Dublin. Gill Books.

6   Dunne, J. (2008) *Lakeshore Loops: Exploring Ireland's lakes*. Dublin. Liberties Press.

7   Magan (2022). *op. cit.*

8   Tohall, P. (1948). The dobhar-dhú: tombstones of Glenade, Co. Leitrim. *Journal of the Royal Society of Antiquaries of Ireland* 78: pp. 127–129.

9   O'Sullivan, A. (2000). *Crannogs*. Irish Treasure Series. Dublin. Town and Country House.

10   Mears, R., & Hillman G.C. (2007). *Wild Food*. London. Hodder and Stoughton.

11   MacCoitir, N. (2006) *Irish Wild Plants: Myths, legends and folklore*. Cork. Collins Press.

12   Jackson, P.W. (2014). *Ireland's Generous Nature: The past and present uses of wild plants in Ireland*. USA. Missouri Botanical Garden Press.

13   Robinson, M.E., Shimwell, D.W., & Cribbin, G. (1999). Re-assessing the logboat from Lurgan townland, Co. Galway, Ireland. *Antiquity* 73: pp. 903–908.

14   Lanting J.N., & Brindley, A.L. (1996). Irish logboats in their European context. *Journal of Irish Archaeology* 7: pp. 85–95.

15   D'Arcy, G. (2016). *The Breathing Burren*. Cork. Collins Press.

16   Kelly-Quinn, M., & Regan, E.C. (2012). *Ireland Red List No. 7: Mayflies* (Ephemeroptera). Dublin, National Parks and Wildlife Service, Department of Arts, Heritage and the Gaeltacht.

17 Wells, J.H. (1978). Results of a census of Northern Ireland heronries in 1977. *Irish Birds* 1: pp. 187–198.

18 Partridge, J.K. (1984). Survey of heronries in Connemara, 1974–1977. *Irish Birds* 2: pp. 457–465.

19 Viney, M. (2009). *Wild Mayo*. Castlebar. Mayo County Council.

20 Huxley, L. (2019). *Lough Carra: A gem worth preserving*. Castlebar. Lough Carra Catchment Association.

21 Doddy, P. (2019). *The Marl Crusts of Lough Carra*. Castlebar. Lough Carra Catchment Association.

22 Partridge, J.K. (1989). Lough Erne's common scoters. *RSPB Conservation Review* 3: pp. 25–28.

23 Tierney, T.D., Dunne, J., & Callahan, T. (2000). The common scoter *Melanitta nigra nigra* breeding in Ireland, range expansion or site relocation? *Irish Birds* 6: pp. 447–452.

24 Heffernan, M.L., & Hunt, J. (2022). Breeding status of common scoter in Ireland, 2020. *Irish Wildlife Manuals* No. 136. Dublin. National Parks and Wildlife Service, Department of Housing, Local Government and Heritage.

25 Hunt, J., Heffernan, M.L., McLoughlin, D., Benson, C., & Huxley, C. (2013) The breeding status of common scoter, *Melanitta nigra*, in Ireland, 2012. *Irish Wildlife Manuals*, No. 66. Dublin. National Parks and Wildlife Service, Department of the Arts, Heritage and the Gaeltacht.

26 Quirke, B. (ed.) (2001). *Killarney National Park: A place to treasure*. Cork. Collins Press.

27   Greene, T. (2022). Lough Neagh: Scars from dredging will take 'decades if not centuries' to recover. *The Irish Times*, 20 December 2022.

28   Poole, W.R., Reynolds, J.D., & Moriarty, C. (1990). Observations on the silver eel migrations of the Burrishoole River System, Ireland, 1959 to 1988. *Hydrobiology* 75: pp. 807–815.

29   Kelly-Quinn, M., & Reynolds, J. (eds) (2020). *Ireland's Rivers*. Dublin. University College Dublin Press.

30   Mac Coitir, N. (2010). *Ireland's Animals: Myths, legends and folklore*. Cork. Collins Press.

31   Greenhalgh, M. (2000). Wild trout in the British Isles – their variety and conservation. *British Wildlife* 12: pp. 114–121.

32   Kelly, F., King, J., Gargan, P., & Roche, W. (2020). Fish in Irish Rivers. In: *Ireland's Rivers* (eds M. Kelly-Quinn & J. Reynolds). Dublin. University College Dublin Press.

33   Gibson, C. (2011). *op. cit.*

34   Mcintyre, P. (2015). *Down to Earth Cookbook*. Belfast. Colourpoint Books.

35   Rosell, R., Harrod, C., Griffiths, D., & McCarthy, T.K. (2004). Conservation of the Irish populations of the pollan *Coregonus autumnalis*. *Biology and Environment: Proceedings of the Royal Irish Academy* 104B: pp. 67–72.

36   Nairn, R., & O'Halloran, J. (2012). *Bird Habitats in Ireland*. Cork. Collins Press.

37   Evans, E.E. (1957). *Irish Folk Ways*. London. Routledge
      & Kegan Paul.

38   Praeger, R.L. (1937). *The Way That I Went: An
      Englishman in Ireland*. Dublin. Hodges, Figgis & Co.
      London: Methuen.

39   Praeger, R.L. (1932). The flora of the turloughs, a
      preliminary note. *Proceedings of the Royal Irish
      Academy* 41B: pp. 37–45.

40   Goodwillie, R., & Reynolds, J.D. (2003) Turloughs. In:
      *Wetlands of Ireland: Distribution, ecology, uses and
      economic value* (ed. M.L. Otte). Dublin. University
      College Dublin Press.

41   Goodwillie, R. (2003). Vegetation of turloughs. In:
      *Wetlands of Ireland: Distribution, ecology, uses and
      economic value* (ed. M.L. Otte). Dublin. University
      College Dublin Press.

42   Praeger, R.L. (1932). *op. cit.*

43   Ní Bhriain, B., Sheehy Skeffington, M., & Gormally, M.
      (1999). *A Study of Plant and Carabid Beetle Communities
      with Respect to Land Management Practices at Two
      Turloughs in South-east Galway*. Unpublished report to
      the Heritage Council, Kilkenny.

44   Nelson, B. (2001). The wetland invertebrates of Ireland.
      British Wildlife 12: pp. 256–263.

45   McDonagh, M. (2006). Geology, not myth, behind
      mystery of disappearing lake. *The Irish Times*, 23 June
      2006.

46 Humphreys, G.R. (1978). Ireland's former premier breeding haunt of aquatic birds. *Irish Birds* 1: pp. 171–187.

47 Alves, J.A., Dias, M.P., Méndez, V., Katrínardóttir, B., & Gunnarsson, T.G. (2016). Very rapid long-distance sea crossing by a migratory bird. *Scientific Reports* 6: 38154.

48 Booth Jones, K., O'Connell, P., Calladine, J., Noble, D., Wolsey, S., Carrington-Cotton, A., & Wernham, C.V. (2020). *Northern Ireland Lowland Breeding Wader Survey*. British Trust for Ornithology Research Report No. 731.

49 Henderson, I.G., Wilson, A.M., Steele, D., & Vickery, J.A. (2002). Population estimates, trends and habitat associations of breeding lapwing, curlew and snipe in Northern Ireland in 1999. *Bird Study* 49: pp. 17–25.

50 Healy, B. (2003). Coastal lagoons. In: *Wetlands of Ireland: Distribution, ecology, uses and economic value* (ed. M.L. Otte). Dublin. University College Dublin Press. pp. 44–78.

Chapter 4: Wet Woodlands

1 House of Commons. Hansard. 18 February 1915. Vol. 69: pp. 1306–7.

2 Cross, J.R. (2012). *Ireland's Woodland Heritage*. Dublin. Department of Arts, Heritage and the Gaeltacht.

3 Cross, J.R., & Collins, K.D. (2017). *Management Guidelines for Ireland's Native Woodlands*. Dublin. National Parks & Wildlife Service and the Forest Service.

4.   Cross, J.R., & Kelly, D.L. (2003). Wetland Woods. In: *Wetlands of Ireland: Distribution, ecology, uses and economic value* (ed. M.L. Otte). Dublin. University College Dublin Press. pp. 160–172.

5   O'Neill, F.H., & Barron, S.J. (2013). *Results of Monitoring Survey of Old Sessile Oak Woods and Alluvial Forests.* Irish Wildlife Manuals, No. 71. Dublin. National Parks and Wildlife Service.

6   Corcoran, K. (2021). *Saving Eden: The Gearagh and Irish nature.* Macroom. Gearagh Press.

7   Brown, A.G., Stone, P., & Harwood, K. (1995). *The Biogeography of a Wooded Anastomosing River: The Gearagh on the River Lee in County Cork, Ireland.* Occasional Paper 32. Leicester University. Department of Geography.

8   White, J. (1985). The Gearagh woodland, Co. Cork. *Irish Naturalists' Journal* 21: pp. 377–424.

9   Kelly, D.L., & Fuller, S. (1988). Ancient woodland in central Ireland: does it exist? In: *Human Influence on Forest Ecosystem Development in Europe* (ed. F Salbitano). pp 363–369. ESF FERN. Bologna. Pitagora Editrice.

10   Balmer, D.E, Gillings, S., Caffrey, B.J., Swann, R.L, Downie, I.S., & Fuller, R.J. (2013). *Bird Atlas 2007–11: The breeding and wintering birds of Britain and Ireland.* Thetford. BTO Books.

11   Barrington, R.M. (1900). *Migration of Birds as Observed at Irish Lighthouses and Lightships.* Dublin and London.

12   Kelly, D.L., & Iremonger, S.F. (1997). Irish wetland woods: the plant communities and their ecology. *Biology and Environment: Proceedings of the Royal Irish Academy* 97B: pp. 1–32.

13   O'Neill, F.H, & Barron, S.J. (2013). *op. cit.*

Chapter 5: Artificial Waters: Ponds, Canals and Constructed Wetlands

1   Williams, P., Biggs, J., & Nicolet, P. (2010). New clean-water ponds – a way to protect biodiversity. *British Wildlife* 22: pp. 77–85.

2   Foster, G. N., Nelson, B. H., & O Connor, Á. (2009) *Ireland Red List No. 1 – Water Beetles*. National Parks and Wildlife Service. Dublin. Department of Environment, Heritage and Local Government.

3   Gioria, M. (2017). *Freshwater Biodiversity in the Irish Agricultural Landscape: The significance of ponds*. STRIVE Report. Wexford. Environmental Protection Agency.

4   Nelson, B., & Thompson, R. (2008). *The Natural History of Ireland's Dragonflies*. Belfast. Museums and Galleries of Northern Ireland.

5   Meehan, S.T. (2013). *IWT National Smooth Newt Survey 2013 Report*. Dublin. Irish Wildlife Trust.

6   Delaney, R. (1992). *A Celebration of 250 Years of Ireland's Inland Waterways*. Belfast. Appletree Press.

7   Roche, N., Aughney, T., Marnell, F., & Lundy, M. (2014). *Irish Bats in the 21st Century*. Virginia. Bat Conservation Ireland.

8   Harty, F. (2017). *Permaculture Guide to Reed Beds: Designing, building and planting your treatment wetland system*. East Meon, Hampshire. Permanent Publications.

9   Becerra Jurado, G., Callanan, M., Gioria, M., Baars, J-R., Harrington, R. & Kelly-Quinn, M. (2009). Comparison of macroinvertebrate community structure and driving environmental factors in natural and wastewater treatment ponds. *Hydrobiologia* 634: pp.153–165.

10   Fisher, K., Nelson, B., and Baars, J.R. (2015). Motorway attenuation ponds make a significant contribution to the landscape biodiversity of mobile aquatic insect groups. Sligo. Proceedings of 25th Environ Conference.

Chapter 6: Rewilding the Waters

1   Meresa, H., Donegan, S., Golian, S., and Murphy, C. (2022). Simulated changes in seasonal and low flows with climate change for Irish catchments. *Water* 14: p. 1556.

2   *Ibid.*

3   Irish Water (2021). *National Water Resources Plan – Framework Plan Technical Appendices: Appendix F Climate Change Impacts on Supplies*. Dublin. Irish Water.

4   Feely, H.B., Giller, P.S., Baars, J.R., and Kelly-Quinn, M.
        (2020) Benthic Macroinvertebrates. In: *Ireland's Rivers*
        (eds M. Kelly-Quinn & J. Reynolds). Dublin. University
        College Dublin Press.

5   Hastie, L.C., Cosgrove, P.J., Ellis, N., and Gaywood,
        M.J. (2003). The threat of climate change to freshwater
        pearl mussel populations. *Ambio* 32: pp. 40–46.

6   Inland Fisheries Ireland. (2020) *River Restoration Works:
        Science-based guidance centred on hydromorphological
        principles in an era of climate change.* Volume 2. *IFISH:
        Fish and Habitats: Science and Management.* Dublin.
        Inland Fisheries Ireland.

7   Pearce, F. (2006). *When the Rivers Run Dry: Water –
        The defining crisis of the twenty-first century.* Boston.
        Beacon Press.

8   Radio Telefís Éireann (2007). Study predicts Dublin
        water crisis. RTÉ News, 22 August 2007.

9   Tanneberger, F., Appulo, L., Ewert, S., Lakner, S., Ó
        Brolcháin, N., Peters, J., & Wichtmann, W. (2021).
        The power of nature-based solutions: how peatlands
        can help us to achieve key EU sustainability objectives.
        Advanced Sustainable Systems 5: adsu.2000146.

10   Giraldus Cambrensis (c.1200). *The History and
        Topography of Ireland.* Translated from the Latin by
        John J. O'Meara (1982 edition). Portlaoise. Dolmen
        Press.

11   D'Arcy, G. (1999). *The Breathing Burren.* Cork. Collins
        Press.

12   Osbourne, L.L., and Kovacic, D.A. (1993). Riparian vegetated buffer strips in water-quality restoration and stream management. *Freshwater Biology* 29: pp. 243–258.

13   Lowrance, R., Todd, R., Fail, J., Hendrickson, O., Leonard, R., & Asmussen, L. (1984). Riparian forests as nutrient filters in agricultural watersheds. *BioScience* 34: pp. 374–377.

14   Wipfli, M.S., & Baxter, C.V. (2010). Linking ecosystems, food webs, and fish production: Subsidies in salmonid watershed. *Fisheries* 35: pp. 373–387.

15   Bennett, A.F. (1999). *Linkages in the Landscape: The role of corridors and connectivity in wildlife conservation.* Gland, Switzerland. IUCN (International Union for Conservation of Nature).

16   McCracken, E. (1971). *The Irish Woods since Tudor Times: Distribution and exploitation.* Newton Abbot. David & Charles.

17   Love, J.A. (1983). *The Return of the Sea Eagle.* Cambridge. Cambridge University Press.

18   Mee, A., Breen, D., Clarke, D., Heardman, C., Lyden, J., McMahon, F., O'Sullivan, P., & O'Toole, L. (2016). Reintroduction of white-tailed eagles *Haliaeetus albicilla* to Ireland. *Irish Birds* 10: pp. 301–314.

19   Wilson, K., Law, A., Gaywood, M., Ramsay, P., & Willby, N. (2020). Beavers: the original engineers of Britain's fresh waters. *British Wildlife* 31: pp. 403–411.

20   Law, A., McLean, F., & Willby, N.J. (2016). Habitat engineering by beaver benefits aquatic biodiversity and ecosystem processes in agricultural streams. *Freshwater Biology* 61: pp. 486–499.

21   Gow, D. (2020). *Bringing Back the Beaver: The story of one man's quest to rewild Britain's waterways*. Chelsea Green Publishing.

22   Giraldus Cambrensis (*c*.1200). *op. cit.*

23   Gostner, W., Alp, M., Schleiss, A. & Robinson, C. (2013). The hydro-morphological index of diversity: a tool for describing habitat heterogeneity in river engineering projects. *Hydrobiologia* 712: pp. 43–60.

24   Feehan, J. (2004). *A Long-lived Wilderness: The future of the north midlands peatland network*. Dublin. Department of Environmental Resource Management, University College Dublin.

Index